Discovering Philosophy:
An Easy Guide to History's Greatest Minds

Compiled and edited by Kevin Scott

© 2024 Kevin Scott. All rights reserved.

Philosophy is often perceived as an intimidating discipline, shrouded in complexity and reserved for academic circles. Yet, at its heart, philosophy addresses questions that are universal to the human condition: What is truth? How should we live? What is the nature of reality, knowledge, and existence? These inquiries touch every life, yet the path to engaging with them often seems hidden behind the dense texts and specialized language of the philosophical canon. This book is an invitation to uncover that path, offering a gateway to some of the greatest thinkers who have shaped human understanding over centuries.

The philosophers presented in these pages are considered essential—canonical figures whose ideas have profoundly influenced not only philosophy but also science, politics, art, and culture. Their thoughts form the foundation of many of the intellectual frameworks we rely on today, whether we realize it or not. From ancient Greece to the modern world, each thinker included here represents a unique response to the timeless questions of existence and meaning, questions that remain as relevant now as they were in their own time.

This collection is designed for readers who may be new to philosophy or who seek a concise overview of its key figures. Each entry offers a brief but insightful biography, situating the philosopher within their historical and intellectual context. More importantly, it distills their central theses—the core ideas that define their contributions to the history of thought. These entries are not exhaustive, nor do they attempt to replace a deeper engagement with the original works. Instead, they are a starting point, a map to the vast terrain of philosophical inquiry.

For the curious reader, this book can serve as a springboard into deeper exploration. Perhaps the skepticism of Pyrrho or the existential angst of Kierkegaard will resonate, prompting further reading. Maybe the rational clarity of Descartes or the revolutionary zeal of Marx will ignite a spark of inspiration. The philosophers here are not presented as static monuments but as living voices, speaking to us across time and inviting us to join the conversation.

In an era where information is abundant but understanding is often superficial, the practice of philosophy offers a rare opportunity to think deeply and critically. By engaging with these thinkers, readers are encouraged to challenge their assumptions, refine their perspectives, and cultivate a sense of wonder about the world. Philosophy is not merely an academic exercise; it is a way of seeing and being, a pursuit of wisdom that enriches our lives and our communities.

This book is meant to be approachable yet profound, concise yet meaningful. It is a guide for those who may not read often, who may have hesitated to explore philosophy because it seemed too daunting. It is also a tribute to the thinkers who have dared to ask the hardest questions and offered us their best answers. Whether you are a student, a lifelong learner, or simply someone curious about the big questions, we hope this collection inspires you to think, question, and explore.

The journey into philosophy begins with a single thought. Let these pages be your first step.

Table of Contents:

1. Thales of Miletus (c. 624 – 546 BCE)
2. Anaximander (c. 610 – 546 BCE)
3. Anaximenes (c. 585 – 525 BCE)
4. Pythagoras (c. 570 – 495 BCE)
5. Siddhartha Gautama (c. 563 BCE – c. 483 BCE)
6. Confucius (c. 551 – 479 BCE)
7. Laozi (c. 6th century BCE)
8. Dharmakirti (c. 6th – 7th century CE)
9. Heraclitus (c. 535 – 475 BCE)
10. Parmenides (c. 515 – 450 BCE)
11. Empedocles (c. 494 – 434 BCE)
12. Anaxagoras (c. 500 – 428 BCE)
13. Protagoras (c. 490 – 420 BCE)
14. Dignaga (c. 480 – 540 CE)
15. Socrates (c. 470 – 399 BCE)
16. Mozi (c. 470 – c. 391 BCE)
17. Democritus (c. 460 – c. 370 BCE)
18. Antisthenes (c. 445 – 365 BCE)
19. Diogenes of Sinope (c. 412 – 323 BCE)
20. Plato (c. 428 – 348 BCE)
21. Asanga (c. 4th – 5th century CE)
22. Aristotle (384 – 322 BCE)
23. Mencius (c. 372 – 289 BCE)
24. Zhuangzi (c. 369 – 286 BCE)
25. Hypatia (c. 360 – 415 CE)
26. Pyrrho (c. 360 – 270 BCE)
27. Epicurus (341 – 270 BCE)
28. Zeno of Citium (c. 334 – 262 BCE)
29. Xunzi (c. 310 – 235 BCE)
30. Chrysippus (c. 279 – 206 BCE)
31. Lucretius (c. 99 – 55 BCE)
32. Philo of Alexandria (c. 20 BCE – 50 CE)
33. Epictetus (c. 50 – 135 CE)
34. Marcus Aurelius (121 – 180 CE)
35. Galen (c. 129 – c. 216 CE)
36. Nagarjuna (c. 150 – 250 CE)

37. Sextus Empiricus (c. 160 – 210 CE)
38. Plotinus (c. 204 – 270 CE)
39. Hypatia (c. 360 – 415 CE)
40. Proclus (412 – 485 CE)
41. Boethius (c. 480 – 524 CE)
42. Vasubandhu (c. 4th century CE)
43. Chandrakirti (c. 600 – 650 CE)
44. Huineng (638 – 713 CE)
45. Shantideva (c. 685 – 763 CE)
46. Shankara (c. 700 – 750 CE)
47. Al-Kindi (c. 801 – 873 CE)
48. Padmasambhava (c. 8th – 9th century CE)
49. Al-Farabi (c. 872 – 950 CE)
50. Avicenna (Ibn Sina) (980 – 1037 CE)
51. Ramanuja (1017 – 1137 CE)
52. Anselm of Canterbury (1033 – 1109 CE)
53. Al-Ghazali (1058 – 1111 CE)
54. Peter Abelard (1079 – 1142 CE)
55. Averroes (Ibn Rushd) (1126 – 1198 CE)
56. Maimonides (1138 – 1204 CE)
57. Dogen (1200 – 1253 CE)
58. Rumi (1207 – 1273 CE)
59. Thomas Aquinas (1225 – 1274 CE)
60. John Duns Scotus (c. 1266 – 1308 CE)
61. William of Ockham (c. 1287 – 1347 CE)
62. Longchenpa (1308 – 1364 CE)
63. Ibn Khaldun (1332 – 1406 CE)
64. Tsongkhapa (1357 – 1419 CE)
65. Nicholas of Cusa (1401 – 1464 CE)
66. Marsilio Ficino (1433 – 1499 CE)
67. Pico della Mirandola (1463 – 1494 CE)
68. Niccolò Machiavelli (1469 – 1527 CE)
69. Wang Yangming (1472 – 1529 CE)
70. John Calvin (1509 – 1564 CE)
71. Michel de Montaigne (1533 – 1592 CE)
72. Giordano Bruno (1548 – 1600 CE)
73. Francis Bacon (1561 – 1626 CE)
74. Tommaso Campanella (1568 – 1639 CE)
75. Hugo Grotius (1583 – 1645 CE)
76. Zera Yacob (1599 – 1692 CE)

77. John Amos Comenius (1592 – 1670 CE)
78. René Descartes (1596 – 1650 CE)
79. Thomas Hobbes (1588 – 1679 CE)
80. Blaise Pascal (1623 – 1662 CE)
81. Anne Conway (1631 – 1679 CE)
82. Baruch Spinoza (1632 – 1677 CE)
83. John Locke (1632 – 1704 CE)
84. Gottfried Wilhelm Leibniz (1646 – 1716 CE)
85. Giovanni Battista Vico (1668 – 1744 CE)
86. Giambattista Vico (1668 – 1744 CE)
87. Christian Wolff (1679 – 1754 CE)
88. George Berkeley (1685 – 1753 CE)
89. Montesquieu (1689 – 1755)
90. Francis Hutcheson (1694 – 1746 CE)
91. Thomas Reid (1710 – 1796 CE)
92. David Hume (1711 – 1776 CE)
93. Jean-Jacques Rousseau (1712 – 1778 CE)
94. Denis Diderot (1713 – 1784 CE)
95. Baron d'Holbach (1723 – 1789 CE)
96. Adam Smith (1723 – 1790 CE)
97. Immanuel Kant (1724 – 1804 CE)
98. Moses Mendelssohn (1729 – 1786 CE)
99. Gotthold Ephraim Lessing (1729 – 1781 CE)
100. Edmund Burke (1729 – 1797 CE)
101. Thomas Paine (1737 – 1809 CE)
102. Johann Gottfried Herder (1744 – 1803 CE)
103. Mary Wollstonecraft (1759 – 1797 CE)
104. Friedrich Schiller (1759 – 1805 CE)
105. Friedrich Schleiermacher (1768 – 1834 CE)
106. Georg Wilhelm Friedrich Hegel (1770 – 1831 CE)
107. Arthur Schopenhauer (1788 – 1860 CE)
108. William Whewell (1794 – 1866 CE)
109. Auguste Comte (1798 – 1857 CE)
110. Ralph Waldo Emerson (1803 – 1882 CE)
111. Ludwig Feuerbach (1804 – 1872 CE)
112. Alexis de Tocqueville (1805 – 1859 CE)
113. Max Stirner (1806 – 1856 CE)
114. John Stuart Mill (1806 – 1873 CE)
115. Charles Darwin (1809 – 1882 CE)
116. Søren Kierkegaard (1813 – 1855 CE)

117. Henry David Thoreau (1817 – 1862 CE)
118. Karl Marx (1818 – 1883 CE)
119. Friedrich Engels (1820 – 1895 CE)
120. Herbert Spencer (1820 – 1903 CE)
121. Fyodor Dostoevsky (1821–1881)
122. Wilhelm Wundt (1832 – 1920 CE)
123. Wilhelm Dilthey (1833 – 1911 CE)
124. Henry Sidgwick (1838 – 1900 CE)
125. Charles Sanders Peirce (1839 – 1914 CE)
126. William James (1842 – 1910 CE)
127. Friedrich Nietzsche (1844 – 1900 CE)
128. Gottlob Frege (1848 – 1925 CE)
129. Vladimir Solovyov (1853 – 1900 CE)
130. Josiah Royce (1855 – 1916 CE)
131. Georg Simmel (1858 – 1918 CE)
132. Edmund Husserl (1859 – 1938 CE)
133. Henri Bergson (1859 – 1941 CE)
134. John Dewey (1859 – 1952 CE)
135. Jane Addams (1860 – 1935 CE)
136. Rabindranath Tagore (1861 – 1941 CE)
137. Alfred North Whitehead (1861 – 1947 CE)
138. George Santayana (1863 – 1952 CE)
139. Max Weber (1864 – 1920 CE)
140. Mahatma Gandhi (1869 – 1948 CE)
141. D.T. Suzuki (1870 – 1966 CE)
142. Nishida Kitaro (1870 – 1945 CE)
143. Bertrand Russell (1872 – 1970 CE)
144. G. E. Moore (1873 – 1958 CE)
145. Ernst Cassirer (1874 – 1945 CE)
146. Max Scheler (1874 – 1928 CE)
147. Ramana Maharshi (1879 – 1950 CE)
148. Pierre Teilhard de Chardin (1881 – 1955 CE)
149. Karl Jaspers (1883 – 1969 CE)
150. Georg Lukács (1885 – 1971 CE)
151. Paul Tillich (1886 – 1965 CE)
152. Ludwig Wittgenstein (1889 – 1951 CE)
153. Gabriel Marcel (1889 – 1973 CE)
154. Rudolf Carnap (1891 – 1970 CE)
155. Antonio Gramsci (1891 – 1937 CE)
156. Mikhail Bakhtin (1895 – 1975 CE)

157. R. Buckminster Fuller (1895 – 1983 CE)
158. Herbert Marcuse (1898 – 1979 CE)
159. Leo Strauss (1899 – 1973 CE)
160. Friedrich Hayek (1899 – 1992 CE)
161. Hans-Georg Gadamer (1900 – 2002 CE)
162. Karl Popper (1902 – 1994 CE)
163. Theodor W. Adorno (1903 – 1969 CE)
164. Hans Jonas (1903 – 1993 CE)
165. Jean-Paul Sartre (1905 – 1980 CE)
166. Hannah Arendt (1906 – 1975 CE)
167. Emmanuel Levinas (1906 – 1995 CE)
168. Maurice Blanchot (1907 – 2003 CE)
169. Simone de Beauvoir (1908 – 1986 CE)
170. Maurice Merleau-Ponty (1908 – 1961 CE)
171. Simone Weil (1909 – 1943 CE)
172. Alfred Ayer (1910 – 1989 CE)
173. Marshall McLuhan (1911 – 1980)
174. E. M. Cioran (1911 – 1995 CE)
175. Wilfrid Sellars (1912 – 1989 CE)
176. Paul Ricoeur (1913 – 2005 CE)
177. David Bohm (1917 – 1992 CE)
178. Elizabeth Anscombe (1919 – 2001 CE)
179. John Rawls (1921 – 2002 CE)
180. Gilles Deleuze (1925 – 1995 CE)
181. Frantz Fanon (1925 – 1961 CE)
182. Michel Foucault (1926 – 1984 CE)
183. Thich Nhat Hanh (1926 – 2022 CE)
184. Noam Chomsky (1928 – present)
185. Alasdair MacIntyre (1929 – present)
186. Jacques Derrida (1930 – 2004 CE)
187. Michel Serres (1930 – 2019 CE)
188. Richard Rorty (1931 – 2007 CE)
189. Charles Taylor (1931 – present)
190. Amartya Sen (1933 – present)
191. Richard Swinburne (1934 – present)
192. Sarah Kofman (1934 – 1994 CE)
193. Alain Badiou (1937 – present)
194. Quentin Skinner (1940 – present)
195. Daniel Dennett (1942 - Present)
196. Julia Kristeva (1941 – present)

197. Giorgio Agamben (1942 – present)
198. Aung San Suu Kyi (1945 – present)
199. Peter Singer (1946 – present)
200. Homi K. Bhabha (1949 – present)
201. Vandana Shiva (1952 – present)
202. Judith Butler (1956 – present)
203. David Chalmers (1966 – present)

Thales of Miletus (c. 624 – 546 BCE)

Thales of Miletus, a pre-Socratic philosopher from the Ionian city of Miletus, is often regarded as the first philosopher in Western thought. He was one of the Seven Sages of Greece and is credited with founding the Milesian school of thought, which sought natural explanations for the phenomena of the world. Thales lived during a period of intellectual exchange between Greece, Egypt, and Babylon, which deeply influenced his thinking. His work represents a shift from mythological to rational explanations of the natural world, emphasizing observation and reason as tools for understanding the cosmos.

Thales is best known for his assertion that water is the fundamental principle ("archê") from which everything in the universe originates. He believed that water, in its various forms—liquid, vapor, and ice—was the primary substance underlying all matter. This idea was revolutionary for its time, as it marked one of the first attempts to explain the world in terms of a single, unifying natural element rather than through mythological narratives. Thales' theory emphasized the essential role of water in sustaining life and its ability to transform, making it a fitting candidate for the primary substance of all things.

Thales' contributions extended beyond metaphysics, particularly in the fields of geometry and astronomy. He is credited with several geometric discoveries, including the concept that a circle is bisected by its diameter and the idea that the base angles of an isosceles triangle are equal. Thales also applied geometry to practical problems, such as calculating the height of the Egyptian pyramids based on their shadows. In astronomy, Thales is said to have predicted a solar eclipse in 585 BCE, further demonstrating his belief in the regularity and predictability of natural events, which underscored his commitment to empirical observation.

Thales' cosmology reflected his naturalistic approach to understanding the universe. He believed that the Earth floated on water, and he explained earthquakes as the result of the Earth's movement on this water. While primitive by modern standards, this explanation represented a significant departure from the prevailing mythological accounts, which attributed natural phenomena to the actions of gods. Thales' insistence on natural causes for events in the natural world helped to lay the foundation for the scientific method, influencing the way future generations would approach the study of the cosmos.

Thales' influence on subsequent philosophers is profound. His rational approach to understanding the natural world through observation and reason laid the groundwork for later pre-Socratic philosophers, including his student Anaximander, who expanded on his ideas. Thales' contributions to natural philosophy, mathematics, and astronomy helped to establish the early foundations of Western science and philosophy, marking him as a pivotal figure in the intellectual history of ancient Greece.

Anaximander (c. 610 – 546 BCE)

Anaximander, a pre-Socratic philosopher from Miletus and a student of Thales, is known for his significant contributions to cosmology, geography, and biology. He lived during a period of philosophical exploration in Ionia, where thinkers were increasingly focused on natural explanations for the universe's origins and structure. Anaximander built on his teacher's ideas but introduced more abstract concepts, moving away from Thales' material-based theories toward metaphysical speculation. His work marks a key moment in the development of early Greek thought, particularly in the realm of cosmology.

Anaximander's most notable contribution to philosophy is his concept of the "apeiron," or the "boundless." Unlike Thales, who identified water as the fundamental substance of the universe, Anaximander proposed that the cosmos originated from an indefinite, infinite substance that was neither water, air, nor any other specific element. The apeiron contained the opposites—such as hot and cold, and wet and dry—that separated out to form the material world. This idea was groundbreaking because it introduced the notion of an abstract, non-material principle that could account for the complexity and diversity of the universe.

Anaximander also developed an early cosmological model that attempted to explain the structure of the universe in terms of natural laws. He proposed that the Earth was a cylindrical object that floated freely in space, suspended by equilibrium, and not supported by any physical structure. He further suggested that the stars, sun, and moon were rings of fire encircling the Earth, visible through openings in these rings. This model represented a significant departure from earlier, more simplistic views of the cosmos and reflected Anaximander's belief in a universe governed by impersonal, natural forces rather than divine intervention.

In addition to his work in cosmology, Anaximander made early contributions to biology and evolutionary theory. He theorized that life originated in water and that humans evolved from fish-like creatures. Anaximander believed that the first animals were born in moisture and gradually adapted to life on land. This early evolutionary idea was revolutionary for its time, as it provided a naturalistic explanation for the origins and development of life, moving away from mythological accounts of creation. Anaximander's emphasis on natural processes as drivers of life's evolution was a precursor to later scientific theories.

Anaximander's influence on later philosophers, particularly Anaximenes and the atomists, was profound. His introduction of the apeiron as a metaphysical principle opened new avenues for understanding the cosmos in abstract terms , and his naturalistic approach to cosmology and biology laid the groundwork for future developments in these fields. Anaximander's work represents a key moment in the evolution of early Greek philosophy, as it marked the transition from tangible, material explanations of the universe to more abstract and theoretical explorations.

Anaximenes (c. 585 – 525 BCE)

Anaximenes, a pre-Socratic philosopher from Miletus and a student of Anaximander, is best known for continuing the Milesian school's quest to identify the fundamental substance of the universe. He lived during a period of growing philosophical inquiry in Ionia, where natural explanations for the cosmos were increasingly sought. Anaximenes, while influenced by Anaximander's abstract ideas, returned to a more concrete and observable element to explain the origins of the universe. His work represents a synthesis of the material focus of Thales and the more abstract metaphysical thinking of Anaximander.

Anaximenes proposed that air was the fundamental principle ("archê") of the universe, rejecting Anaximander's indefinite apeiron in favor of a more tangible substance. He believed that air, through processes of rarefaction and condensation, could transform into all other elements. When air is rarefied, it becomes fire, and when condensed, it becomes water, and eventually earth. This dynamic process allowed Anaximenes to explain the diversity of matter while maintaining that all things originated from a single substance. His choice of air reflected his desire to root his philosophy in the observable world, making it more accessible than Anaximander's abstract apeiron.

Anaximenes also developed a cosmological model based on his belief in air as the primary substance. He suggested that the Earth was flat and floated on a cushion of air, while the stars, sun, and moon were composed of air in various states. According to Anaximenes, these celestial bodies were carried around the Earth by air currents. His cosmological model built on Anaximander's ideas but introduced a more physical and dynamic element, reflecting his broader belief in the unity and transformation of all things through air. This model represented an early attempt to explain the movement of celestial bodies through natural processes.

In addition to his cosmological ideas, Anaximenes developed a theory of change that relied on the processes of rarefaction and condensation. He believed that these processes were responsible for all changes in the natural world, from the formation of clouds and wind to the transformation of one element into another. By focusing on air's ability to change form, Anaximenes offered an early explanation of the mechanisms behind observable changes in nature. His theory laid the groundwork for later explorations into the nature of matter and transformation.

Anaximenes' influence on later philosophers, particularly in the development of material monism, was significant. His emphasis on air as a dynamic, transforming substance contributed to the ongoing philosophical quest to identify a single underlying principle of the cosmos. Anaximenes' contributions to cosmology, metaphysics, and natural philosophy played a pivotal role in shaping early Greek thought and helped to bridge the gap between the material and abstract approaches of his predecessors.

Pythagoras (c. 570 – 495 BCE)

Pythagoras, a philosopher and mathematician from the island of Samos, is best known for founding the Pythagorean school, a religious and philosophical community combining mathematics, mysticism, and ethics. He spent much of his life in Croton, a Greek colony in southern Italy, where his followers developed his ideas into a comprehensive system of thought. Living during a period of intellectual and spiritual exploration, Pythagoras was deeply influenced by earlier Greek, Egyptian, and Babylonian traditions. His philosophy centered on the belief that the universe could be understood through numbers and harmonious relationships.

At the heart of Pythagorean philosophy is the idea that numbers are the essence of all reality. Pythagoras and his followers believed that the structure of the cosmos could be explained through mathematical principles, with numbers as the building blocks of both the material and spiritual worlds. This mathematical mysticism extended to all areas of life, as the Pythagoreans believed that studying numbers revealed the universe's underlying harmony. For Pythagoras, numbers were not merely abstract symbols but the key to understanding the divine order governing existence.

Pythagoras is most famous for the Pythagorean theorem, which established the relationship between the sides of a right triangle. However, for Pythagoras, this theorem was not just a mathematical tool but a demonstration of the cosmos's underlying order. The Pythagoreans also introduced the concept of the "music of the spheres," which held that celestial movements followed mathematical ratios, producing a harmonious sound imperceptible to human ears. This reflected Pythagoras' broader belief that the universe operates according to mathematical laws mirrored in both the physical and spiritual realms.

In addition to his mathematical theories, Pythagoras espoused a philosophy of ethics and spiritual purification. He believed in the immortality of the soul and the doctrine of reincarnation, asserting that the soul underwent a cycle of rebirths based on its moral conduct. The Pythagorean way of life emphasized self-discipline, moral virtue, and ascetic practices, such as vegetarianism, as part of the quest for spiritual purity. Pythagoras taught that living in harmony with the universe's principles purified the soul and ultimately released it from reincarnation.

Pythagoras' influence extended beyond mathematics and mysticism. His ideas about the interconnectedness of numbers, nature, and ethics shaped later philosophical developments, particularly in Plato's thought, which embraced Pythagorean notions of harmony and the relationship between the material and immaterial worlds. The emphasis on mathematics in understanding the cosmos laid the groundwork for future scientific inquiry. Although much of Pythagoras' original teachings have been lost, his legacy endures in mathematics, philosophy, and spirituality, making him one of the most influential thinkers of the ancient world.

Siddhartha Gautama (c. 563 BCE – c. 483 BCE)

Siddhartha Gautama, known as the Buddha, was born in the Shakya clan in the region that is now Nepal. The son of a king, he lived a sheltered life of luxury, but his encounters with suffering—seeing old age, sickness, and death—led him to renounce his princely life and seek enlightenment. At the age of 29, he left his home to become a wandering ascetic. After years of practicing severe asceticism and meditation, he attained enlightenment under the Bodhi tree in Bodh Gaya, becoming the Buddha, or "Awakened One." He spent the rest of his life teaching the Dharma or the path to end suffering. His teachings became the foundation of Buddhism, a major philosophical and religious tradition in Asia.

The context in which Siddhartha's philosophy arose was one of widespread religious diversity in ancient India. At the time, Indian society was shaped by Vedic practices and the growing influence of Upanishadic thought, which emphasized concepts like Brahman (the universal soul) and Atman (the individual soul). Siddhartha rejected the rigid caste system of the Vedic religion, as well as the idea that spiritual liberation could only be attained through rituals or extreme asceticism. Instead, his teachings focused on a Middle Way between sensual indulgence and self-mortification, which aimed to overcome suffering by understanding and practicing ethical conduct, mental discipline, and wisdom.

Central to Gautama's philosophy is the concept of dukkha, which is often translated as "suffering" or "unsatisfactoriness." He taught that all life is characterized by dukkha, and this suffering stems from desire or craving. However, the Buddha also provided a solution through the Four Noble Truths: (1) Life is suffering, (2) The cause of suffering is craving, (3) The cessation of suffering is possible, and (4) The path to cessation is the Noble Eightfold Path. This path includes right understanding, right thought, right speech, right action, right livelihood, right effort, right mindfulness, and right concentration. Through this method, individuals can attain Nirvana, a state of liberation from the cycle of birth and death (samsara).

Another critical element of Gautama's philosophy is the concept of Anatta, or no-self. Contrary to the prevailing beliefs in a permanent soul (Atman), the Buddha taught that there is no unchanging, eternal self. Instead, individuals are composed of five aggregates (skandhas): form, sensation, perception, mental formations, and consciousness. These are in constant flux, and clinging to them as a permanent self leads to suffering. Understanding this truth, he believed, is essential for liberation.

The Buddhist ethical framework is deeply interwoven with his philosophical insights. Gautama emphasized compassion, non-violence, and the cultivation of positive mental states. The practice of meditation plays a crucial role in developing these qualities, as it allows practitioners to quiet their minds, gain insight into the nature of reality, and ultimately reach enlightenment. His teachings spread rapidly across India and later into Central, East, and Southeast Asia, profoundly shaping religious and philosophical thought in those regions.

Confucius (c. 551 – 479 BCE)

Confucius, also known as Kong Fuzi, was a Chinese philosopher and educator who lived during the late Zhou dynasty, a time of political instability and social unrest. Born in the state of Lu, Confucius dedicated his life to teaching and to the pursuit of moral integrity, social harmony, and virtuous governance. His teachings, later compiled into the Analects by his disciples, formed the basis of Confucianism, a system of ethical and political thought that became deeply ingrained in Chinese culture. Confucius' ideas emerged in response to the chaotic state of society during his time, and he sought to restore social order through a return to traditional values.

At the heart of Confucius' philosophy is the concept of "ren," often translated as "benevolence" or "humaneness." Ren represents the ideal moral character that individuals should cultivate in their relationships with others. Confucius believed that a society governed by ren would naturally be harmonious, as people would act with kindness, compassion, and empathy. He argued that rulers, in particular, should embody ren, leading by example and inspiring virtuous behavior in their subjects. For Confucius, personal morality was deeply intertwined with social stability, and he believed that a well-ordered society could only be achieved through the cultivation of virtuous individuals.

In addition to ren, Confucius emphasized the importance of "li," or ritual propriety, in maintaining social order. Li encompassed a wide range of practices, from ceremonial rites to everyday manners, and Confucius believed that observing these rituals fostered respect for tradition and authority. By adhering to li, individuals would internalize the values of respect, duty, and harmony, which were essential for the proper functioning of society. Confucius saw rituals as a way to reinforce moral behavior and social cohesion, arguing that when people observe proper conduct, they contribute to the overall stability of the state.

Confucius also introduced the concept of the "junzi," or the "gentleman," who embodies moral virtue, wisdom, and self-discipline. The junzi, in Confucius' view, is the ideal leader who governs not through force or coercion but through moral example. A ruler who embodies the qualities of a junzi would inspire loyalty and virtuous behavior among the people, thereby creating a harmonious and well-ordered society. Confucius believed that leadership was not about status or power but about the cultivation of moral character and the ability to inspire others through ethical behavior.

Confucius' teachings on morality, governance, and social order profoundly shaped Chinese culture and political philosophy. His emphasis on the role of virtue in leadership and the importance of education in cultivating moral individuals became central tenets of Confucianism, which influenced Chinese government and society for centuries. Confucianism became the official state philosophy during the Han dynasty, and its ideas continue to resonate in East Asian culture today. Confucius' legacy as a philosopher of ethics and political order remains one of the most enduring in human history.

Laozi (c. 6th century BCE)

Laozi, also known as Lao Tzu, is traditionally considered the founder of Daoism (Taoism), one of the major philosophical and religious traditions in China. Little is known about Laozi's life, and much of his biography is shrouded in legend. According to tradition, Laozi was an archivist in the Zhou dynasty who became disillusioned with the corruption of society and withdrew from public life. Before departing for the western frontier, Laozi is said to have written the Tao Te Ching, a foundational text of Daoism. Laozi's thought arose in response to the political turmoil of the time, offering an alternative to Confucian ideas of social order and governance.

At the heart of Laozi's philosophy is the concept of the Dao (Tao), often translated as the "Way." The Dao is an indefinable, all-encompassing force that governs the natural world and the cosmos. Unlike Confucianism, which emphasizes human relationships and societal roles, Daoism encourages individuals to align themselves with the natural flow of the Dao. Laozi believed that the Dao is best understood not through intellectual effort but through simplicity, humility, and non-interference. The Dao is ever-present and operates through a principle of effortless action, or "wu wei," which involves acting in accordance with the natural order without forcing outcomes.

Wu wei, or "non-action," is one of the key principles in Laozi's thought. It does not mean inactivity but rather acting in a way that is harmonious with the natural flow of events. Laozi argued that human beings often disrupt the natural balance of the world by imposing their will on it. He believed that true wisdom lies in allowing things to unfold naturally, without unnecessary interference or striving. This concept contrasts sharply with Confucianism, which promotes active moral cultivation and intervention in social affairs. For Laozi, the best ruler or leader is one who governs with minimal action, allowing the people to live in harmony with the Dao.

Laozi also criticized rigid societal structures and artificial distinctions, believing that they lead to conflict and disharmony. He was skeptical of laws, rituals, and hierarchical systems, which he saw as obstacles to a peaceful and natural way of life. In the Tao Te Ching, Laozi advocates for simplicity, humility, and a return to a more natural way of living. He argued that people should live in accordance with nature and the spontaneous unfolding of events, rather than trying to control or manipulate their environment. His teachings promote a lifestyle of simplicity, contentment, and non-attachment to material wealth or social status.

Laozi's ideas had a profound influence on Chinese philosophy, religion, and culture. Daoism, as articulated by Laozi, emphasizes living in harmony with nature, humility, and non-intervention, offering a counterbalance to Confucian ideals of social order and moral responsibility. Daoism would later develop into a religious movement, incorporating practices such as meditation, alchemy, and rituals aimed at attaining harmony with the Dao. Laozi's teachings, particularly on the importance of simplicity and non-action, continue to influence not only Chinese culture but also global philosophies related to nature, mindfulness, and environmentalism.

Dharmakirti (c. 6th – 7th century CE)

Dharmakirti was a highly influential Indian philosopher and logician, primarily associated with the Yogachara and Sautrāntika schools of Buddhism. Born in South India, Dharmakirti was a disciple of the famous logician Dignaga and continued his master's work by developing Buddhist logic and epistemology. His time was marked by intense philosophical debates between various schools of Indian thought, including Buddhism, Hinduism, and Jainism. His philosophical work emerged as a response to these intellectual challenges, particularly focusing on the nature of perception, inference, and the ultimate nature of reality.

Dharmakirti's epistemology revolves around the theory of valid cognition (pramāṇa). He argued that there are only two reliable means of knowledge: perception (pratyakṣa) and inference (anumāna). Perception provides direct knowledge, while inference is based on logical reasoning. Dharmakirti emphasized that perception is always free from conceptual elaboration, which makes it a direct encounter with reality. This idea formed the core of his critique against other schools of thought, particularly Nyaya and Mimamsa, which posited a more expansive range of epistemological tools. His view was that other forms of knowledge, such as testimony or analogy, ultimately depend on either perception or inference.

In terms of metaphysics, Dharmakirti argued for the Buddhist concept of momentariness (kṣaṇikatva). According to this view, all phenomena are transient, existing only for a moment before being replaced by new ones. This doctrine had implications for understanding causality, as Dharmakirti proposed that causes and their effects are momentary and that only similar kinds of phenomena can produce one another. This is a key feature of his rejection of the concept of permanent substances, as upheld by Hindu schools like Nyaya and Vedanta. For Dharmakirti, all that exists are momentary events conditioned by previous causes.

Dharmakirti also made significant contributions to Buddhist ethics. He advocated for a form of consequentialism, where ethical actions are judged by their results, particularly in terms of reducing suffering and promoting liberation from the cycle of birth and death (samsara). His ethical philosophy is intertwined with his epistemology, as valid cognition was seen as essential for understanding the nature of reality, which in turn leads to ethical living. By understanding the impermanence and interdependent nature of all things, individuals could make ethical decisions aligned with the ultimate goal of enlightenment.

Overall, Dharmakirti's influence extended beyond Buddhism into Indian philosophy as a whole. His ideas were hotly debated by Hindu and Jain philosophers, and his logical methods were adopted and adapted by later thinkers, both Buddhist and non-Buddhist. His works, particularly the "Pramanavarttika," became foundational texts in Buddhist philosophy, especially in Tibet, where they continue to be studied to this day.

Heraclitus (c. 535 – 475 BCE)

Heraclitus, a pre-Socratic philosopher from Ephesus, is best known for his doctrine of change and the unity of opposites. Living in a time of intellectual ferment in Ionia, Heraclitus challenged the views of earlier thinkers, such as Pythagoras and the Milesians, who sought to identify a stable, unchanging principle behind the universe. Heraclitus' work represents a radical departure from the belief in a static cosmos, as he emphasized the inherent instability and flux of all things. Often referred to as the "Weeping Philosopher" due to his melancholic view of human nature, Heraclitus saw change as the essential nature of reality.

Central to Heraclitus' philosophy is the idea that change is constant and fundamental to the universe. He famously stated, "You cannot step into the same river twice," emphasizing that everything is in a state of perpetual flux. For Heraclitus, the world is characterized by a process of becoming, where nothing remains fixed or permanent. This view directly contrasts with earlier philosophers who believed in the existence of an unchanging substance underlying the diversity of the natural world. Heraclitus argued that the only constant in the universe is change itself, making stability an illusion.

Another key aspect of Heraclitus' thought is the unity of opposites. He believed that opposites, such as life and death, war and peace, and day and night, are not mutually exclusive but are interconnected and define each other. This tension between opposites is what drives the continuous process of change in the universe. Heraclitus argued that conflict and strife are necessary for harmony, as they create the balance that underpins the cosmos. This idea of unity through opposition was a significant departure from earlier thinkers who saw conflict as a source of disorder rather than a fundamental aspect of the natural world.

Heraclitus also introduced the concept of the Logos, a rational principle that governs the universe. The Logos is an impersonal, universal law that ensures the coherence and order of the cosmos amid the constant flux. While the world is in a state of perpetual change, the Logos provides a structure within which this change occurs. Heraclitus believed that most people fail to recognize the Logos because they are preoccupied with their individual perspectives. Only through deep reflection can one understand the underlying order that governs the universe and embrace the inevitability of change.

Heraclitus' philosophy had a profound influence on later thinkers, particularly the Stoics, who adopted his concept of the Logos as a central part of their worldview. His emphasis on the ever-changing nature of reality also resonated with later existential and process philosophers. Although his work survives only in fragments, Heraclitus' ideas continue to be a vital part of Western philosophical tradition, offering a vision of a universe defined by change, conflict, and the pursuit of understanding through the recognition of underlying patterns.

Parmenides (c. 515 – 450 BCE)

Parmenides, a pre-Socratic philosopher from Elea in southern Italy, is regarded as the founder of the Eleatic school of thought. His most significant work, a poem titled On Nature, outlines his views on metaphysics and ontology. Parmenides lived during a time when Greek philosophers were beginning to question earlier cosmological theories and explore the nature of existence itself. In contrast to Heraclitus, who emphasized change, Parmenides is known for his radical claim that change is impossible, and that reality is one, unchanging, and eternal. His work marks a pivotal moment in the history of Western metaphysics.

The central argument of Parmenides' philosophy is that "what is, is," meaning that only being or existence is real, and non-being or nothingness cannot exist. This leads him to deny the reality of change and motion, which he argues are illusory. According to Parmenides, for something to change, it must come into being from nothing or pass into non-being, both of which are logically impossible. Therefore, the world of sensory experience, where things appear to change, is deceptive. Parmenides maintained that only reason can reveal the truth about reality, which is that it is eternal, unchanging, and indivisible.

Parmenides further developed this argument by distinguishing between the way of truth and the way of opinion. The way of truth, based on reason, reveals that being is eternal, unified, and unchanging. The way of opinion, by contrast, is based on sensory perception and leads to false conclusions about the world, such as the belief in change, multiplicity, and time. Parmenides rejected the evidence of the senses as unreliable and argued that only through rational thought could one access the true nature of reality. This distinction between reason and perception was a significant departure from earlier philosophers, who had relied more heavily on empirical observation.

Another important aspect of Parmenides' philosophy is his conception of being as a single, undivided whole. He argued that if reality is one, it cannot be divided into separate entities or parts. This led him to conclude that the apparent multiplicity of things in the world is an illusion, and that true reality is an unchanging, homogeneous sphere of being. Parmenides' emphasis on the unity and indivisibility of being challenged the views of earlier thinkers who believed in a cosmos composed of many different elements and forces.

Parmenides' ideas had a profound influence on later philosophers, particularly Plato and Aristotle, who grappled with his conception of being. His rejection of change and multiplicity forced subsequent thinkers to develop new approaches to metaphysics, balancing the insights of Parmenides with the reality of the changing world. Although Parmenides' work survives only in fragments, his contributions to the study of being and the limits of sensory perception remain foundational in the history of Western philosophy.

Empedocles (c. 495 BCE – c. 435 BCE)

Empedocles was a pre-Socratic philosopher, poet, and mystic from Acragas (modern Agrigento) in Sicily. A figure of both intellectual and political significance, he is said to have been involved in his city's governance, advocating for democratic reforms against the tyranny of oligarchs. His era was one of intense philosophical innovation, where thinkers sought to explain the natural world without resorting to mythology. Empedocles was heavily influenced by the Pythagorean emphasis on harmony and by earlier Ionian philosophers, particularly Parmenides and Heraclitus. His philosophical and mystical teachings were disseminated through two epic poems, On Nature and Purifications, though only fragments survive.

Empedocles is best known for his cosmological theory of the four elements: earth, air, fire, and water. He proposed that these elements are the fundamental constituents of all matter and cannot be created or destroyed. This notion, which he referred to as "roots," represented an early attempt to provide a unified framework for understanding the diversity of the natural world. He introduced the opposing cosmic forces of Love (Philia) and Strife (Neikos), which act as agents of unity and division, respectively, shaping the cycles of creation and destruction.

In addition to his materialist cosmology, Empedocles also ventured into biology and the origin of life. He described a quasi-evolutionary process where random combinations of body parts emerged and survived based on their functionality. While not a fully developed evolutionary theory, this idea marked a significant departure from teleological explanations of nature. Empedocles also offered an explanation for sensory perception, suggesting that external objects emit effluences that interact with corresponding pores in the human body. This mechanistic view of sensation contributed to the development of ancient epistemology and foreshadowed later scientific theories.

Empedocles' philosophical work was deeply intertwined with his mystical and religious beliefs. He claimed to be a divine figure and a spiritual guide, reportedly performing miracles such as controlling the winds and reviving the dead. He adhered to the Pythagorean doctrine of reincarnation, teaching that souls are punished for their transgressions by being reincarnated in various forms until purified. His poem Purifications emphasized the ethical dimensions of life, urging individuals to avoid the killing of animals and to strive for spiritual enlightenment. This fusion of philosophical inquiry with religious practice made him a unique figure in Greek thought.

Empedocles' legacy lies in his synthesis of materialist and mystical perspectives. His concept of the four elements influenced later philosophers such as Aristotle, who integrated it into his own theories of nature. Meanwhile, the dual forces of Love and Strife prefigured ideas of dynamic balance in later metaphysical systems. Although some of his claims were deemed extravagant or self-aggrandizing, his work bridged the gap between mythological cosmologies and rational explanations, leaving an indelible mark on both philosophy and science. His vision of a cyclical universe governed by fundamental principles remains a cornerstone of pre-Socratic thought.

Anaxagoras (c. 500 – 428 BCE)

Anaxagoras was a pre-Socratic philosopher from Clazomenae in Ionia, who later moved to Athens, becoming one of the most influential thinkers of his time. He was the first philosopher to bring philosophy to Athens, where his ideas deeply influenced figures like Socrates and Pericles. Anaxagoras is best known for introducing the concept of nous (mind) as the organizing principle of the cosmos, and for his pluralistic view of the universe, which departed from the earlier monistic approaches of thinkers like Thales and Anaximenes. His work marks a significant advancement in Greek thought, moving toward more sophisticated metaphysical and cosmological theories.

Anaxagoras proposed that everything in the universe is composed of infinitesimally small particles, which he called "seeds" (spermata). Unlike earlier philosophers who sought a single fundamental substance to explain the diversity of matter, Anaxagoras argued that all things contain a mixture of different particles, but that certain types of particles dominate in each substance. For example, a piece of gold contains not only gold particles but also particles of stone, wood, and other materials, though the gold particles predominate. This theory allowed Anaxagoras to account for the diversity and complexity of the natural world without relying on the notion of a single underlying substance.

To explain how these particles are arranged and organized, Anaxagoras introduced the concept of nous (mind). Nous is an infinite, eternal, and intelligent force that governs the cosmos, directing the movement and arrangement of particles to form the objects and phenomena we observe. Unlike the passive elements, nous is an active and dynamic principle that imposes order on the chaotic mixture of particles. Anaxagoras believed that nous was responsible for the creation and organization of the universe, making it one of the earliest concepts of an intelligent force guiding the cosmos. This idea would later influence philosophers like Plato and Aristotle.

Anaxagoras also contributed to early scientific thought, particularly in the fields of astronomy and geology. He was one of the first philosophers to suggest that the sun was a fiery mass larger than the Peloponnesus, challenging traditional Greek views of the sun as a small, divine chariot. Anaxagoras also theorized that the moon reflected the sun's light and that the stars were distant fiery objects. His naturalistic explanations of celestial phenomena often clashed with religious beliefs, leading to his eventual prosecution for impiety in Athens. Nevertheless, his willingness to question established views and provide rational explanations for natural events was groundbreaking.

Anaxagoras' influence on later philosophy and science was profound. His concept of nous as an intelligent, ordering principle was a precursor to later ideas about the role of mind and reason in the universe. His pluralistic approach to matter also laid the groundwork for the development of atomism and other theories of the composition of matter. Anaxagoras' blend of metaphysical speculation and scientific inquiry made him a pivotal figure in the transition from mythological to rational explanations of the natural world.

Protagoras (c. 490 – 420 BCE)

Protagoras, a pre-Socratic philosopher from Abdera, Thrace, is widely regarded as one of the most important figures in the development of Sophism, a movement that emphasized rhetoric, relativism, and skepticism. He lived during a time when the Greek city-states were experiencing intellectual flourishing, particularly in Athens, where Protagoras spent much of his career. He was a contemporary of Socrates and Pericles and was highly sought after as a teacher of rhetoric and practical wisdom. Protagoras is most famous for his relativistic claim that "man is the measure of all things."

Protagoras' famous statement—"man is the measure of all things"—captures his belief in the subjective nature of truth and knowledge. He argued that knowledge and truth are not absolute but are relative to the individual's perception. This means that what is true for one person may not be true for another, as truth is dependent on individual experience and perspective. This relativistic approach stood in stark contrast to the ideas of philosophers like Parmenides and Plato, who sought to identify universal truths. For Protagoras, human perception and experience shaped reality, and there was no objective truth beyond this.

In addition to his theory of relativism, Protagoras is known for his contributions to the philosophy of ethics and morality. He believed that moral values were also relative and shaped by societal norms and conventions rather than being grounded in any absolute or divine law. This view led to the idea that laws and customs should be evaluated based on their practical benefits to society rather than their adherence to some universal moral code. Protagoras emphasized the importance of education in developing good citizens who could participate effectively in the democratic processes of the city-state.

Protagoras also played a key role in the development of rhetorical theory, particularly in the context of legal and political debate. He taught his students the art of persuasion, focusing on the skillful use of language to influence others. Protagoras believed that effective communication was essential for success in public life, especially in democratic Athens, where persuasion was crucial in both the assembly and the courts. His emphasis on rhetoric made him a controversial figure, as critics like Plato accused the Sophists of using their skills for manipulation rather than the pursuit of truth.

Protagoras' legacy is complex, as he was both celebrated for his rhetorical prowess and criticized for his relativism. His ideas laid the groundwork for later philosophical discussions on the nature of truth, ethics, and language. Although much of his work has been lost, Protagoras' influence can be seen in the development of humanism, skepticism, and pragmatism in Western thought. His relativistic approach to knowledge and morality challenged the search for universal truths and paved the way for a more flexible understanding of human experience.

Dignaga (c. 480 – 540 CE)

Dignaga was one of the most influential figures in the development of Buddhist logic and epistemology. Born in southern India, Dignaga was originally trained in Hinayana teachings, but he later became a student of Vasubandhu and was profoundly influenced by the Mahayana tradition. His works on logic, perception, and inference set the stage for a new era of Buddhist philosophical inquiry. Dignaga's texts, such as the Pramanasamuccaya (Compendium of Valid Cognition), had a lasting influence not only in Buddhist philosophy but also in Indian and Tibetan intellectual traditions.

Dignaga's philosophy arose in response to both internal Buddhist debates and external challenges from other Indian philosophical schools, such as the Nyaya school of Hindu philosophy. At the time, Buddhist thinkers were engaged in discussions about the nature of knowledge, perception, and reality, leading Dignaga to develop a sophisticated system of logic to defend Buddhist metaphysics. His focus on valid cognition (pramana) sought to establish a reliable means of distinguishing valid knowledge from erroneous perception, laying the groundwork for later epistemological developments in both Buddhist and Indian philosophy.

At the core of Dignaga's epistemology is the distinction between perception (pratyaksha) and inference (anumana) as two types of valid cognition. According to Dignaga, perception is direct, non-conceptual experience of objects, free from mental constructs. Inference, on the other hand, involves reasoning based on perception and allows individuals to derive knowledge about things that are not directly perceived. This distinction helped clarify how humans engage with the world and make judgments about reality. Dignaga's focus on the reliability of these two means of knowledge was central to his epistemological theory.

Dignaga's theory of perception was particularly important in refuting the realist philosophies of the time, which posited the existence of an external world independent of perception. In contrast, Dignaga argued that what we perceive as the external world is a construction of consciousness and that the mind plays an active role in shaping our experiences. His work on mental representations influenced later Buddhist thinkers who sought to reconcile the nature of reality with human cognition. Dignaga's insights into the constructed nature of perception also prefigured modern philosophical debates about phenomenology and constructivism.

One of Dignaga's most significant contributions was his theory of apoha (exclusion), which he developed to explain how words and concepts relate to reality. According to this theory, words do not correspond to inherent essences in objects but function by excluding everything that they are not. For instance, the word "cow" does not signify an essential cow-ness but rather excludes all non-cow entities. This radical rethinking of language and conceptual thought had far-reaching implications for both Buddhist and Indian philosophy, challenging essentialist views of language and meaning and influencing later thinkers such as Dharmakirti and Madhyamaka philosophers.

Socrates (c. 470 – 399 BCE)

Socrates, one of the most influential figures in Western philosophy, was born in Athens during a period of political instability and intellectual growth. Despite leaving no written works of his own, his ideas were preserved by his students, particularly Plato. Socrates is best known for his method of inquiry, the Socratic method, which involved asking probing questions to stimulate critical thinking and expose contradictions in the beliefs of others. He spent much of his life engaging in public debates and discussions, challenging conventional wisdom and questioning the moral values of Athenian society.

Socrates' philosophy centered on the pursuit of wisdom and the examination of human life. He famously declared that "the unexamined life is not worth living," emphasizing the importance of self-reflection and ethical inquiry. Socrates believed that true wisdom lay in recognizing one's own ignorance, as this recognition opened the path to genuine knowledge. He rejected the Sophist approach of relativism, arguing that there were objective truths, particularly in matters of morality. For Socrates, virtue was the highest good, and knowledge of virtue was essential for living a good life.

One of Socrates' key contributions to philosophy was his concept of ethical intellectualism, which holds that knowledge is the foundation of virtuous action. He believed that if people truly understood what was good, they would naturally choose to act in accordance with it. In this sense, Socrates viewed moral wrongdoing as a result of ignorance rather than willful evil. He also emphasized the unity of the virtues, arguing that qualities such as courage, justice, and temperance were interconnected and could not be separated from the pursuit of knowledge.

Socrates' method of inquiry, known as the Socratic method, involved asking a series of questions to lead his interlocutors to a deeper understanding of the issues being discussed. This method was designed to expose contradictions in their beliefs and to encourage them to think critically about their assumptions. The Socratic method has had a lasting impact on the development of critical thinking and is still used in education and legal training today. Socrates' focus on dialogue and questioning set him apart from earlier philosophers who were more concerned with providing definitive answers.

Socrates' philosophical career came to a tragic end when he was put on trial for impiety and corrupting the youth of Athens. He was sentenced to death by drinking hemlock, a fate he accepted with calmness and dignity. His trial and execution are depicted in Plato's Apology, where Socrates defends his role as a gadfly to the Athenian state, challenging its citizens to pursue virtue and wisdom. Socrates' death solidified his legacy as a martyr for philosophy, and his ideas continue to influence discussions on ethics, politics, and education.

Mozi (c. 470 – c. 391 BCE)

Mozi, also known as Mo Tzu, was a Chinese philosopher who founded Mohism, a philosophical school that challenged the dominant Confucian worldview in ancient China. Mozi lived during the Warring States period, a time of great social and political upheaval. His philosophy arose as a response to the chaos of his era, offering an alternative to both Confucianism and Daoism. Unlike Confucius, who emphasized hierarchical relationships and ritual propriety, Mozi focused on universal love, meritocracy, and practical solutions to social problems.

At the core of Mozi's philosophy is the concept of "universal love" (jian ai), which advocates for impartial care and concern for all people, regardless of their social status or familial ties. Mozi believed that many of the problems in society, such as war, poverty, and inequality, were caused by people prioritizing their own families and interests over the common good. In contrast to Confucianism, which placed a strong emphasis on filial piety and loyalty to one's kin, Mozi argued that people should extend their love and care to all individuals equally. He saw universal love as the foundation for peace and social harmony.

Mozi was also a strong advocate for meritocracy, arguing that leaders should be chosen based on their abilities and moral character rather than their noble birth. He believed that rulers should act as moral exemplars and that their legitimacy derived from their ability to care for their subjects and promote the common good. In this sense, Mozi's philosophy was highly practical and focused on addressing the needs of the population. He rejected the lavish rituals and ceremonies promoted by Confucianism, viewing them as wasteful and unnecessary distractions from the real work of governance.

In addition to his ethical and political ideas, Mozi made significant contributions to military theory. He was a proponent of defensive warfare and developed strategies for protecting cities from attack. Mozi believed that war was one of the greatest evils in society and that it arose from rulers' selfishness and aggression. He argued that rulers should prioritize the welfare of their people over territorial expansion and personal glory. His writings on military strategy emphasized the importance of preparedness, discipline, and the moral responsibility of rulers to avoid unnecessary conflict.

Mozi's philosophy of universal love, meritocracy, and anti-war sentiment made him a unique figure in Chinese thought. While Mohism never gained the same influence as Confucianism, Mozi's ideas had a significant impact on Chinese political theory and ethics. His emphasis on practicality, egalitarianism, and the welfare of the people set him apart from other philosophers of his time, and his critiques of Confucianism provided a valuable alternative perspective in the intellectual landscape of ancient China.

Democritus (c. 460 – c. 370 BCE)

Democritus, a pre-Socratic philosopher from Abdera in Thrace, is best known for his development of the atomic theory of the universe. He was a student of Leucippus, with whom he shared the belief that the cosmos is composed of indivisible, eternal particles called atoms. Democritus lived during a time when Greek philosophy was evolving from mythological explanations of the world to more rational and scientific theories. His ideas about the nature of matter and the universe represented a major departure from earlier philosophical views, emphasizing the material and mechanistic nature of reality.

At the core of Democritus' philosophy is the theory that the universe is made up of tiny, indivisible particles called atoms (atomos), which move through the void. These atoms are eternal, indestructible, and vary in shape and size, and their combinations form the different objects and phenomena we observe. Democritus believed that everything in the universe, from the stars to human beings, is the result of the random movement and combination of atoms. His atomic theory was a significant advancement in natural philosophy, as it provided a mechanistic explanation for the diversity and complexity of the natural world.

Democritus argued that qualities like warmth, coldness, taste, and color are subjective, meaning they exist only in human perception and not inherently in objects. This view, often referred to as "secondary qualities," positioned Democritus as an early figure in the philosophical tradition that distinguishes between the reality of objects and the way humans experience them. He believed that atoms themselves do not have these perceptual qualities; rather, they possess only size, shape, and motion. These qualities combine in various ways to create the phenomena we experience through our senses, which makes Democritus an early materialist.

In addition to his atomic theory, Democritus made contributions to ethics and epistemology. He believed that human happiness, or eudaimonia, was achieved through moderation and the cultivation of the soul. Democritus proposed that tranquility, or "cheerfulness" (euthymia), was the highest good and that it could be attained by living a balanced life and controlling one's desires. In his view, happiness was not the result of external pleasures but of maintaining an inner harmony. This ethical approach was consistent with his atomism, as he believed that the soul itself was composed of finer, more spherical atoms, and that its balance was essential for personal well-being.

Though much of Democritus' work has been lost, his atomic theory became a cornerstone of later scientific thought, particularly influencing figures like Epicurus and, much later, modern scientists such as John Dalton and Albert Einstein. His materialistic view of the universe, combined with his ethical and epistemological insights, made him one of the most important thinkers of the pre-Socratic era. His contributions to the understanding of the physical world and the nature of human perception continue to resonate in both philosophy and science today.

Antisthenes (c. 445 – 365 BCE)

Antisthenes, a pupil of Socrates, was a Greek philosopher who founded the Cynic school of philosophy. Born in Athens, Antisthenes was initially a student of the sophist Gorgias but later became a disciple of Socrates, adopting and adapting his teacher's ethical teachings. Antisthenes lived during a period of political upheaval in Athens following the Peloponnesian War, and his philosophy arose as a reaction to the social and moral decline he observed in Athenian society. His emphasis on simplicity, self-sufficiency, and virtue laid the groundwork for the later development of Cynicism.

Antisthenes' philosophy was deeply influenced by Socratic thought, particularly the idea that virtue is the only true good. Like Socrates, Antisthenes believed that external possessions and material wealth were irrelevant to happiness and that virtue alone was sufficient for a fulfilling life. He argued that living in accordance with nature, rather than societal conventions, was the key to achieving true happiness. This focus on living a virtuous life through self-discipline and rejecting unnecessary desires became a central tenet of Cynicism, a philosophy that would later be epitomized by Diogenes of Sinope.

One of the defining features of Antisthenes' thought was his rejection of pleasure as a legitimate goal in life. He viewed pleasure as a distraction from the pursuit of virtue and believed that indulging in physical pleasures weakened the soul. Instead, Antisthenes advocated for asceticism and self-control, arguing that true freedom came from mastering one's desires rather than being enslaved by them. This austere approach to life set him apart from other philosophical schools of his time, which often valued pleasure, such as the Hedonists and the later Epicureans.

In addition to his ethical views, Antisthenes was critical of traditional education and rhetoric, believing that these practices often led people away from virtue and toward the pursuit of fame or wealth. He emphasized the importance of direct, honest speech and simplicity in communication, rejecting the elaborate rhetorical techniques used by the Sophists. Antisthenes believed that wisdom was not found in intellectual debates or abstract reasoning but in practical living and the cultivation of moral character.

Antisthenes' influence on later philosophy was significant, particularly in the development of Cynicism. His ideas about living in accordance with nature, rejecting societal conventions, and the importance of self-sufficiency were adopted and expanded by Diogenes of Sinope, who became the most famous Cynic. Antisthenes' commitment to living a life of virtue and simplicity left a lasting impact on Hellenistic philosophy and later influenced Stoicism, which shared many of Cynicism's ethical principles.

Diogenes of Sinope (c. 412 – 323 BCE)

Diogenes of Sinope, one of the most famous figures of the Cynic school of philosophy, is best known for his radical rejection of social conventions and materialism. Born in Sinope, on the coast of the Black Sea, Diogenes was exiled from his home city for defacing currency. He eventually made his way to Athens, where he became a student of Antisthenes, the founder of Cynicism. Diogenes' philosophy arose in response to what he saw as the moral corruption and superficiality of Athenian society. He advocated for a life of simplicity, self-sufficiency, and virtue, often through provocative and unconventional behavior.

At the heart of Diogenes' philosophy is the idea of living in accordance with nature. He believed that human beings had become corrupted by society's artificial values and that the only way to achieve happiness was to return to a more natural, unadorned way of life. Diogenes famously lived in a large ceramic jar (often misinterpreted as a barrel) and owned very few possessions, embodying his belief that material wealth and comfort were unnecessary for a fulfilling life. His ascetic lifestyle was a direct challenge to the materialism and decadence of Athenian society.

Diogenes is also known for his sharp wit and provocative actions, which he used to expose the hypocrisy and pretensions of others. He would often perform public stunts to demonstrate his philosophical ideas, such as walking around Athens with a lantern in broad daylight, claiming to be looking for an honest man but never finding one. Through these acts, Diogenes sought to criticize the moral decay he observed in Athenian society and to encourage people to question their values and live more authentically. He believed that wisdom and virtue could only be achieved through self-discipline and a rejection of societal norms.

Another important aspect of Diogenes' philosophy was his rejection of social hierarchies and distinctions. He believed that all human beings were equal in their ability to live virtuously and that societal divisions based on wealth, status, or power were artificial and meaningless. Diogenes treated both the wealthy and the poor with equal disdain, often mocking the powerful for their vanity and corruption. His egalitarian views made him a controversial figure in Athens, where social hierarchies were deeply ingrained.

Diogenes' influence on later philosophical traditions, particularly Stoicism, was significant. His emphasis on living in accordance with nature, rejecting societal conventions, and cultivating personal virtue had a profound impact on Stoic thinkers like Zeno of Citium, who founded Stoicism in the early 3rd century BCE. Diogenes' unconventional lifestyle and relentless pursuit of truth continue to be admired by those who value simplicity, authenticity, and moral courage.

Plato (c. 428 – 348 BCE)

Plato, a student of Socrates and teacher of Aristotle, is one of the most influential figures in Western philosophy. Born into a wealthy and aristocratic family in Athens, Plato was deeply affected by the execution of his mentor, Socrates, and this event significantly shaped his philosophical outlook. Plato founded the Academy, one of the first institutions of higher learning in the Western world, where he taught and developed his philosophical ideas. His work emerged during a time of political instability in Athens, and much of his philosophy addressed questions of justice, governance, and the nature of knowledge.

One of Plato's most significant contributions to philosophy is his Theory of Forms. According to Plato, the physical world is not the true reality but merely a shadow of a higher, unchanging realm of Forms, or Ideas. These Forms represent the perfect, eternal versions of objects and concepts, such as beauty, justice, and equality, which exist independently of the material world. Plato argued that the objects we perceive through our senses are mere imitations of these perfect Forms. The most famous illustration of this theory is the Allegory of the Cave, where prisoners mistake shadows on a wall for reality, unaware of the true forms casting those shadows.

Plato's epistemology is closely tied to his Theory of Forms. He believed that true knowledge is not derived from sensory experience but from intellectual insight into the realm of Forms. In this view, the philosopher, through reason and contemplation, can access the eternal truths of the Forms, whereas ordinary people, relying on their senses, are trapped in a world of illusions. This distinction between knowledge (episteme) and opinion (doxa) is central to Plato's philosophy. For Plato, philosophy is the process of guiding the soul out of ignorance and toward an understanding of the ultimate realities.

In addition to his metaphysical and epistemological contributions, Plato made significant contributions to political philosophy. In his most famous work, The Republic, Plato outlines his vision of an ideal state ruled by philosopher-kings—wise and virtuous rulers who have ascended to an understanding of the Forms, particularly the Form of the Good. Plato believed that only those who had attained true knowledge of justice and goodness were fit to govern, as they would be able to create a harmonious and just society. In this ideal state, individuals would be divided into three classes: rulers, soldiers, and producers, each contributing to the common good according to their abilities and nature.

Plato's influence on Western thought is immeasurable. His ideas on metaphysics, epistemology, ethics, and politics laid the groundwork for much of subsequent philosophy, particularly in the development of idealism. His student, Aristotle, would later challenge and refine many of Plato's theories, but Plato's impact remained central in shaping philosophical discourse for centuries. Plato's works continue to be studied for their profound insights into the nature of reality, knowledge, and human society, making him one of the foundational figures of Western philosophy.

Asanga (c. 4th – 5th century CE)

Asanga was a major figure in the development of Mahayana Buddhism, particularly through his contributions to the Yogachara school, also known as the Mind-Only (Cittamatra) school. Born in the Gandhara region (modern-day Afghanistan/Pakistan), he was initially trained in Hinayana Buddhism but became dissatisfied with its teachings. Withdrew to meditate and study, Asanga is said to have received teachings directly from the Bodhisattva Maitreya, which became central to his philosophy. Asanga's works, along with those of his brother Vasubandhu, became foundational texts for Yogachara and profoundly influenced Buddhist thought in India, China, and Tibet.

Asanga's philosophy emerged during the rise of Mahayana Buddhism, which emphasized the Bodhisattva path and the collective goal of guiding all sentient beings toward enlightenment. In contrast to earlier Buddhist teachings focused on individual enlightenment (arhatship), Asanga's Yogachara teachings explored the nature of consciousness and its role in shaping reality. His work also addressed philosophical challenges within Buddhist thought, particularly the nature of reality and metaphysics, during a time of heightened intellectual inquiry in India.

Central to Asanga's philosophy is the concept of vijnapti-matra, or "consciousness-only." Yogachara holds that all phenomena are projections of consciousness, with the external world being a construction of the mind. Consciousness, in this system, is divided into eight categories, with the alaya-vijnana (storehouse consciousness) being the most significant. This storehouse retains imprints of past experiences that shape future perceptions and actions. According to Asanga, purifying the mind by transforming these imprints is essential to achieving enlightenment, as delusions must be overcome to realize the true nature of reality.

Another major contribution of Asanga is his articulation of the Bodhisattva ideal, prioritizing Buddhahood for the benefit of all sentient beings. For Asanga, a Bodhisattva is motivated by compassion (karuna) and guided by wisdom (prajna), practicing the six perfections (paramitas): generosity, ethics, patience, effort, meditation, and wisdom. His teachings emphasized that personal liberation is inseparable from the well-being of others, placing compassion at the core of his ethical philosophy.

Asanga also introduced the Three Natures doctrine (trisvabhava), which explains how individuals construct reality. These three natures are the imagined (parikalpita), dependent (paratantra), and perfected (parinishpanna). The imagined nature involves the mistaken belief in an independent external reality, while the dependent nature recognizes the interdependent origination of all things. The perfected nature represents the ultimate realization of reality as free from dualistic projections. This doctrine, central to Yogachara, sought to bridge experience and the true nature of consciousness.

Aristotle (384 – 322 BCE)

Aristotle, a student of Plato and tutor to Alexander the Great, is one of the most important figures in Western philosophy. Born in Stagira, a small town in northern Greece, Aristotle moved to Athens to study at Plato's Academy, where he spent 20 years. Although he began as a follower of Plato, Aristotle later developed his own philosophical system, which diverged significantly from his teacher's ideas. Aristotle's work spanned a wide range of subjects, including metaphysics, ethics, politics, biology, and logic, and his comprehensive approach to philosophy laid the foundation for many fields of study.

Aristotle's metaphysics differs sharply from Plato's Theory of Forms. While Plato posited a realm of perfect, unchanging Forms existing beyond the physical world, Aristotle rejected this dualism and argued that the forms, or essences, of things exist within the objects themselves. According to Aristotle, every object is a combination of matter and form. Matter is the substance that makes up an object, while form is its essential nature or structure. For example, the form of a tree is what makes it a tree, while its matter is the physical substance from which it is made. This theory of hylomorphism (the unity of form and matter) underpins much of Aristotle's philosophy.

Aristotle also developed a comprehensive system of logic, which remained the standard for centuries. His Organon, a collection of works on logic, introduced the method of syllogistic reasoning, where conclusions are drawn from two or more premises. For example, in the syllogism "All men are mortal; Socrates is a man; therefore, Socrates is mortal," Aristotle's method demonstrates how rational arguments can lead to valid conclusions. His work on logic was a major contribution to the development of deductive reasoning and scientific inquiry, influencing later philosophers and scientists.

In ethics, Aristotle introduced the concept of the "Golden Mean," a moral philosophy based on moderation and balance. He argued that virtue lies between two extremes: for example, courage is the mean between cowardice and recklessness. Aristotle's ethical philosophy is based on the idea that the ultimate goal of human life is to achieve eudaimonia, or flourishing, through the cultivation of virtues. For Aristotle, living a virtuous life meant developing good habits and making choices in accordance with reason. His ethical theory emphasized practical wisdom and the importance of context in moral decision-making.

Aristotle's influence on Western philosophy is profound and far-reaching. His writings on metaphysics, logic, ethics, and politics shaped the intellectual landscape of the Middle Ages and the Renaissance. In the sciences, Aristotle's work in biology, astronomy, and physics laid the groundwork for scientific inquiry, although many of his theories were later revised or replaced. Nevertheless, Aristotle's method of systematic observation, analysis, and classification set the standard for empirical investigation, and his philosophy continues to be studied and debated to this day.

Mencius (c. 372 – 289 BCE)

Mencius, also known as Mengzi, was a Chinese philosopher and the most famous follower of Confucius. Born in the state of Zou during the Warring States period, Mencius lived in a time of political chaos and moral decline. He studied Confucian teachings and became an advocate for the Confucian ideal of a just and virtuous society. Mencius traveled extensively, advising rulers on matters of governance and ethics, and his dialogues were later recorded in the Book of Mencius, which became one of the core texts of Confucianism. Mencius' philosophy arose in response to the turbulent political climate of his time, and he sought to restore order through the cultivation of virtue.

At the heart of Mencius' philosophy is the belief that human nature is inherently good. He argued that all people are born with innate moral tendencies, such as compassion, righteousness, and a sense of propriety. According to Mencius, these virtues are like seeds that, when nurtured, can grow into full moral character. He believed that moral cultivation was essential for both individuals and rulers, as it led to the development of ren (benevolence) and yi (righteousness), which were necessary for creating a harmonious society. Mencius' view of human nature was more optimistic than that of later Confucians, such as Xunzi, who believed that human nature was inherently selfish.

Mencius also emphasized the importance of virtuous leadership. He believed that rulers should govern through moral example rather than force or coercion. A ruler who embodied the virtues of ren and yi would naturally inspire loyalty and respect from the people, leading to a stable and prosperous state. Mencius was a strong advocate for the Mandate of Heaven, the belief that a ruler's right to govern was based on their moral conduct. If a ruler became corrupt or tyrannical, they would lose the Mandate of Heaven, and the people would be justified in overthrowing them. This idea provided a moral justification for rebellion against unjust rulers.

In addition to his views on governance, Mencius developed a theory of moral psychology. He believed that humans possess an inherent moral sense, which can be cultivated through self-reflection and education. Mencius used the analogy of a child falling into a well to illustrate his point: anyone witnessing such an event would feel an instinctive sense of compassion, which demonstrates the innate goodness of human nature. However, Mencius acknowledged that external circumstances, such as poverty or social disorder, could corrupt these moral instincts, making moral education and virtuous leadership all the more important.

Mencius' contributions to Confucian thought had a lasting impact on Chinese philosophy and governance. His emphasis on the innate goodness of human nature and the importance of moral leadership shaped the development of Confucianism and influenced Chinese political theory for centuries. Mencius' teachings on the Mandate of Heaven and the moral responsibilities of rulers became central to the Confucian tradition, and his ideas continue to be studied and revered in both China and the wider world today.

Zhuangzi (c. 369 – 286 BCE)

Zhuangzi, also known as Chuang Tzu, was a Chinese philosopher and one of the most significant figures in Daoism, second only to Laozi. He lived during the Warring States period, a time of social and political chaos, and his work reflects a deep skepticism toward the rigid social structures and moral codes of his era. Zhuangzi's teachings are recorded in the Zhuangzi, a text that blends humor, parables, and philosophical discourse to convey Daoist principles. His philosophy arose in opposition to both Confucianism and Mohism, offering an alternative vision of life based on spontaneity, freedom, and harmony with the Dao.

Central to Zhuangzi's philosophy is the concept of the Dao, or the Way, which he understood as the underlying force that governs the universe. Unlike Confucius, who emphasized social order and moral responsibility, Zhuangzi advocated for a life lived in accordance with the natural flow of the Dao, free from the constraints of social conventions and human-made distinctions. He believed that the Dao could not be fully grasped through intellectual effort or rigid moral codes, but rather through intuitive understanding and spontaneous action. For Zhuangzi, the highest form of wisdom was to embrace the uncertainties of life and to move harmoniously with the ever-changing nature of the world.

One of Zhuangzi's key ideas is the concept of wu wei, or "non-action," which involves acting in a way that is effortless and in harmony with the Dao. He believed that people often create suffering for themselves by trying to control or impose their will on the world. Instead, Zhuangzi encouraged individuals to let go of their desires and attachments, allowing things to unfold naturally. He used various parables and stories to illustrate this point, such as the tale of the butcher who skillfully carves an ox by following the natural lines of the animal's body, rather than forcing the knife through it. This story exemplifies how mastery and wisdom come from aligning oneself with the Dao, rather than through force or control.

Zhuangzi also rejected the rigid distinctions between right and wrong, good and bad, and other dualities that dominated Confucian and Mohist thought. He argued that these distinctions were artificial and limited human understanding. In one of his most famous stories, Zhuangzi dreams that he is a butterfly, only to awaken and question whether he is a man who dreamed of being a butterfly or a butterfly dreaming of being a man. This parable highlights Zhuangzi's belief that reality is subjective and that human perspectives are inherently limited. For Zhuangzi, true freedom comes from transcending these narrow distinctions and embracing the fluid, ever-changing nature of existence.

Zhuangzi's philosophy of spontaneity, non-attachment, and freedom from societal constraints has had a profound influence on Chinese thought and culture. His rejection of rigid moral codes and his emphasis on living in harmony with the Dao provided a counterbalance to the more structured philosophies of Confucianism and Mohism. Zhuangzi's teachings continue to resonate with those who seek a life of simplicity, spontaneity, and freedom, making him one of the most enduring figures in Daoist philosophy.

Hypatia (c. 360 – 415 CE)

Hypatia of Alexandria was a renowned mathematician, astronomer, and philosopher, and is often considered the last great thinker of the ancient classical world. Born in Alexandria, Egypt, she was the daughter of Theon, a prominent mathematician, who trained her in the intellectual traditions of Greek philosophy and science. Hypatia rose to prominence as the head of the Neoplatonic school in Alexandria, where she taught philosophy, mathematics, and astronomy. Her intellectual career occurred during a time of religious conflict and political instability, as the Roman Empire was transitioning toward Christianity, and her association with the pagan intellectual elite made her a target of hostility.

Hypatia was deeply influenced by Neoplatonism, the philosophical system developed by Plotinus, which emphasized the existence of a transcendent, ineffable source of all reality called the One. As a Neoplatonist, Hypatia taught that the material world is a mere reflection of higher, immaterial realities, and that the goal of philosophy is to ascend from the physical realm to the divine through contemplation and intellectual rigor. She believed that the study of mathematics and astronomy, with their emphasis on abstract and universal truths, provided a pathway to understanding the divine order of the cosmos.

In addition to her philosophical teachings, Hypatia made significant contributions to mathematics and astronomy, although much of her original work has been lost. She is known to have written commentaries on Diophantus's Arithmetica and Ptolemy's Almagest, helping to preserve and transmit these important scientific texts to later generations. Hypatia also worked on refining the astrolabe, an instrument used to measure the positions of stars and planets, and may have contributed to early understandings of conic sections. Her scientific work reflected the Neoplatonic belief in the unity of all knowledge, where mathematics, philosophy, and science were seen as interconnected pursuits leading to the same ultimate truths.

Hypatia's prominence as a female philosopher and scientist made her a unique figure in a male-dominated intellectual world, and she became a symbol of reason, knowledge, and the classical tradition. However, her association with the pagan intellectual elite of Alexandria, combined with her close ties to the city's political leadership, eventually led to her downfall. In 415 CE, amid growing tensions between the Christian bishop Cyril and the Roman governor Orestes, Hypatia was brutally murdered by a Christian mob. Her death marked the decline of the classical intellectual tradition in Alexandria and the triumph of Christian orthodoxy over the pagan philosophical schools.

Despite the tragic end to her life, Hypatia's legacy has endured as a symbol of intellectual courage and the pursuit of knowledge. She is remembered not only for her contributions to philosophy, mathematics, and astronomy but also for her role as a female scholar in a world where women were rarely afforded such opportunities. Hypatia's life and work continue to inspire scholars, particularly in the fields of women's history and the history of science, as a reminder of the enduring value of reason, inquiry, and intellectual freedom.

Pyrrho (c. 360 – 270 BCE)

Pyrrho of Elis was an ancient Greek philosopher and the founder of Pyrrhonism, a school of skepticism that profoundly influenced later philosophical traditions. Pyrrho's life unfolded during the era of Greek expansion following the conquests of Alexander the Great, and it is said that he traveled with Alexander's army to India, where he encountered Eastern philosophers, possibly including practitioners of Indian Buddhism. This exposure to Eastern thought may have contributed to his development of radical skepticism. Upon his return to Greece, Pyrrho articulated a philosophy of doubt that challenged the certainty of knowledge, emphasizing the impossibility of achieving definitive truth.

At the core of Pyrrho's philosophy is the principle of epoché, or the suspension of judgment. Pyrrho argued that for every argument, there exists an equally compelling counterargument, making it impossible to determine which is correct. As a result, human beings should refrain from making absolute judgments about the nature of reality. Pyrrho believed that since nothing could be known for certain, the best course of action was to suspend judgment on all matters. This state of epoché was thought to lead to ataraxia, or mental tranquility, as it freed individuals from the anxiety that comes with trying to discern truth in an uncertain world.

Pyrrho's skepticism extended beyond theoretical concerns about knowledge to practical matters of daily life. He argued that because we cannot be sure of what is truly good or bad, humans should not become emotionally attached to their desires or aversions. Instead, Pyrrho advised that people should live in accordance with appearances, acting according to what seems immediately present, without forming dogmatic beliefs. This ethical stance, rooted in indifference to outcomes, was designed to protect individuals from the emotional disturbances caused by attachment to things beyond their control.

Pyrrho's philosophy challenged not only the claims of knowledge made by other philosophers but also the very foundations of human reasoning and perception. He believed that the senses were unreliable and that reason itself was incapable of providing certainty. This radical skepticism placed him in opposition to philosophical traditions that sought to discover truth through reason, such as the Platonic and Aristotelian schools. However, Pyrrho's focus on achieving mental tranquility through the suspension of judgment found resonance in later philosophical developments, particularly in the Hellenistic period.

Pyrrhonism, as formalized by later philosophers like Sextus Empiricus, became one of the major schools of skepticism in antiquity. While Pyrrho himself left no written works, his influence was preserved through the writings of his followers. His skepticism was a precursor to later developments in Western philosophy, including the works of David Hume and Michel de Montaigne. Pyrrho's legacy endures as a challenge to the idea that humans can ever attain certain knowledge and a reminder of the importance of intellectual humility in the face of uncertainty.

Epicurus (341 – 270 BCE)

Epicurus was a Greek philosopher who founded the school of Epicureanism, which advocated for the pursuit of a tranquil and happy life through the cultivation of pleasure and the avoidance of pain. Born on the island of Samos, Epicurus moved to Athens, where he established his philosophical community, known as "The Garden." This school was one of the few that welcomed men, women, and slaves alike, making it unique in its inclusivity. Epicurus' philosophy arose in the Hellenistic period, a time of great political instability following the conquests of Alexander the Great. His teachings offered an escape from the uncertainties of life by focusing on personal happiness and inner peace.

At the heart of Epicurean philosophy is the idea that the highest good is pleasure, which he defined as the absence of pain in both the body and the soul. However, Epicurus did not advocate for hedonistic excess but for a life of moderation and simplicity. He argued that the most pleasurable life is one free from unnecessary desires and that true pleasure comes from the avoidance of physical pain (aponia) and mental disturbance (ataraxia). By focusing on simple, sustainable pleasures, such as friendship, intellectual contemplation, and moderation, Epicurus believed individuals could achieve a state of inner tranquility.

Epicurus also espoused a materialistic view of the universe, heavily influenced by the atomistic theory of Democritus. He believed that everything, including the soul, is composed of atoms moving through the void. In this mechanistic universe, there is no room for divine intervention or supernatural forces. Epicurus famously rejected the fear of the gods and the afterlife, arguing that the gods, if they existed, were indifferent to human affairs. This belief in a natural, impersonal universe freed his followers from the fear of divine retribution and the anxieties associated with death, allowing them to focus on achieving happiness in the present life.

In addition to his ethical and metaphysical teachings, Epicurus placed a strong emphasis on friendship as a key component of a happy life. He believed that meaningful relationships provided emotional security and were essential to achieving ataraxia. In his community, The Garden, Epicurus and his followers practiced these ideals, living together in a close-knit, supportive environment. Friendship, for Epicurus, was not just a source of pleasure but a fundamental aspect of human flourishing.

Epicureanism became one of the most influential schools of thought in the Hellenistic world, rivaling Stoicism in its appeal. Although often misunderstood as advocating for unrestrained pleasure-seeking, Epicurus' philosophy was deeply concerned with the cultivation of a peaceful and virtuous life. His teachings on the nature of pleasure, the rejection of fear, and the importance of friendship have continued to resonate throughout the centuries, influencing later thinkers such as the Roman poet Lucretius and shaping modern humanistic and materialistic philosophies.

Zeno of Citium (c. 334 – 262 BCE)

Zeno of Citium was a Hellenistic philosopher from Cyprus who founded the Stoic school of philosophy in Athens around 300 BCE. After surviving a shipwreck and arriving in Athens, Zeno became interested in philosophy and studied under several teachers, including Crates of Thebes, a leading Cynic philosopher. Zeno's Stoicism arose during a time of social and political turmoil in the Greek world, as the city-states struggled to maintain their independence in the wake of Alexander the Great's conquests. His philosophy, which emphasized virtue, reason, and emotional resilience, provided individuals with a framework for achieving inner peace amid external chaos.

At the core of Zeno's philosophy is the idea that the universe is governed by a rational, divine principle called the Logos. Zeno taught that everything in the cosmos, including human beings, is part of this divine order, and that true happiness (eudaimonia) comes from living in accordance with nature and the Logos. He believed that the key to achieving happiness was to align one's will with the rational order of the universe, accepting whatever happens as part of a larger, purposeful plan. This acceptance of fate, known as amor fati, became a central tenet of Stoic thought.

Zeno's ethical teachings emphasized the cultivation of virtue as the highest good. He argued that external circumstances, such as wealth, health, and social status, were "indifferent" in the pursuit of happiness, meaning that they neither contributed to nor detracted from true well-being. What truly mattered, according to Zeno, was the development of one's moral character and the ability to live in accordance with reason. The four cardinal virtues of Stoicism—wisdom, courage, justice, and temperance—formed the foundation of Zeno's ethical system, and he believed that living virtuously was the only path to true happiness.

In addition to his ethical and metaphysical teachings, Zeno introduced the concept of apatheia, or freedom from destructive emotions. He argued that emotions such as fear, anger, and desire arise from false judgments about what is valuable in life. By training oneself to view external events with detachment and to focus solely on virtue, Zeno believed that individuals could achieve emotional resilience and inner peace. This emphasis on emotional control and rational detachment became one of the defining features of Stoic philosophy.

Zeno's Stoicism laid the groundwork for one of the most influential philosophical movements of the Hellenistic and Roman periods. His teachings on virtue, rationality, and emotional resilience resonated with individuals seeking to navigate the uncertainties of life in a chaotic world. Zeno's legacy was carried on by later Stoic philosophers, such as Cleanthes, Chrysippus, Epictetus, and Marcus Aurelius, who expanded and refined his ideas, ensuring that Stoicism would remain a central part of Western philosophical thought for centuries to come.

Xunzi (c. 310 – 235 BCE)

Xunzi was a Confucian philosopher who lived during the Warring States period in ancient China, a time of political instability and philosophical debate. He studied in the Jixia Academy and became a major thinker who directly challenged the views of his Confucian predecessor, Mencius. While Mencius believed in the innate goodness of human nature, Xunzi argued that humans are born inherently selfish and that morality must be cultivated through education and strict social structures. His philosophy emerged in response to the chaos of his time, reflecting his belief in the necessity of order and control to maintain a stable society.

Xunzi's central philosophical idea is that human nature (xing) is innately selfish, driven by desires for pleasure, comfort, and survival. He believed that without proper education and guidance, people would naturally act in ways that harm others and destabilize society. Unlike Mencius, who thought that moral virtues were intrinsic and merely needed to be nurtured, Xunzi saw moral development as an artificial construct that must be imposed on humans through ritual (li) and law (fa). For Xunzi, rituals were essential to civilize and discipline human desires, allowing individuals to live in harmony with each other.

Another important aspect of Xunzi's philosophy is his emphasis on education. He argued that through rigorous learning and the practice of Confucian rituals, people could be transformed from selfish beings into virtuous individuals. This process required a conscious effort to follow moral principles and social norms, which Xunzi saw as vital for creating a peaceful and prosperous society. His view of education was not just about intellectual development but about shaping moral character and instilling a deep respect for social hierarchies and traditions.

Xunzi also critiqued mystical elements in Chinese philosophy, particularly those of Daoism, which he believed promoted passivity and irresponsibility. He rejected the Daoist idea of returning to a natural, spontaneous state, arguing instead that civilization and human effort were necessary for progress. Xunzi believed that people should actively cultivate themselves and society through hard work, rituals, and governance. His pragmatic approach made him influential in the development of the Legalist school of thought, which later influenced the authoritarian rule of the Qin dynasty.

Although Xunzi was largely overshadowed by Mencius in later Confucian thought, his ideas played a crucial role in shaping Chinese political philosophy, particularly in emphasizing the role of statecraft and law. His belief that human nature requires regulation through strict social structures and education deeply influenced Chinese governance and the development of Confucian legalism.

Chrysippus (c. 279 – 206 BCE)

Chrysippus of Soli was a Stoic philosopher and is often regarded as the second founder of Stoicism due to his significant contributions in systematizing and expanding the doctrine. He was born in Soli, Cilicia, and later moved to Athens, where he became a student of Cleanthes, the second head of the Stoic school after Zeno of Citium. Chrysippus' philosophical career occurred during a time of intellectual rivalry among different schools of thought in Athens, particularly between the Stoics, Epicureans, and Skeptics. Chrysippus' efforts to solidify Stoicism's foundations made it the most influential philosophical school in the Hellenistic period.

At the heart of Chrysippus' philosophy was the belief that the universe is an orderly and rational system governed by the Logos, the divine reason that pervades all things. He developed Zeno's concept of the Logos further, arguing that everything in the universe is predetermined by divine reason, including human actions. However, unlike other deterministic thinkers, Chrysippus introduced the idea of "compatibilism," the notion that human beings could exercise free will within the framework of this determinism. He believed that while everything is governed by fate, humans could still choose to align their will with the rational order of the universe, thus achieving moral responsibility.

Chrysippus also made significant contributions to Stoic logic, which became an essential part of Stoic philosophy. He refined the Stoic theory of logic by introducing propositional logic, which dealt with whole propositions rather than individual terms, as in Aristotelian logic. Chrysippus' work on conditional statements and logical paradoxes contributed to the development of formal logic, which would later influence medieval and modern philosophy. His rigorous approach to logic helped Stoicism defend its doctrines against attacks from rival schools, particularly the Skeptics, who questioned the possibility of knowledge.

In ethics, Chrysippus emphasized the Stoic belief that virtue is the only true good and that everything else, such as wealth, health, or pleasure, is indifferent. He taught that the path to happiness lies in living in accordance with nature and reason, which involves accepting both the good and bad events in life with equanimity. For Chrysippus, the sage, or wise person, is someone who has attained this perfect harmony with nature and who remains untroubled by external circumstances. This ideal of emotional resilience and moral fortitude became a central tenet of Stoic ethics.

Chrysippus' work had a lasting influence on Stoicism and ensured its survival as a dominant philosophical school in the Hellenistic and Roman periods. His writings, though mostly lost, were widely regarded as the authoritative texts on Stoicism by later Stoics such as Seneca, Epictetus, and Marcus Aurelius. Chrysippus' contributions to logic, ethics, and metaphysics helped shape the development of Stoicism into a comprehensive philosophical system that would influence Western thought for centuries.

Lucretius (c. 99 – 55 BCE)

Lucretius, a Roman poet and philosopher, is best known for his epic philosophical poem De Rerum Natura (On the Nature of Things), which outlines the key principles of Epicureanism. Little is known about Lucretius' life, but his work emerged during the late Roman Republic, a period marked by political turmoil and social unrest. Lucretius sought to popularize and explain the Epicurean worldview to a Roman audience, offering a rational explanation of the universe as an antidote to the fear of death and the gods. His poem represents one of the most comprehensive accounts of Epicurean philosophy in Latin.

At the core of Lucretius' philosophy is the Epicurean belief in atomism, the idea that the universe is composed of indivisible particles called atoms that move through the void. Lucretius explains that all things, including the human soul, are made up of these atoms, and that the processes of creation and destruction are the result of their random interactions. He argues that everything in the universe, from the stars to human beings, follows natural laws and is not subject to divine intervention. This materialistic view of the cosmos frees individuals from the fear of the gods, who, Lucretius contends, are indifferent to human affairs.

Lucretius also addresses the Epicurean view of death, which is central to his ethical philosophy. He argues that death is nothing to fear because it is simply the dissolution of the atoms that make up the body and soul. Since the soul is material and perishes along with the body, there is no consciousness after death, and therefore no pain or suffering. This argument, known as the "symmetry argument," posits that death should be viewed with the same indifference as the time before one's birth, when one did not exist. By eliminating the fear of death, Lucretius believes that individuals can achieve peace of mind and live more fulfilling lives.

In addition to his metaphysical and ethical teachings, Lucretius provides a naturalistic explanation of various phenomena, such as the movements of the stars, the weather, and the origins of life. He seeks to demonstrate that all events in the natural world can be explained through the interaction of atoms, without resorting to supernatural explanations. Lucretius' goal is to dispel the ignorance and superstitions that he believed caused fear and misery in people's lives. By understanding the natural world through reason and observation, individuals can live in harmony with nature and achieve the tranquility that Epicurus advocated.

Lucretius' De Rerum Natura had a profound influence on later Roman thinkers, as well as Renaissance philosophers and scientists such as Galileo and Isaac Newton. His atomistic and naturalistic worldview anticipated many developments in modern science, particularly in physics and biology. Though his work was not widely appreciated in his own time, Lucretius' poetic articulation of Epicurean philosophy has left a lasting legacy in both literature and philosophy.

Philo of Alexandria (c. 20 BCE – 50 CE)

Philo of Alexandria was a Hellenistic Jewish philosopher whose work attempted to harmonize Greek philosophy, particularly Platonism and Stoicism, with Jewish religious thought. Born into a wealthy and influential Jewish family in Alexandria, Egypt, Philo lived during a period of cultural and intellectual exchange between the Greek and Jewish worlds. Alexandria was a major center of learning, and Philo was deeply influenced by the philosophical traditions that flourished there. His works, which include extensive commentaries on the Hebrew Bible, sought to demonstrate that Greek philosophy and Jewish theology were not only compatible but mutually reinforcing.

Philo's philosophy is best known for its use of allegory to interpret the Hebrew scriptures. He believed that the literal meaning of the Bible often concealed deeper, philosophical truths that could be uncovered through allegorical reading. For Philo, the stories of the Bible were not just historical events but symbolic representations of spiritual and metaphysical realities. For example, Philo interpreted the account of the creation in Genesis as an allegory for the creation of the rational soul and the development of human intellect. This approach allowed him to integrate Platonic and Stoic ideas into his understanding of Jewish theology.

One of Philo's key contributions to philosophy is his concept of the Logos, which he identified with the divine reason that orders the universe. Drawing on Platonic and Stoic thought, Philo described the Logos as an intermediary between God and the material world. The Logos, according to Philo, is both the creative principle through which God fashioned the universe and the means by which humans can come to know God. This idea of the Logos as a bridge between the divine and the material would later influence early Christian theology, particularly in the development of the doctrine of the Incarnation.

Philo's ethical philosophy was also deeply influenced by Greek thought, particularly Stoicism. He believed that the highest goal of human life was to live in accordance with reason and to cultivate virtue, which he saw as the path to achieving unity with the divine. For Philo, the virtuous life involved overcoming the passions and desires of the body in order to focus on the contemplation of God and the pursuit of wisdom. His ethical teachings reflect a synthesis of Stoic ideas about self-discipline and Jewish teachings about obedience to God's will.

Philo's work had a lasting influence on both Jewish and Christian thought. His allegorical interpretation of scripture provided a model for later Christian theologians such as Origen, and his concept of the Logos played a crucial role in the development of Christian doctrine. Although Philo's attempt to harmonize Greek philosophy with Judaism was not widely accepted by his Jewish contemporaries, his writings have been preserved and continue to be studied for their insights into the relationship between faith and reason.

Epictetus (c. 50 – 135 CE)

Epictetus was a Stoic philosopher born into slavery in the Roman Empire, likely in Hierapolis, Phrygia. He gained his freedom early in life and went on to become one of the most influential Stoic teachers of his time. After studying under the Stoic philosopher Musonius Rufus, Epictetus established his own school in Nicopolis, where he taught Stoicism to students from all over the empire. His teachings were recorded by his student Arrian in works such as the Discourses and the Enchiridion, which became foundational texts of Stoic philosophy. Epictetus lived during a period of political instability in the Roman Empire, and his philosophy provided practical guidance for navigating the uncertainties of life.

At the heart of Epictetus' philosophy is the distinction between what is within our control and what is outside of our control. He taught that while external events, such as wealth, health, and social status, are beyond our control, our thoughts, beliefs, and actions are entirely within our power. Epictetus argued that true freedom and happiness come from focusing on what we can control—our own mind and actions—while accepting everything else with equanimity. This core principle of Stoic thought is known as the dichotomy of control, and it became central to Epictetus' teachings on how to live a virtuous and fulfilling life.

Epictetus also emphasized the Stoic belief in the importance of living in accordance with nature and reason. He taught that human beings, as rational creatures, are capable of understanding the natural order of the universe, which is governed by the Logos. For Epictetus, virtue consists in aligning one's will with the rational and divine order of the cosmos, accepting whatever happens as part of a larger, purposeful plan. This acceptance of fate, known as amor fati, is a hallmark of Stoic philosophy, and Epictetus believed that it was essential for achieving tranquility and freedom from destructive emotions.

Another key aspect of Epictetus' teachings is his focus on the development of self-discipline and emotional resilience. He believed that individuals could train themselves to respond to life's challenges with reason and composure, rather than being overwhelmed by fear, anger, or desire. Epictetus emphasized the importance of cultivating an inner fortress of virtue, which could withstand the external turmoil of the world. His practical advice on how to deal with adversity, such as illness, poverty, or even death, has made his philosophy enduringly relevant for those seeking guidance in difficult times.

Epictetus' influence on later Stoic thinkers, including Marcus Aurelius, was profound, and his works have continued to resonate with philosophers, military leaders, and modern practitioners of Stoicism. His emphasis on personal responsibility, resilience, and the pursuit of virtue has made him one of the most accessible and practical Stoic philosophers. Even today, Epictetus' teachings on the dichotomy of control and the importance of focusing on one's own actions continue to inspire those seeking to live a more purposeful and balanced life.

Marcus Aurelius (121 – 180 CE)

Marcus Aurelius, born in Rome in 121 CE, was a Roman emperor and Stoic philosopher. He ruled as the last of the so-called "Five Good Emperors" and is remembered not only for his leadership but also for his philosophical work Meditations, which was written as a personal journal during his military campaigns. Marcus lived in a time of political turbulence, military conflict, and the spread of new religions like Christianity. His Stoic philosophy, however, reflects a deeply personal attempt to maintain inner peace and moral virtue amid the chaos of the empire.

Central to Marcus Aurelius' philosophy is the Stoic belief in rationality and virtue as the keys to living a good life. He believed that the universe is governed by a rational principle, the Logos, and that humans, as rational beings, must live in harmony with this natural order. For Marcus, virtue was the only true good, and he emphasized the importance of wisdom, justice, courage, and self-discipline. He taught that external events are beyond our control, and the only thing we can truly control is our response to these events. This perspective is evident in his writings, where he frequently reminds himself to accept fate and maintain equanimity in the face of adversity.

Marcus also stressed the interconnectedness of all things and the importance of empathy and compassion in human relationships. He viewed humanity as part of a larger cosmic whole and believed that each person has a role to play within this greater order. This belief in universal brotherhood led Marcus to emphasize the need for justice and the responsibility of rulers to act in the best interests of their people. He was deeply concerned with the welfare of his subjects and saw his role as emperor not as a position of privilege but as a duty to serve the common good.

A significant aspect of Marcus Aurelius' Stoicism is the concept of apatheia, or freedom from passion. He believed that emotions such as anger, fear, and desire cloud judgment and prevent individuals from acting rationally. Marcus practiced and advocated for emotional detachment, arguing that true freedom comes from mastering one's emotions and desires. His writings are filled with reflections on mortality, the impermanence of life, and the need to live virtuously in the present moment, without being distracted by fleeting pleasures or anxieties about the future.

Marcus Aurelius' Meditations has had a lasting influence on both philosophy and leadership. His Stoic reflections on duty, virtue, and self-discipline continue to resonate with readers, and his work remains a cornerstone of Stoic philosophy. His ability to balance the demands of ruling an empire with his philosophical pursuits has made him a model of the philosopher-king, and his writings offer timeless guidance for those seeking to live a life of purpose and integrity.

Galen (c. 129 – c. 216 CE)

Galen was a Greek physician, philosopher, and prolific writer born in Pergamon (modern-day Turkey). He is considered one of the most influential figures in the history of medicine and philosophy, with his work spanning a variety of fields, including anatomy, physiology, pathology, and logic. Galen lived during the height of the Roman Empire, and his intellectual environment was shaped by the works of earlier Greek philosophers like Aristotle, Hippocrates, and Plato. He worked as a physician to Roman emperors, and his writings on both medicine and philosophy dominated Western medical thought for over a millennium.

Galen's contributions to philosophy are closely intertwined with his medical theories, as he believed in a deep connection between physical health and moral character. He upheld a Platonic tripartite view of the soul, arguing that the soul is divided into three parts: the rational, the spirited, and the appetitive. According to Galen, health is achieved when these aspects are balanced, which he connected to the four humors theory of Hippocrates. He argued that an imbalance in the bodily humors (blood, phlegm, black bile, and yellow bile) could lead to both physical and mental illness. This blend of medicine and philosophy placed Galen in the tradition of thinkers who saw ethics and health as intertwined.

In addition to his medical contributions, Galen was a Stoic philosopher, though he was critical of some Stoic doctrines. He rejected the Stoic belief that emotions should be completely suppressed, instead arguing that emotions could be managed through reason and that moderate emotional responses were natural and healthy. This idea placed him at odds with more austere Stoic thinkers, such as Epictetus. Galen believed that philosophy should be practical, providing guidance for living a good and healthy life, and that philosophy and medicine were deeply connected in this pursuit.

Galen was also a logician, contributing to the development of scientific methodology. He emphasized the importance of observation and experimentation, which he applied in his anatomical studies. His extensive dissections of animals, particularly pigs and monkeys, laid the groundwork for anatomical knowledge in Europe for centuries. Although some of his anatomical theories were later disproven, his methodological rigor in combining philosophy with empirical study was groundbreaking for his time. He sought to apply logical reasoning to the study of the body and disease, viewing medicine as a science deeply intertwined with philosophy.

Galen's legacy is vast, particularly in the fields of medicine and philosophy. His writings were translated into Latin and Arabic, influencing both the medieval Islamic world and Renaissance Europe. While many of his specific medical theories were eventually replaced, his holistic approach to health and his integration of philosophy and medicine shaped medical education and philosophical thought for centuries. His idea that physical and mental health are interconnected continues to influence modern holistic approaches to medicine.

Nagarjuna (c. 150 – 250 CE)

Nagarjuna was an influential Indian philosopher and the founder of the Madhyamaka school of Mahayana Buddhism. He lived during a time when Buddhism was undergoing significant development, with new schools of thought emerging that emphasized different interpretations of Buddhist doctrine. Born in southern India, Nagarjuna's work focused on the concept of sunyata, or emptiness, and he is widely regarded as one of the most important Buddhist thinkers after the Buddha himself. His philosophy played a crucial role in shaping Mahayana Buddhism, particularly in its metaphysical and epistemological dimensions.

Nagarjuna's central philosophical contribution is his doctrine of sunyata, which asserts that all phenomena are empty of inherent existence. He argued that everything, including the self, is dependent on other things for its existence, and therefore nothing possesses independent or intrinsic essence. This idea of dependent origination was not new to Buddhism, but Nagarjuna developed it into a comprehensive metaphysical framework. According to Nagarjuna, emptiness is not a nihilistic denial of existence but rather a middle path that avoids the extremes of eternalism (the belief in permanent, unchanging essences) and annihilationism (the belief that nothing exists at all).

In his major work, Mulamadhyamakakarika (Fundamental Verses on the Middle Way), Nagarjuna used dialectical reasoning to deconstruct the categories of thought that people use to understand the world. He employed a method known as prasanga, a form of reductio ad absurdum, to demonstrate the contradictions inherent in common views about reality. For Nagarjuna, even the concept of emptiness itself must not be reified; it is a tool for understanding the nature of reality, not an ultimate truth. This paradoxical view emphasized that all views, including the view of emptiness, are provisional and subject to deconstruction.

Nagarjuna's philosophy also had profound implications for Buddhist ethics and the path to enlightenment. By realizing the emptiness of all phenomena, including the self, practitioners can overcome attachment and delusion, which are the root causes of suffering. Nagarjuna taught that recognizing emptiness leads to the cessation of clinging and the cultivation of compassion, as one comes to understand the interconnectedness of all beings. His emphasis on emptiness as a way of seeing beyond the illusions of ordinary existence became a foundational aspect of Mahayana Buddhist practice, influencing later thinkers such as Chandrakirti and Shantideva.

Nagarjuna's legacy continues to shape Buddhist philosophy, particularly in East Asian and Tibetan traditions. His insights into the nature of reality, knowledge, and the self have had a lasting impact on Buddhist metaphysics and soteriology. Nagarjuna's emphasis on emptiness as the key to understanding the nature of existence and attaining liberation remains a central theme in Mahayana Buddhism today.

Sextus Empiricus (c. 160 – 210 CE)

Sextus Empiricus was a Greek philosopher and physician, best known for his role as a leading figure in Pyrrhonian skepticism. He lived during the height of the Roman Empire and was part of a philosophical tradition that emphasized the suspension of judgment and the questioning of dogmatic beliefs. As a follower of Pyrrho, Sextus Empiricus played a crucial role in reviving and systematizing Pyrrhonism, particularly through his works Outlines of Pyrrhonism and Against the Mathematicians. His writings became the most comprehensive accounts of ancient skepticism and influenced later philosophical developments, particularly in the Renaissance.

At the heart of Sextus Empiricus' philosophy is the principle of epoché, or the suspension of judgment. He argued that for every proposition, there exists an equally plausible counter-proposition, making it impossible to determine which is true. This recognition of the equal strength of opposing arguments led Sextus to advocate for withholding assent from all dogmatic beliefs. Instead of striving for certainty, Pyrrhonian skeptics maintain a state of ataraxia, or mental tranquility, by accepting the impossibility of knowledge and refraining from making definitive judgments about reality.

Sextus Empiricus extended his skepticism to all areas of human knowledge, including ethics, science, and metaphysics. He challenged the foundations of knowledge, questioning whether humans have the cognitive faculties to accurately perceive and understand the world. He argued that perceptions are subjective and vary from person to person, making it difficult to establish any universal truth. By demonstrating the limitations of human reasoning, Sextus undermined the claims of dogmatic philosophers who believed they could attain certain knowledge through reason or empirical observation.

Sextus also critiqued the moral philosophies of his contemporaries, arguing that ethical systems based on fixed principles were inherently flawed. He believed that since we cannot know what is truly good or bad, it is better to live according to appearances and conventions without becoming attached to any particular moral framework. This ethical skepticism was intended to free individuals from the anxiety that comes from trying to live according to absolute moral standards. Sextus emphasized that by suspending judgment on ethical matters, people could achieve a more peaceful and balanced way of life.

The influence of Sextus Empiricus extended far beyond antiquity. His skeptical arguments were rediscovered during the Renaissance and had a profound impact on early modern thinkers such as Michel de Montaigne, David Hume, and René Descartes. His works challenged the foundations of knowledge and inspired new approaches to epistemology and skepticism in the modern era. Sextus Empiricus remains a central figure in the history of skepticism, with his philosophy continuing to inspire debates about the nature of knowledge and belief.

Plotinus (c. 204 – 270 CE)

Plotinus was a Hellenistic philosopher and the founder of Neoplatonism, a philosophical system that sought to synthesize Platonic thought with mystical and religious elements. He was born in Lycopolis, Egypt, and later studied philosophy in Alexandria before moving to Rome, where he established a school of philosophy. Plotinus' work emerged during a time of great religious and philosophical diversity in the Roman Empire, and his ideas were influenced by earlier Greek thinkers, particularly Plato and Aristotle. His most significant contribution to philosophy is his development of the concept of the One, the ultimate source of all existence.

At the heart of Plotinus' philosophy is the idea of the One, an ineffable and transcendent reality that is the source of all being. According to Plotinus, the One is beyond all categories of thought and cannot be grasped by the intellect or described in language. It is pure unity, without division or multiplicity, and all things emanate from it. Plotinus described the process of emanation as a kind of overflowing, where the One, in its abundance, produces the Nous (intellect), the Soul, and finally the material world. Each level of reality is progressively less perfect, with the material world being the farthest from the One.

Plotinus also developed a theory of knowledge that emphasized the importance of turning inward to discover the divine within oneself. He believed that the human soul is part of the same reality as the One and that through contemplation and spiritual practice, individuals can ascend to higher levels of understanding and eventually unite with the One. This process of self-realization involves purifying the soul of its attachment to the material world and cultivating a life of virtue and wisdom. For Plotinus, the ultimate goal of human life is to achieve mystical union with the One, which he described as an experience of indescribable bliss and transcendence.

In addition to his metaphysical and epistemological teachings, Plotinus emphasized the importance of ethics and virtue in the pursuit of the good life. He believed that by living in accordance with reason and the divine order, individuals could align themselves with the higher realities of the Nous and the One. Plotinus' ethical philosophy was deeply influenced by Plato's idea of the Good, and he saw the cultivation of virtue as essential for achieving the soul's ascent to the divine. This emphasis on virtue and the contemplative life became a central feature of Neoplatonism.

Plotinus' philosophy had a profound impact on the development of Western thought, particularly in the areas of metaphysics, mysticism, and ethics. His ideas influenced later Christian, Islamic, and Jewish thinkers, including St. Augustine, who incorporated elements of Neoplatonism into Christian theology. Plotinus' vision of a transcendent, ineffable source of all being continues to inspire philosophical and spiritual traditions, making him one of the most important figures in the history of philosophy.

Hypatia (c. 360 – 415 CE)

Hypatia was a prominent philosopher, mathematician, and astronomer in late antiquity, known for her work in Neoplatonism and her role as one of the leading intellectuals of Alexandria. Born in Alexandria, Egypt, around 360 CE, she was the daughter of Theon, a renowned mathematician and astronomer who trained her in both disciplines. Hypatia eventually surpassed her father in reputation, becoming a celebrated teacher and scholar. She lived during a period of social and religious turmoil, as the Roman Empire transitioned from its pagan past to Christianity, a context that shaped her intellectual career and led to her tragic death.

Hypatia is most closely associated with the Neoplatonic school of thought, which built on Plato's teachings and explored the nature of reality, the soul, and the cosmos. Neoplatonism emphasized a transcendent, unified reality from which all things emanate, with the goal of achieving union with this higher reality through intellectual and spiritual discipline. Like her predecessors Plotinus and Iamblichus, Hypatia's philosophy was rooted in this metaphysical framework, but she also engaged with the practical applications of Platonic thought, particularly in mathematics and astronomy.

In addition to her work in philosophy, Hypatia made significant contributions to mathematics and astronomy. She is believed to have written commentaries on the works of Diophantus, an ancient mathematician known for algebra, and Ptolemy's Almagest, an influential astronomical text. Her mathematical works aimed to make complex ideas more accessible to students, and she worked on devices such as the astrolabe to aid in celestial measurements. Her reputation as a brilliant teacher attracted students from across the Mediterranean, further solidifying her legacy.

Hypatia's public life as a philosopher and teacher in Alexandria placed her at the center of the city's political and religious tensions. Her philosophical school, one of the few remaining centers of pagan learning, stood out in a city that was a melting pot of pagans, Christians, and Jews. Her association with Orestes, the Roman prefect of Alexandria, who was in conflict with Cyril, the bishop of Alexandria, made her a target of political and religious hostility. As a symbol of pagan philosophy, she was perceived as an obstacle to Christian dominance.

In 415 CE, Hypatia was murdered by a Christian mob, an act seen as both religious and political. Her death marked the end of an era for Alexandria's intellectual community and symbolized the decline of pagan philosophy in the face of Christian power. Despite this tragic end, Hypatia's legacy endures as a philosopher, mathematician, and teacher, representing the intellectual achievements of antiquity and the complex interplay of reason, faith, and politics in the ancient world.

Proclus (412 – 485 CE)

Proclus was a Neoplatonist philosopher born in Constantinople and later educated in Alexandria and Athens, where he became the head of the Platonic Academy. His life unfolded during the late Roman Empire, a period marked by significant political, religious, and intellectual change, including the growing influence of Christianity. Proclus sought to preserve and expand upon the legacy of earlier Neoplatonists, such as Plotinus and Iamblichus, while engaging with both classical Greek philosophy and contemporary Christian thought. As one of the last major pagan philosophers, Proclus' work was a defense of the Platonic tradition against the rise of Christianity.

Proclus' philosophical system was highly structured and hierarchical, building on the Neoplatonic idea of emanation from a single, transcendent source known as the One. He believed that all levels of reality, from the material world to the highest divine realms, were connected in a chain of being, with each level emanating from the one above it. This hierarchy included the One, the Nous (Divine Intellect), the World Soul, and finally the physical world. Proclus expanded on this by adding further layers of intermediaries, including divine beings and souls, making his metaphysical system one of the most complex and detailed in Neoplatonism.

In addition to his metaphysics, Proclus made significant contributions to theology, particularly in his discussions of the gods and their relation to the cosmos. He believed that the gods were not merely mythological figures but were real metaphysical entities that played an active role in the governance of the universe. Proclus developed a system of theurgy, or divine rites, which he believed allowed individuals to connect with these divine beings and ascend toward the One. His theurgical practices were influenced by the Chaldean Oracles and earlier Neoplatonic thought, and they represented an attempt to bridge the gap between philosophical contemplation and religious ritual.

Proclus was also deeply interested in mathematics and its relationship to metaphysics. Like many Neoplatonists, he saw mathematics as a bridge between the physical and the intellectual worlds, offering insight into the eternal truths of the cosmos. Proclus wrote extensive commentaries on works such as Euclid's Elements, and he viewed geometry and arithmetic as essential tools for understanding the structure of reality. His mathematical writings reflect his broader belief that the universe is governed by rational, intelligible principles, and that through the study of these principles, one can attain knowledge of the divine.

Proclus' influence extended far beyond his lifetime, particularly through the transmission of his works to the Byzantine and Islamic worlds, and later to medieval Europe. His commentaries on Plato's dialogues were particularly influential in the development of Christian and Islamic philosophy, especially in the works of thinkers like Pseudo-Dionysius the Areopagite. Though Proclus' paganism made him a controversial figure in a Christianized world, his Neoplatonic system continued to shape theological and metaphysical thought for centuries.

Boethius (c. 480 – 524 CE)

Boethius, born into an aristocratic Roman family, was a philosopher, statesman, and theologian whose work bridged the classical and medieval worlds. Educated in Greek philosophy, Boethius became a high-ranking official under the Ostrogothic King Theodoric but later fell from favor and was imprisoned. It was during his imprisonment that Boethius wrote his most famous work, The Consolation of Philosophy, a dialogue between himself and Lady Philosophy, which has been regarded as one of the most influential texts of the Middle Ages. Boethius lived during the collapse of the Western Roman Empire and sought to preserve classical learning in the face of political and cultural decline.

The Consolation of Philosophy is a deeply personal reflection on the nature of fortune, suffering, and happiness. In this work, Boethius grapples with the apparent injustice of his imprisonment and explores the relationship between fate, divine providence, and human free will. Drawing on the Stoic and Neoplatonic traditions, Boethius argues that true happiness is not found in external goods such as wealth, power, or honor, which are subject to the whims of fortune. Instead, happiness comes from within, through the cultivation of virtue and the pursuit of wisdom. This Stoic acceptance of fate, combined with a belief in the ultimate goodness of divine providence, forms the philosophical core of The Consolation.

Boethius' philosophical thought was also deeply influenced by his Christian faith, though The Consolation of Philosophy itself does not directly engage with Christian doctrine. He believed that reason and faith were not opposed but complementary paths to truth. In his theological works, Boethius sought to reconcile Greek philosophy with Christian theology, particularly in his efforts to clarify the nature of the Trinity. His treatises on logic, theology, and metaphysics, especially De Trinitate and De Fide Catholica, laid the groundwork for later Scholasticism, influencing thinkers such as Thomas Aquinas.

One of Boethius' most significant contributions to the intellectual world was his work as a translator and commentator on Greek philosophy. He translated key works of Aristotle and Plato into Latin, making them accessible to the medieval European world. Boethius also wrote influential works on logic, including commentaries on Aristotle's Categories and De Interpretatione, which helped preserve Aristotelian logic during the early Middle Ages. His ambition to translate all of Plato and Aristotle's works into Latin was never fully realized, but his efforts were critical in transmitting classical philosophy to the medieval West.

Boethius' legacy is enduring, as The Consolation of Philosophy became one of the most widely read and studied texts throughout the Middle Ages and Renaissance. His integration of classical philosophy with Christian thought helped shape the intellectual culture of medieval Europe, and his writings on logic and theology laid the foundations for later developments in Scholasticism. Boethius stands as a pivotal figure in the transmission of classical knowledge to the medieval world, ensuring the survival of ancient philosophical traditions during a time of great cultural and political upheaval.

Vasubandhu (c. 4th century CE)

Vasubandhu was an influential Indian philosopher and a central figure in the development of Mahayana Buddhism, particularly in the Yogacara school. He was originally associated with the Sarvastivada school of early Buddhism but later became a major proponent of Mahayana doctrines. Vasubandhu lived during a period of intense doctrinal debate and intellectual development in Indian Buddhism, and his works, such as the Abhidharmakosha and the Triṃśikā-vijñaptimātratā, significantly shaped Buddhist thought. Along with his brother Asanga, Vasubandhu is considered one of the founders of Yogacara, a school that emphasized the nature of consciousness and the illusion of external reality.

Vasubandhu's early work, Abhidharmakosha, was a comprehensive treatise on Sarvastivada Abhidharma, which sought to systematize Buddhist teachings on the nature of reality, karma, and mental phenomena. This text provided detailed analyses of the constituent elements of existence (dharmas) and their relationships. However, Vasubandhu later critiqued the very doctrines he had previously expounded, shifting toward the Mahayana perspective, which emphasized the emptiness (sunyata) of all phenomena. His rejection of Sarvastivada realism in favor of Mahayana concepts marked a significant turning point in his philosophical career.

The Yogacara school, which Vasubandhu helped develop, is based on the doctrine of vijñaptimātratā, or "consciousness-only." This teaching asserts that what we perceive as the external world is not independent reality but rather a projection of consciousness. Vasubandhu argued that all experiences are mental constructs and that the belief in an external, objective world is a fundamental ignorance. This view aligns with the Mahayana concept of emptiness, which holds that all phenomena are devoid of intrinsic existence. By understanding the illusory nature of perception, practitioners can overcome attachment and delusion, ultimately leading to liberation.

In addition to his metaphysical contributions, Vasubandhu wrote extensively on Buddhist ethics, psychology, and soteriology. He emphasized the importance of meditation and mental discipline as the means to transform consciousness and achieve enlightenment. His analysis of the mind's workings, particularly in his Twenty Verses on Consciousness-Only (Vimśatikā) and Thirty Verses (Trimśikā), laid the groundwork for later Buddhist philosophy, including the development of Buddhist logic and epistemology. Vasubandhu's detailed exploration of the stages of mental development and the obstacles to enlightenment made his works essential reading for Mahayana practitioners.

Vasubandhu's influence on Buddhist thought is profound, extending beyond India to Tibet, China, and Japan, where his works became central to the development of Buddhist philosophy. His contributions to the Yogacara school helped shape the Mahayana tradition, particularly in its understanding of the mind, perception, and the path to enlightenment. Vasubandhu's writings continue to be studied and revered in both the academic and religious contexts of Buddhist practice.

Chandrakirti (c. 600 – 650 CE)

Chandrakirti was an Indian Buddhist philosopher and a prominent figure in the Madhyamaka school, following in the footsteps of Nagarjuna, the school's founder. Chandrakirti lived during a period of vibrant intellectual exchange and debate within Indian Buddhism, particularly regarding the nature of reality, emptiness (sunyata), and the path to enlightenment. His works, especially his commentary on Nagarjuna's Mulamadhyamakakarika called the Prasannapada, played a crucial role in clarifying and defending the Madhyamaka doctrine against its critics, establishing him as one of the key interpreters of Nagarjuna's thought.

Chandrakirti's philosophy is centered on the Madhyamaka concept of sunyata, or emptiness, which posits that all phenomena lack inherent existence. He argued that everything we perceive is dependent on causes and conditions, and thus cannot possess an independent, self-sustaining essence. For Chandrakirti, recognizing the emptiness of all things is essential for overcoming attachment and delusion, which are the root causes of suffering. His writings elaborated on Nagarjuna's teachings by using reasoned arguments to demonstrate the absurdity of assuming that anything has an independent, intrinsic nature.

One of Chandrakirti's most significant contributions to Madhyamaka philosophy is his critique of the Yogacara school's doctrine of vijñaptimātratā ("consciousness-only"). While the Yogacara school argued that external objects do not exist independently of consciousness, Chandrakirti contended that even consciousness itself is empty of inherent existence. He believed that the Yogacara perspective did not go far enough in deconstructing the illusions of reality and that the true realization of emptiness required the recognition that both subject and object are equally devoid of inherent essence. This critique helped distinguish the Madhyamaka school's radical approach to emptiness from other Buddhist philosophical systems.

In his ethical teachings, Chandrakirti emphasized the role of compassion (karuna) and the Bodhisattva path in the pursuit of enlightenment. He argued that understanding emptiness should not lead to nihilism or disengagement from the world, but rather to a deeper commitment to alleviating the suffering of all sentient beings. Chandrakirti believed that the realization of emptiness was inseparable from the cultivation of compassion, and that the highest expression of wisdom was the Bodhisattva's dedication to helping others achieve liberation. His works thus integrated the philosophical insights of Madhyamaka with the ethical imperatives of Mahayana Buddhism.

Chandrakirti's influence on Tibetan Buddhism, particularly the Gelug school founded by Tsongkhapa, has been profound. His commentaries and interpretations of Nagarjuna's teachings are considered authoritative, and his arguments continue to be studied by scholars and practitioners alike. Chandrakirti's integration of rigorous philosophical analysis with compassionate ethical practice remains a cornerstone of Mahayana Buddhist thought.

Huineng (638 – 713 CE)

Huineng was a Chinese monk and the sixth patriarch of Chan (Zen) Buddhism, regarded as one of the most influential figures in the development of Chinese Zen. He was born into a poor family in Guangdong province and became a Buddhist monk after a transformative experience while hearing the Diamond Sutra. His simple background and unconventional path to becoming a patriarch of Chan Buddhism are notable, as he broke the traditional image of monastic elitism. His teachings, later compiled in the Platform Sutra, laid the foundation for the Southern School of Chan, which emphasized sudden enlightenment over gradual cultivation.

Huineng's rise to prominence occurred during a period of intense debate within the Chan tradition. His main philosophical rival, Shenxiu, advocated for a gradual path to enlightenment through constant effort and meditation. Huineng, however, championed the idea that enlightenment is immediate and inherent in all beings. He taught that all sentient beings possess the Buddha-nature, and enlightenment occurs the moment one realizes this truth. This notion of "sudden enlightenment" became central to his school's teachings, setting it apart from other Chan sects that emphasized gradual progress.

The Platform Sutra of Huineng articulates his core teachings on the non-duality of mind and reality. He believed that the mind, in its purest form, is already enlightened but becomes clouded by delusion and attachment. For Huineng, the practice of meditation and other Buddhist rituals was not about purifying the mind or achieving something new but realizing the mind's inherent purity. His famous analogy compares the mind to a mirror that is inherently clean but appears dirty due to dust. The dust does not change the nature of the mirror, just as delusion does not change the enlightened nature of the mind.

Huineng's approach to meditation differed from his contemporaries. He rejected the practice of seated meditation as a means to enlightenment, arguing that true meditation occurs when one is free from attachment in every action, whether sitting, standing, or walking. This view encouraged his followers to integrate Chan practice into everyday life, making the path to enlightenment accessible to all, regardless of monastic or lay status. It democratized Chan Buddhism, which had previously been more associated with monastic elites.

Huineng's influence on Chinese Buddhism is profound, and his ideas laid the groundwork for the development of the Southern School of Chan, which eventually became the dominant form of Zen in China. His teachings on sudden enlightenment, non-duality, and the inherent purity of the mind continue to resonate in both Chinese and Japanese Zen traditions today.

Shantideva (c. 685 – 763 CE)

Shantideva was an Indian Buddhist monk and philosopher, best known for his text, Bodhicaryavatara (The Way of the Bodhisattva), which is considered one of the great masterpieces of Mahayana Buddhist literature. He was born into a royal family in Saurashtra, India, but renounced worldly life to become a monk in the monastic university of Nalanda. His time was marked by the flourishing of Mahayana Buddhism, which emphasized the Bodhisattva path—an altruistic path focused on attaining enlightenment not just for oneself but for all sentient beings. Despite his humble and withdrawn demeanor in the monastery, his teachings would later resonate across cultures and eras as profound guides for ethical and spiritual development.

The Bodhicaryavatara is Shantideva's most significant contribution to Buddhist philosophy, outlining the path a Bodhisattva should follow. It stresses the development of bodhicitta, or the mind of enlightenment, as the foundation of all spiritual practice. The text is a manual for developing the six perfections (paramitas) of generosity, ethics, patience, effort, concentration, and wisdom. Shantideva's philosophy, therefore, revolves around the ideal of compassion, which he sees as the central motivator for the Bodhisattva's quest for enlightenment.

In addition to compassion, Shantideva emphasizes the practice of mindfulness and meditation. He teaches that one must remain vigilant in guarding the mind against destructive emotions like anger, greed, and pride. His reflections on anger, in particular, are profound, as he sees it as one of the most destructive forces, capable of undoing the positive karmic results of a lifetime's worth of good deeds. His recommendation is to practice patience and understanding, even toward those who cause harm, because they are, in reality, suffering themselves.

Shantideva's approach to emptiness (shunyata) is deeply rooted in the Madhyamaka tradition of Nagarjuna. He argues that all phenomena lack inherent existence, a realization that can help the practitioner overcome attachment and aversion. By understanding that both the self and the external world are empty of independent, intrinsic existence, one can cultivate greater compassion for others, as suffering is seen as arising from misunderstanding this fundamental truth. This insight into emptiness does not lead to nihilism, but rather to a compassionate engagement with the world.

Shantideva's work continues to be a guiding light in Mahayana Buddhism, especially within the Tibetan tradition. His emphasis on compassion, patience, and the philosophical understanding of emptiness has inspired countless practitioners on their spiritual paths, making him one of the most revered figures in the history of Buddhist philosophy. His teachings are still studied and recited today, reflecting their timeless relevance and their capacity to speak to the challenges of human existence.

Shankara (c. 700 – 750 CE)

Shankara, also known as Adi Shankaracharya, was a highly influential Indian philosopher and theologian who consolidated the doctrine of Advaita Vedanta. Born in Kaladi, Kerala, Shankara lived during a period of growing competition between various schools of Hindu philosophy, as well as the rising influence of Buddhism and Jainism in India. He is best known for his teachings on non-duality (Advaita), which argue that the individual soul (Atman) and the ultimate reality (Brahman) are identical. Shankara's works and travels across India aimed to revive and unify the Hindu tradition under the Vedantic philosophy, while also refuting rival schools of thought.

Central to Shankara's philosophy is the concept of non-duality, or Advaita, which posits that there is only one ultimate reality—Brahman—and that the perception of a separate individual self (Atman) is an illusion. Shankara argued that the apparent multiplicity and diversity of the world, as well as the distinction between the self and the external world, arise from ignorance (avidya). This ignorance leads to the mistaken belief in dualities such as self and other, subject and object, and ultimately causes suffering. According to Shankara, the realization that the self and Brahman are one is the key to liberation (moksha).

In his Brahmasutra Bhashya (commentary on the Brahma Sutras), Shankara elaborated on his interpretation of the Upanishads, the foundational texts of Vedanta. He argued that the highest knowledge (jnana) is the realization that the Atman is identical to Brahman, which transcends all categories of time, space, and causation. For Shankara, liberation is not attained through ritual actions (karma) or devotional practices (bhakti) alone, but through direct knowledge and insight into the true nature of reality. He emphasized that while ritual and devotion may help prepare the mind for enlightenment, they are ultimately secondary to the knowledge of non-duality.

Shankara also refuted other philosophical schools, particularly the dualistic and pluralistic systems of thought, such as those found in Samkhya, Yoga, and Nyaya-Vaisheshika. He criticized these schools for their belief in the real existence of a multiplicity of substances and for their assertion that the self is distinct from the ultimate reality. Shankara's dialectical approach involved demonstrating the logical inconsistencies in these views and asserting that only Brahman is real, while the world of forms and distinctions is maya, or illusion. His critiques were aimed at affirming the unity of Brahman as the sole, unchanging reality.

In addition to his philosophical works, Shankara is credited with founding several monastic orders and establishing mathas (monasteries) across India, which became centers for the teaching and propagation of Advaita Vedanta. His efforts to consolidate the Hindu tradition and promote the teachings of non-duality had a lasting impact on Indian philosophy and spirituality. Shankara's Advaita Vedanta remains one of the most influential schools of Hindu thought, and his teachings continue to inspire spiritual seekers and scholars alike. His legacy endures through his writings, as well as through the monastic institutions that carry forward his vision of non-dualistic philosophy.

Al-Kindi (c. 801 – 873 CE)

Al-Kindi, known as the "Philosopher of the Arabs," was born in Kufa, Iraq, and became one of the earliest and most influential figures in the translation and adaptation of Greek philosophy in the Islamic world. He lived during the Abbasid Caliphate, a period when the intellectual center of the Muslim world was flourishing, especially in Baghdad. Al-Kindi played a crucial role in integrating Greek philosophical ideas, particularly those of Aristotle and Plato, into Islamic thought. He was appointed by the Abbasid caliphs to oversee the translation of Greek works into Arabic and is credited with more than 260 works on philosophy, mathematics, medicine, and astronomy.

Al-Kindi's philosophy was grounded in the belief that reason and revelation could be harmonized. He argued that human reason, when properly cultivated, could lead to truths that did not conflict with the teachings of Islam. Al-Kindi was heavily influenced by Neoplatonism, adopting its hierarchical vision of the cosmos, with the One (or God) at the highest level. He viewed the material world as an emanation from a higher reality and believed that human intellect could ascend toward divine knowledge. For Al-Kindi, philosophy was not merely an abstract pursuit but a means of coming closer to God through rational understanding.

One of Al-Kindi's most significant contributions to Islamic philosophy was his work on metaphysics, where he tackled the nature of God, creation, and the soul. He argued for the existence of a single, eternal, and immaterial God who created the universe out of nothing (ex nihilo). This idea contrasted with the Aristotelian concept of an eternal universe, and Al-Kindi worked to reconcile the two. He maintained that while the universe has a temporal beginning, it is sustained through a continuous act of divine will. This view helped lay the groundwork for later Islamic metaphysical discussions on the nature of creation and divine omnipotence.

Al-Kindi also contributed to the fields of epistemology and ethics, emphasizing the importance of knowledge and wisdom. He believed that the human intellect was capable of acquiring knowledge through both sensory experience and rational contemplation. However, he distinguished between different kinds of knowledge: lower forms, derived from the senses, and higher forms, which involved the contemplation of eternal truths. In ethics, Al-Kindi advocated for moderation and self-discipline, suggesting that human happiness lies in intellectual and spiritual fulfillment rather than material wealth or physical pleasure.

Al-Kindi's work had a lasting impact on the development of Islamic philosophy, particularly in how later thinkers, such as Al-Farabi and Avicenna, approached the relationship between philosophy and religion. His efforts to introduce and adapt Greek philosophical ideas to the Islamic world established a foundation for centuries of intellectual inquiry. His legacy as a polymath and philosopher who bridged different intellectual traditions continues to be appreciated in both the Islamic and Western philosophical traditions.

Padmasambhava (c. 8th – 9th century CE)

Padmasambhava, also known as Guru Rinpoche, is one of the most venerated figures in Tibetan Buddhism and is credited with introducing Buddhism to Tibet in the 8th century. Born in India, his early life is shrouded in legend, with stories of him being miraculously born from a lotus flower. His arrival in Tibet occurred during a time when the Tibetan king, Trisong Detsen, invited Buddhist scholars to Tibet to help establish the religion in the face of indigenous opposition. Padmasambhava's teachings and tantric practices were instrumental in overcoming these obstacles and spreading Buddhism throughout the region. He is often regarded as a second Buddha in Tibetan Buddhism, symbolizing his unparalleled role in shaping the spiritual landscape of Tibet.

Padmasambhava's teachings are deeply rooted in Vajrayana (Tantric) Buddhism. Vajrayana emphasizes the use of esoteric practices and rituals to achieve enlightenment more swiftly than in other Buddhist paths. Padmasambhava introduced a range of tantric practices, including the use of mantras, mudras, and mandalas, to help practitioners engage with the deeper, transformative aspects of the mind. His teachings focus on the idea that enlightenment can be achieved in this very lifetime, using the body, speech, and mind as vehicles for transformation through tantric rituals.

Central to Padmasambhava's philosophy is the concept of the "Great Perfection" (Dzogchen). Dzogchen emphasizes the innate purity of the mind and the realization that all beings possess Buddha-nature inherently. The mind, in its natural state, is already enlightened, and the path to awakening involves recognizing this fundamental truth. Padmasambhava taught that through Dzogchen practices, practitioners could directly experience their enlightened nature without the need for extensive study or gradual practice, making it a direct path to liberation.

Padmasambhava is also renowned for his mastery over spirits and local deities, which played a crucial role in his efforts to establish Buddhism in Tibet. According to Tibetan tradition, he subdued hostile forces and integrated local deities into the Buddhist pantheon. This process helped to assimilate indigenous Tibetan beliefs into Buddhism, allowing the new religion to flourish without completely displacing the local culture. His ability to harmonize Buddhism with local traditions is seen as one of his most enduring contributions.

The legacy of Padmasambhava is vast, and his influence can be seen across Tibetan Buddhism, particularly within the Nyingma school, where he is regarded as the founder. His teachings on Dzogchen, tantric practices, and the assimilation of Tibetan culture into Buddhism laid the foundation for the flourishing of Vajrayana Buddhism in Tibet. He remains a deeply revered figure, with many Tibetan Buddhist texts, rituals, and practices attributed to his wisdom, and his life is celebrated annually during the Guru Rinpoche festivals held throughout Tibet and Himalayan regions.

Al-Farabi (c. 872 – 950 CE)

Al-Farabi, also known as "the Second Teacher" after Aristotle, was born in Farab, in what is now Kazakhstan, and later moved to Baghdad, where he became one of the most prominent philosophers of the Islamic Golden Age. He lived during a period of intense intellectual exchange, when Greek philosophy was being translated into Arabic and integrated into Islamic thought. Al-Farabi's work focused on logic, political philosophy, and metaphysics, and he played a key role in shaping the philosophical discourse of the Islamic world. His ability to synthesize Platonic, Aristotelian, and Islamic ideas earned him a lasting reputation as a philosopher who bridged different intellectual traditions.

One of Al-Farabi's central philosophical concerns was the relationship between philosophy and religion. He believed that both philosophy and religion aimed at the same truth, but they approached it in different ways: philosophy through reason and religion through symbolic representation. According to Al-Farabi, the highest goal of human life is to attain knowledge of the First Cause (or God), and both philosophy and religion are paths to this ultimate knowledge. He viewed the prophet and the philosopher as complementary figures—the prophet communicates truth to the masses through symbolic laws, while the philosopher seeks to understand the underlying reality through rational inquiry.

In his political philosophy, Al-Farabi is most famous for his concept of the ideal state, which he described in his works Al-Madina al-Fadila (The Virtuous City). Drawing on Plato's Republic, Al-Farabi envisioned a society governed by a philosopher-king, a ruler whose wisdom and knowledge of divine truths would guide the city toward justice and harmony. Al-Farabi believed that the role of the philosopher-king was not only to create laws but to cultivate virtue in the citizens. He saw politics as an extension of ethics, where the goal of the state was to create conditions for its citizens to achieve moral and intellectual perfection.

Al-Farabi also made important contributions to logic and metaphysics, particularly in his interpretation of Aristotle. He expanded on Aristotle's theory of the intellect, distinguishing between the potential intellect, the active intellect, and the acquired intellect. Al-Farabi's theory of the active intellect suggested that it was a divine intermediary that allowed humans to achieve knowledge of universal truths. His metaphysical system sought to explain how the material world emanated from the First Cause, using a hierarchical model similar to that of Neoplatonism. His work on the intellect and metaphysics would later influence Islamic philosophers like Avicenna and Averroes.

Al-Farabi's synthesis of Greek and Islamic thought had a profound influence on both the Islamic world and medieval European philosophy. His works were translated into Latin, and his ideas on political philosophy, logic, and metaphysics became central to the intellectual traditions of both East and West. As a key figure in the development of Islamic philosophy, Al-Farabi's contributions continue to resonate in discussions on the relationship between reason, religion, and governance.

Avicenna (Ibn Sina) (980 – 1037 CE)

Avicenna, known in the Islamic world as Ibn Sina, was born in Afshana, near Bukhara, in present-day Uzbekistan. He is one of the most significant figures in the history of Islamic philosophy and medicine, producing over 450 works on topics ranging from philosophy and theology to medicine and astronomy. Avicenna lived during the height of the Islamic Golden Age, a period of flourishing intellectual and cultural activity, and his work became foundational for both Islamic and Western philosophical traditions. His Canon of Medicine remained a key medical text in Europe and the Islamic world for centuries, while his philosophical writings, particularly The Book of Healing and The Metaphysics of the Shifa, had a lasting impact on medieval European scholasticism.

Central to Avicenna's philosophy is his concept of Being and his metaphysical distinction between essence and existence. He argued that in the material world, the essence of a thing (what it is) is distinct from its existence (that it is). However, in the case of God, essence and existence are identical—God's essence is to exist, and therefore God is the necessary being from which all contingent beings derive. Avicenna's Proof of the Necessary Existent became one of his most famous contributions to Islamic metaphysics, influencing later Islamic and Christian philosophers like Thomas Aquinas.

Avicenna's theory of the intellect is another major contribution to Islamic philosophy. Building on Aristotle, he developed a hierarchical model of the intellect, distinguishing between the material, potential, active, and acquired intellects. Avicenna argued that human knowledge begins with sensory experience but progresses through the active intellect to reach universal truths. The active intellect, in his view, acts as an intermediary between the human mind and the divine, illuminating the intelligible forms necessary for human understanding. This theory of the intellect became foundational for later Islamic thinkers, including Averroes, and was also influential in medieval Christian philosophy.

In addition to his work on metaphysics and epistemology, Avicenna made significant contributions to ethics and psychology. He believed that the soul is distinct from the body and that its ultimate goal is to achieve knowledge and union with the divine intellect. Avicenna's ethical system emphasized the development of intellectual and moral virtues, which he saw as essential for achieving happiness and fulfilling one's potential as a rational being. His ideas on the soul and intellect were deeply influential in both Islamic mysticism and Western medieval thought, particularly in the works of Scholastic philosophers like Albertus Magnus and Thomas Aquinas.

Avicenna's legacy as both a philosopher and a physician continues to resonate today. His works were translated into Latin in the 12th century, becoming central texts in European universities. His synthesis of Aristotelian philosophy with Islamic theology provided a framework that shaped the intellectual traditions of both East and West, earning him a place among the greatest philosophers of the medieval world.

Ramanuja (1017 – 1137 CE)

Ramanuja was an Indian philosopher and theologian who is widely regarded as the most important proponent of the Vishishtadvaita (Qualified Non-dualism) school of Vedanta. Born in Tamil Nadu, India, Ramanuja was deeply influenced by the teachings of the earlier Vedantic scholar Yamunacharya. Ramanuja lived during a time when Advaita Vedanta, led by Shankara, dominated Indian philosophical discourse. His philosophy arose as a reaction to Shankara's non-dualism (Advaita), which he believed neglected the role of personal devotion and the reality of multiplicity within the universe. Ramanuja's theological contributions were not just philosophical but also deeply rooted in the ritual and devotional practices of the Vaishnavite tradition.

Ramanuja's central philosophical concept is Vishishtadvaita, which holds that while Brahman (the ultimate reality) is one, it is also qualified by attributes. He argued that the individual soul (atman) and the universe are real and distinct from Brahman, but they are also dependent on Brahman. In this way, Ramanuja's view contrasted with Shankara's Advaita, which posited that the atman and Brahman are ultimately identical and that the perception of distinction is due to ignorance. For Ramanuja, the relationship between the soul and Brahman is one of qualified unity, where the soul is part of Brahman but retains its individual identity.

A key element of Ramanuja's philosophy is his emphasis on bhakti (devotion) as the primary means to attain liberation (moksha). While Shankara's Advaita Vedanta emphasized jnana (knowledge) as the path to realizing the non-duality of Brahman, Ramanuja argued that devotion to a personal God (Vishnu) was the most direct and accessible path to liberation for the average person. He believed that through devotion, one could cultivate a personal relationship with God, which would ultimately lead to union with Brahman. Ramanuja's perspective democratized spiritual practice by making liberation attainable not just for scholars but for laypeople through devotion and service.

Ramanuja also rejected the idea of maya, or illusion, which was central to Shankara's philosophy. According to Shankara, the world of multiplicity is an illusion, and only Brahman is real. Ramanuja, on the other hand, affirmed the reality of the world and the diversity within it. He argued that the world is a manifestation of Brahman's divine nature and that it should be engaged with through righteous action and devotion. This positive view of the world emphasized its divine origin and its integral role in spiritual practice, making his philosophy more accessible to theistic practitioners.

Ramanuja's contributions to Indian philosophy had a lasting impact, particularly within the Vaishnavism tradition. His emphasis on devotion and personal experience of God shaped the development of devotional practices in Hinduism, and his critique of non-dualism provided a robust alternative to Shankara's Advaita. His ideas continue to influence contemporary Hindu philosophy and devotional practice, fostering a vision of spirituality where love, devotion, and personal connection to God are central to the path of liberation.

Anselm of Canterbury (1033 – 1109 CE)

Anselm of Canterbury, an Italian-born Benedictine monk, philosopher, and theologian, served as Archbishop of Canterbury from 1093 until his death in 1109. He is best known for his development of the "ontological argument" for the existence of God, which remains a fundamental topic in philosophy of religion. Anselm lived during the early medieval period, a time when Christian theology was heavily influenced by Augustinian thought and monastic scholarship. His intellectual context was shaped by the emerging Scholastic tradition, which sought to reconcile Christian faith with reason, and his writings reflected this synthesis.

Anselm's ontological argument, articulated in his work Proslogion, is perhaps his most famous contribution to philosophy. He argued that the very concept of God implies God's existence. Anselm defined God as "that than which nothing greater can be conceived," and claimed that it is greater to exist both in the mind and in reality than solely in the mind. Therefore, if God exists in the mind, He must also exist in reality, because a God who exists in reality would be greater than one who only exists as an idea. This argument was a significant attempt to demonstrate the existence of God through purely rational reflection, without recourse to empirical evidence.

Beyond his ontological argument, Anselm made significant contributions to theology, particularly in his doctrine of atonement. In his work Cur Deus Homo (Why God Became Man), Anselm introduced the "satisfaction theory" of atonement, which sought to explain why Christ's incarnation and crucifixion were necessary for human salvation. He argued that human sin dishonored God and that justice required some form of restitution. Since humans were incapable of providing adequate satisfaction for this dishonor, God became incarnate in the person of Jesus Christ, who offered his life as a perfect satisfaction. This theory of atonement influenced subsequent Christian theology and became a dominant explanation of Christ's redemptive work in Western Christianity.

Anselm's philosophy also engaged deeply with epistemology, particularly with the relationship between faith and reason. His famous phrase, "faith seeking understanding" (fides quaerens intellectum), encapsulates his belief that faith is the starting point for philosophical inquiry but that reason plays a crucial role in deepening one's understanding of divine truths. He believed that while faith in God is foundational, reason can help elucidate and defend the principles of the Christian faith. This approach laid the groundwork for later Scholastic thinkers, including Thomas Aquinas, who similarly sought to harmonize faith and reason.

Anselm's legacy in both philosophy and theology is substantial, particularly in the fields of metaphysics, logic, and religious epistemology. His ontological argument has been both highly influential and widely debated, with later philosophers like René Descartes, Immanuel Kant, and Alvin Plantinga offering their own interpretations or critiques. Anselm's work represents a significant moment in the development of medieval thought, where reason and faith were seen not as opposing forces but as complementary means of understanding the divine.

Al-Ghazali (1058 – 1111 CE)

Al-Ghazali, also known as Algazel in the West, was an influential Islamic philosopher, theologian, and mystic, whose works reshaped Islamic thought during the medieval period. Born in Tus, in present-day Iran, Al-Ghazali lived during the Abbasid Caliphate's intellectual zenith. He initially studied Islamic jurisprudence and philosophy, and his early career was marked by engagement with the rationalist traditions of Islamic philosophy, particularly the works of Avicenna and the broader Islamic Neoplatonic tradition. However, after experiencing a personal spiritual crisis, Al-Ghazali withdrew from public life, eventually adopting Sufism, and became one of its most significant proponents.

Al-Ghazali's philosophical and theological thought is best captured in his critique of Islamic philosophers in Tahafut al-Falasifa (The Incoherence of the Philosophers). In this work, he systematically attacked the metaphysical positions of philosophers like Avicenna and Al-Farabi, particularly their views on the eternity of the world and the nature of causality. Al-Ghazali argued that philosophers could not prove the necessity of cause and effect relationships, introducing what would later be known as occasionalism—the idea that God is the direct cause of all events. This rejection of rationalist metaphysics marked a major shift in Islamic philosophy, moving it away from Aristotelian and Neoplatonic influences and toward a more theological, fideistic approach.

A central theme in Al-Ghazali's work is the relationship between reason and faith. While Al-Ghazali was initially steeped in philosophical methods, he came to believe that rational inquiry alone was insufficient for understanding the deepest truths about God and the universe. He argued that philosophy could only take one so far, and that true knowledge could only be attained through divine revelation and mystical experience. In his later work, Ihya Ulum al-Din (The Revival of the Religious Sciences), Al-Ghazali integrated Islamic theology with Sufism, emphasizing the importance of spiritual practices, such as prayer and meditation, in attaining direct knowledge of God.

Al-Ghazali's embrace of Sufism marked a turning point in Islamic thought, as he sought to reconcile orthodox Islamic theology with the mysticism of Sufism. He believed that true knowledge of God was experiential, rather than intellectual, and that the ultimate goal of human life was to draw closer to God through inner purification and mystical experience. His emphasis on inner spirituality and his critique of philosophy had a profound impact on Islamic intellectual life, leading to a greater acceptance of Sufism and a diminished role for speculative philosophy.

Al-Ghazali's influence extended beyond the Islamic world, with his works being translated into Latin and studied by medieval European philosophers. His critique of causality, in particular, influenced later developments in philosophy, including the works of David Hume. Al-Ghazali's integration of mysticism, theology, and philosophy helped shape the future trajectory of Islamic thought, making him one of the most important figures in the history of Islamic philosophy.

Peter Abelard (1079 – 1142 CE)

Peter Abelard, a French philosopher and theologian, was one of the most renowned intellectual figures of the 12th century. Born in Brittany, Abelard became famous for his dialectical skills and his controversial approach to theology. He taught at the Cathedral School of Notre-Dame in Paris, where his debates with other prominent scholars, particularly William of Champeaux, made him a leading figure in Scholasticism. Abelard's tumultuous personal life, including his infamous love affair with Héloïse, has often overshadowed his intellectual achievements, but his contributions to logic, ethics, and theology remain central to medieval thought.

One of Abelard's most significant contributions to philosophy was his development of conceptualism, a middle ground between the extreme positions of realism and nominalism in the medieval debate over universals. Realists, following Plato, argued that universals (such as "humanness") exist independently of particular things, while nominalists claimed that universals were merely names with no real existence. Abelard proposed that universals exist as concepts in the mind but do not have independent, external existence. This conceptualist view allowed him to navigate between the two extremes and became an important part of Scholastic philosophy.

In addition to his work on universals, Abelard made substantial contributions to ethics, particularly in his Ethica (often referred to as Scito Te Ipsum, or Know Thyself). He argued that morality is determined not by the external action itself but by the intention behind it. Abelard held that an action is only sinful if the agent knowingly and willingly acts against their conscience. This emphasis on intention rather than the action itself was a significant departure from earlier ethical theories and paved the way for later discussions on moral culpability in medieval and modern ethics.

Abelard's Sic et Non (Yes and No) was another groundbreaking work that demonstrated his method of dialectical reasoning. In this work, Abelard presented seemingly contradictory statements from Church Fathers on theological issues, encouraging his students to resolve the contradictions through reasoned analysis. This method was innovative in that it encouraged critical thinking and inquiry rather than mere acceptance of authority. Abelard's use of dialectic had a lasting impact on Scholasticism, and his method of posing questions and seeking logical solutions influenced the development of medieval theological debate.

Despite his intellectual achievements, Abelard's life was marked by controversy. His views on theology and the nature of the Trinity led to charges of heresy, and he was condemned at the Council of Soissons in 1121. Nevertheless, his philosophical and theological works had a profound influence on later thinkers, including Thomas Aquinas. Abelard's emphasis on reason and logic in theology, as well as his contributions to ethics and dialectic, solidified his place as one of the most important philosophers of the medieval period.

Averroes (Ibn Rushd) (1126 – 1198 CE)

Averroes, also known as Ibn Rushd, was a prominent Andalusian philosopher, jurist, and physician, born in Córdoba, in what is now Spain. He is best known for his extensive commentaries on Aristotle, through which he sought to reconcile Greek philosophy with Islamic thought. Averroes lived during a time of intellectual flourishing in the Islamic West, particularly in Al-Andalus, where scholars engaged with both Islamic and classical Greek traditions. His work significantly influenced the transmission of Aristotelian philosophy to the Latin West, shaping the development of Western European philosophy during the Middle Ages and the Renaissance.

Averroes' primary philosophical project was to defend the compatibility of philosophy and religion, particularly through his interpretation of Aristotle's works. He argued that both philosophy and Islamic revelation aimed at the same truth but used different methods to reach it. Philosophy employed rational inquiry and logical argumentation, while religion used symbolic language and revelation. In his The Decisive Treatise, Averroes argued that it was not only permissible but necessary for learned Muslims to study philosophy, as reason was a gift from God that could aid in the understanding of divine truth. He believed that there was no contradiction between reason and faith when properly understood.

One of Averroes' most significant contributions to philosophy was his theory of the "double truth." He posited that there are two distinct ways of understanding the world: one based on philosophical reason and the other on religious faith. These two modes of understanding could coexist without necessarily conflicting. While this idea was controversial in both the Islamic and Christian worlds, it offered a framework for reconciling philosophical inquiry with religious belief. Averroes contended that philosophical truths, such as those found in Aristotle, could coexist with religious truths, provided that they were interpreted correctly.

Averroes also made major contributions to metaphysics, particularly in his discussion of the nature of the intellect. He expanded on Aristotle's theory of the active intellect, arguing that the human intellect was not an individual, personal faculty but a shared, universal intellect. This doctrine, known as "monopsychism," suggested that all human beings share the same active intellect, which exists independently of individual minds. This theory, however, was later criticized by Christian philosophers like Thomas Aquinas, who rejected the idea of a universal intellect. Nevertheless, Averroes' interpretations of Aristotle's metaphysics became highly influential, especially in the Latin West, where they were studied by medieval Christian scholars.

Averroes' work had a profound impact on both the Islamic and Western intellectual traditions. His commentaries on Aristotle were translated into Latin and Hebrew, significantly shaping the development of medieval Scholasticism and the Renaissance. Though his ideas were not universally accepted within the Islamic world, his efforts to reconcile reason and faith left a lasting legacy, influencing philosophers such as Thomas Aquinas and Spinoza. Averroes remains a key figure in the history of philosophy, particularly for his role in preserving and transmitting classical Greek thought to the medieval West.

Maimonides (1138 – 1204 CE)

Maimonides, born Moses ben Maimon in Córdoba, Spain, was one of the most influential Jewish philosophers, legal scholars, and physicians of the medieval period. After his family fled religious persecution, they settled in Egypt, where Maimonides eventually became the personal physician to the Sultan of Egypt. He is best known for his works on Jewish law and philosophy, particularly his monumental work The Guide for the Perplexed, which sought to reconcile Aristotelian philosophy with Jewish theology. Maimonides lived during a time of significant cultural and intellectual exchange between Jewish, Christian, and Islamic scholars, and his works reflect the philosophical currents of his time.

In The Guide for the Perplexed, Maimonides tackled the relationship between reason and revelation, arguing that the truths of philosophy and the truths of the Hebrew Bible could be harmonized. He believed that both reason and divine revelation were valid paths to understanding the nature of God and the universe. Like Averroes, Maimonides was influenced by Aristotle's philosophy, particularly in his views on metaphysics and ethics. He argued that while the Hebrew Bible used symbolic language to communicate complex metaphysical truths to the masses, the philosopher could uncover deeper meanings through rational inquiry and allegorical interpretation.

One of Maimonides' key philosophical contributions is his negative theology, or apophatic theology. He maintained that God's essence is entirely beyond human comprehension and that humans can only describe what God is not, rather than what God is. For Maimonides, any positive descriptions of God would limit the infinite nature of the divine. Thus, he argued that God should be understood in negative terms—for example, God is not material, not finite, and not subject to time. This approach allowed Maimonides to uphold the transcendence of God while acknowledging the limitations of human knowledge.

Maimonides also made significant contributions to ethics and political philosophy, particularly in his view of the human goal as intellectual perfection. He argued that the ultimate purpose of human life is to cultivate the intellect and achieve knowledge of God. For Maimonides, moral virtue was essential for developing the intellect, but intellectual virtue, or knowledge of the divine, was the highest goal. His ethical system was heavily influenced by Aristotle, particularly the idea that virtue is a mean between extremes. Maimonides believed that by cultivating virtues and pursuing knowledge, humans could fulfill their purpose and attain true happiness.

Maimonides' influence extended far beyond the Jewish community, as his works were widely studied by Christian and Islamic philosophers. His synthesis of Aristotelian philosophy and Jewish theology had a profound impact on the development of Scholastic thought, particularly on figures like Thomas Aquinas. Maimonides' contributions to Jewish law, philosophy, and medicine solidified his reputation as one of the greatest intellectual figures of the medieval period. His legacy continues to be felt in both religious and philosophical circles today.

Dogen (1200 – 1253 CE)

Dogen was a Japanese Zen Buddhist teacher and the founder of the Soto school of Zen in Japan. He was born in Kyoto to an aristocratic family but lost his parents at a young age, prompting him to seek answers to existential questions. His quest for enlightenment led him to study various forms of Buddhism, and eventually, he traveled to China, where he studied under the Zen master Rujing. It was during this time that he had a profound realization that became the foundation of his teachings, centered around the concept of "just sitting" (shikantaza) as the core of Zen practice. Dogen returned to Japan with a mission to share his insights, determined to reform the Buddhist practice of his time and bring it back to its meditative essence.

Dogen's philosophy was deeply influenced by his time in China and his study of the Chan (Zen) tradition. Upon returning to Japan, he emphasized the importance of direct experience in meditation, rejecting intellectualism and ritualism that had permeated Japanese Buddhism at the time. His teachings revolved around zazen, or seated meditation, which he saw not as a means to an end but as an expression of enlightenment itself. This radical approach distinguished his teachings from other schools of Zen that treated meditation as a path toward achieving enlightenment.

One of Dogen's key philosophical concepts is "genjokoan," which refers to the idea that enlightenment is not a distant goal but is manifested in the present moment through the ordinary activities of life. He taught that all beings, in their inherent nature, are already enlightened, but they fail to realize it due to delusion. Through the practice of zazen, one could realize this inherent enlightenment in the here and now. This view challenged the traditional Buddhist notion of enlightenment as something to be attained after years of practice and brought a sense of immediacy and accessibility to his teachings.

Dogen's understanding of time, known as "uji" or "being-time," is another significant aspect of his philosophy. He argued that time is not a linear progression of past, present, and future but is experienced directly in the present moment. Each moment is a complete expression of being, and thus, every action, no matter how mundane, contains the potential for enlightenment. This idea reinforced his teaching that the practice of zazen in each moment is itself the realization of enlightenment. For Dogen, existence and time were inseparable, making every moment a sacred opportunity for awakening.

Dogen's writings, particularly his masterwork Shobogenzo (Treasury of the True Dharma Eye), continue to be studied by Zen practitioners and scholars. His emphasis on the unity of practice and enlightenment, as well as his unique interpretation of time and existence, has made him one of the most influential figures in the history of Zen Buddhism. His teachings remain a cornerstone of Soto Zen, inspiring practitioners to find enlightenment in the simplicity of everyday life.

Rumi (1207 – 1273 CE)

Rumi, born Jalal ad-Din Muhammad Balkhi, was a Persian poet, Islamic scholar, and Sufi mystic whose works have had a lasting impact on both Islamic thought and world literature. Born in present-day Afghanistan, Rumi later moved to Konya in modern-day Turkey, where he became a renowned teacher and mystic. He is best known for his poetic works, particularly the Masnavi, a six-volume spiritual epic that explores themes of divine love, the soul's journey toward God, and the human experience of separation and union with the divine. Rumi's teachings arose in the context of Sufism, the mystical tradition of Islam, which emphasizes direct personal experience of God through love and devotion.

Central to Rumi's philosophy is the concept of divine love (ishq), which he viewed as the driving force behind all creation. He believed that every soul yearns for union with God, and this longing is expressed through love. Rumi's poetry often uses metaphors of earthly love to illustrate the deeper, spiritual love that binds the human soul to the divine. For Rumi, love is both the means and the goal of the spiritual path—it is through love that the soul transcends the ego and realizes its oneness with God. This theme of love as a transformative force permeates much of his work.

Another key aspect of Rumi's philosophy is the idea of fana, or the annihilation of the self in God. In Sufi thought, fana refers to the dissolution of the individual ego and the realization of the divine within oneself. Rumi taught that the soul must transcend the illusion of separation and ego in order to experience unity with the divine. This process of annihilation is not a loss of identity but a realization of the soul's true nature as part of the divine reality. Rumi's poetry often reflects this mystical journey, using imagery of fire, water, and the cosmos to describe the soul's transformation.

Rumi's works also emphasize the importance of spiritual practice, particularly through dhikr (remembrance of God) and music. As a Sufi mystic, Rumi believed that spiritual practices, such as chanting and music, could help individuals draw closer to God. His association with the whirling dervishes, a Sufi order that practices a form of ecstatic dance, reflects his belief in the physical embodiment of spiritual devotion. Rumi saw the act of whirling as a symbolic representation of the soul's journey toward the divine, where the spinning of the body mirrors the movement of the cosmos and the soul's rotation around the divine center.

Rumi's influence has extended far beyond the Islamic world, with his poetry being translated into numerous languages and embraced by readers from various religious and cultural backgrounds. His exploration of love, the soul, and the divine has made him one of the most celebrated mystical poets in history. Today, Rumi's works continue to inspire spiritual seekers and artists alike, and his teachings on love and unity resonate across cultures and religions.

Thomas Aquinas (1225 – 1274 CE)

Thomas Aquinas, born in Roccasecca, Italy, in 1225, was a Dominican friar and one of the most influential philosophers and theologians of the Middle Ages. Educated in the Benedictine tradition, Aquinas later studied at the University of Naples, where he was exposed to Aristotelian philosophy. Despite his family's opposition, he joined the Dominican Order and studied under Albertus Magnus in Cologne and Paris. Aquinas lived during a period when the integration of Aristotle's philosophy with Christian theology was a significant intellectual endeavor, especially within the Scholastic tradition. His most famous work, Summa Theologica, is a comprehensive exploration of theology, ethics, and metaphysics.

Aquinas is best known for his attempt to reconcile faith and reason, asserting that both could coexist and complement each other. He argued that while human reason could discover certain truths about God, such as His existence, divine revelation was essential for understanding deeper theological mysteries, like the Trinity and the Incarnation. This synthesis of Aristotelian logic with Christian doctrine marked a crucial development in Scholasticism, where philosophical inquiry supported theological understanding. Aquinas believed that reason was a gift from God and that the pursuit of knowledge through both faith and reason led to the ultimate truth.

Aquinas' Five Ways is one of his most significant contributions, providing five logical arguments for the existence of God. These include the argument from motion, the argument from causality, the argument from contingency, the argument from degrees of perfection, and the teleological argument (design). Drawing heavily from Aristotelian principles, Aquinas demonstrated that the existence of change and causality in the world pointed to the necessity of a first cause, which he identified as God. His metaphysical arguments for God's existence laid the groundwork for future discussions on natural theology and greatly influenced Christian philosophy.

Aquinas' ethical system was grounded in Aristotelian virtue ethics but expanded with Christian theology. He argued that the ultimate goal of human life is union with God, and achieving this goal required cultivating both intellectual and moral virtues. He incorporated Aristotle's virtues and added the theological virtues of faith, hope, and charity, which he believed were necessary for achieving eternal happiness with God. Aquinas also emphasized that human reason and natural law guided ethical behavior, but divine grace was essential for spiritual salvation. His ethical thought became central to Christian moral theology and influenced Western philosophical discussions on virtue and morality.

In his political philosophy, Aquinas developed a theory of natural law that deeply influenced Western legal and ethical thought. He posited that natural law, derived from divine eternal law, was discernible through human reason and provided the basis for moral conduct and human legislation. He argued that human laws must align with natural law to be just and that unjust laws lacked moral authority. Aquinas' views on natural law, justice, and the proper relationship between church and state shaped later discussions on human rights and legal theory, making him a pivotal figure in both medieval and modern thought.

John Duns Scotus (c. 1266 – 1308 CE)

John Duns Scotus was born in Duns, Scotland, and became one of the most influential philosophers and theologians of the High Middle Ages. A member of the Franciscan Order, he was educated at Oxford and later taught at the University of Paris, where he gained a reputation for his complex and subtle arguments, earning the title Doctor Subtilis (the Subtle Doctor). Scotus lived during a time when the philosophical and theological dominance of Thomas Aquinas was being questioned, particularly in the Franciscan tradition. His works, primarily concerned with metaphysics, theology, and ethics, provided a rigorous alternative to Thomistic philosophy.

One of Scotus' most important contributions to metaphysics is his theory of "formal distinction," which offers a middle ground between Aquinas' real distinction (where two things are separate) and mere conceptual distinction (existing only in the mind). For Scotus, entities like God's attributes or a soul's faculties are formally distinct, meaning they are conceptually separable but not actually separate in reality. This theory became essential in theological debates, particularly concerning the nature of the Trinity and Christ's Incarnation, where divine attributes must be distinguished without implying actual division. His formal distinction was a nuanced response to earlier metaphysical problems and influenced later medieval thought.

Scotus also developed the concept of haecceity, or "thisness," a major advancement in metaphysical individualism. Whereas Aquinas emphasized universals, Scotus argued that individual beings are unique due to their haecceity, a property that gives them their individual identity. This move emphasized the uniqueness of each entity in contrast to earlier Aristotelian views that focused on universal qualities. The concept of haecceity laid the foundation for later discussions on individuation and identity, particularly within theology and philosophy.

In ethics, Scotus is known for his defense of voluntarism, which holds that God's will is supreme and not subordinate to divine reason or moral law. While Aquinas emphasized that God's actions align with His intellect and reason, Scotus argued that God's will is absolutely free and not constrained by any external standards. For Scotus, morality is contingent on God's will, meaning that what is morally right or wrong is determined by God's commands. This voluntarist approach had profound implications for the understanding of divine omnipotence and moral obligation, challenging the Thomistic emphasis on natural law.

Scotus' thought significantly influenced later philosophy, especially within the Franciscan tradition. His metaphysical and ethical ideas provided a counterpoint to Thomism and shaped the theological debates of his time. His emphasis on individuality and the role of divine will in morality left a lasting legacy, influencing philosophers such as William of Ockham. Scotus remains a key figure in medieval philosophy, contributing to enduring debates on metaphysics, ethics, and theology.

William of Ockham (c. 1287 – 1347 CE)

William of Ockham, born in Ockham, Surrey, was an English Franciscan friar, philosopher, and theologian, best known for his principle of parsimony, often called Ockham's Razor. He studied and taught at Oxford but faced significant controversy later in his life, especially when he was summoned to Avignon to defend himself against accusations of heresy. Ockham lived during a time of intense intellectual and political tension between the papacy and secular rulers, and his writings reflect his challenges to both ecclesiastical authority and intellectual orthodoxy. Ockham's work in metaphysics, logic, and political theory made him one of the most influential thinkers of the late medieval period.

Ockham's Razor, his most famous contribution, asserts that one should not multiply entities beyond necessity, meaning the simplest explanation or theory with the fewest assumptions is preferable. Ockham applied this principle to his critique of the dominant metaphysical views of his time, particularly those of the Scholastics who followed Aristotle. He argued that universals (abstract entities like "humanity" or "redness") did not exist independently of the mind but were merely mental concepts. This nominalist view stood in contrast to the realism of philosophers like Thomas Aquinas, who believed in the real existence of universals.

Ockham also made significant contributions to epistemology, particularly in his development of empirical knowledge. He argued that humans know individual things directly through sensory experience and that knowledge of universals comes only from abstraction, not from direct experience. This emphasis on empirical knowledge and the rejection of unnecessary metaphysical entities laid the groundwork for later developments in empiricism, influencing philosophers like John Locke and David Hume. Ockham's insistence on the limits of human knowledge also led him to critique speculative theology and metaphysics, emphasizing that certain divine truths can only be known through faith, not reason.

In political philosophy, Ockham argued for a separation of powers between the church and the state, particularly in his conflict with Pope John XXII. In works such as Dialogus, Ockham contended that the pope did not have the authority to interfere in secular political matters and that secular rulers had a right to govern independently. Ockham's political writings, combined with his philosophical views on the limits of papal authority, contributed to the broader intellectual movement that sought to limit the political power of the church. His political thought helped lay the foundation for later secular theories of governance and contributed to the development of modern political philosophy.

Ockham's influence extended far beyond his lifetime, especially in the areas of logic, metaphysics, and political thought. His nominalism and emphasis on empirical knowledge were significant departures from the dominant philosophical traditions of his time, and his political ideas challenged the authority of the papacy. Ockham's legacy can be seen in the development of later philosophical movements, particularly in the rise of empiricism and the eventual separation of church and state in modern political thought.

Longchenpa (1308 – 1364 CE)

Longchenpa, also known as Longchen Rabjampa, was a prominent Tibetan philosopher and scholar of the Nyingma school of Tibetan Buddhism. He was born in the central region of Tibet during a period of significant Buddhist scholastic activity and religious development. His life was dedicated to the study, practice, and systematization of the Dzogchen teachings, which were central to the Nyingma tradition. Longchenpa is widely regarded as one of the greatest scholars of Dzogchen, and his writings and teachings continue to influence Tibetan Buddhism to this day. He is also remembered for his meditative depth and the profound spiritual realization he embodied, inspiring countless practitioners.

Longchenpa's philosophy is deeply rooted in Dzogchen, or the "Great Perfection," which teaches that the nature of reality and the mind is innately pure and that enlightenment is already present within all beings. He elaborated on these teachings by developing a systematic presentation of Dzogchen, focusing on the idea that the ultimate nature of all phenomena is emptiness (shunyata), and that enlightenment is the recognition of this inherent emptiness. His works, such as the Seven Treasuries and the Trilogy of Natural Ease, provide extensive commentaries and instructions on Dzogchen practice, emphasizing the direct realization of the mind's natural state.

One of Longchenpa's key contributions was his synthesis of Dzogchen with other Buddhist teachings, such as Madhyamaka and Yogachara. He harmonized the philosophical rigor of Madhyamaka's emptiness teachings with the experiential, contemplative practices of Dzogchen. This integration allowed practitioners to understand the ultimate emptiness of phenomena while simultaneously recognizing the innate clarity and awareness of the mind. Longchenpa emphasized that both conceptual understanding and direct experience are necessary for spiritual realization.

Longchenpa also focused on the importance of relaxation and naturalness in spiritual practice. He taught that striving for enlightenment or forcing spiritual progress would only create obstacles, as it implies a dualistic mindset. Instead, Longchenpa advocated for resting in the natural state of the mind, free from effort and artificiality. This approach, known as lhundrup or "natural perfection," became central to his interpretation of Dzogchen and remains a core teaching in the Nyingma school. His emphasis on naturalness resonated with practitioners seeking an accessible yet profound path to spiritual realization.

Longchenpa's legacy endures through his vast body of written work, which continues to be studied and revered in Tibetan Buddhist traditions. His synthesis of Dzogchen with broader Buddhist philosophical traditions helped solidify Dzogchen as one of the most profound and respected paths within Tibetan Buddhism. His teachings emphasize the immediacy of enlightenment and the importance of resting in the natural, effortless state of the mind. Longchenpa remains a guiding figure for practitioners of the Nyingma school, bridging timeless wisdom with practical spiritual guidance.

Ibn Khaldun (1332 – 1406 CE)

Ibn Khaldun, born in Tunis in 1332, was an influential historian, sociologist, and philosopher whose work laid the foundations for modern disciplines like historiography and sociology. He was educated in Islamic law, theology, and philosophy and served in various political roles throughout North Africa and Spain before eventually retiring to write his most famous work, the Muqaddimah (Introduction). Ibn Khaldun lived during a period of political instability and fragmentation in the Islamic world, and his experiences in government informed his analysis of the rise and fall of civilizations. His innovative approach to history and society made him one of the most original thinkers of the medieval Islamic world.

In his Muqaddimah, Ibn Khaldun introduced the concept of asabiyyah (social cohesion), which he believed was the key factor behind the success and decline of civilizations. He argued that strong asabiyyah—often found in nomadic or tribal societies—enabled groups to come together, conquer, and establish powerful states. However, as these groups settled and became accustomed to luxury and ease, their social solidarity weakened, leading to their eventual decline. Ibn Khaldun's cyclical view of history was revolutionary, as it focused on social and economic factors rather than divine will or individual rulers to explain the dynamics of historical change.

Another key aspect of Ibn Khaldun's thought is his analysis of economic and political structures. He believed that economics played a crucial role in shaping political power and that the wealth of a state depended on its labor force and the proper management of resources. He also recognized the detrimental effects of excessive taxation, arguing that it would eventually weaken a state's economy and lead to its downfall. His approach to economic and political theory was empirical, based on observation and experience, which set him apart from other thinkers of his time who often relied on more abstract or theological explanations.

Ibn Khaldun's methodology was also groundbreaking in terms of historical writing. He emphasized the importance of critical examination of sources and the need for historians to be objective and skeptical of traditional narratives. He argued that historical events should be analyzed with attention to context and causality, rather than simply accepted at face value. This focus on empirical analysis and the rejection of uncritical reliance on tradition established a new standard for historiography, one that prefigured the scientific approach to history that would emerge in the modern era. His contributions to historical method have earned him the title of the "father of sociology" and "father of historiography."

Ibn Khaldun's work had a profound influence on later Islamic thought and was eventually translated into various European languages during the Renaissance. His emphasis on social dynamics, economics, and political structures as the driving forces of history was revolutionary for its time and continues to resonate in modern social science. His legacy endures as a pioneer in the study of civilizations and historical processes, and his Muqaddimah remains a foundational text in the fields of history, sociology, and political theory.

Tsongkhapa (1357 – 1419 CE)

Tsongkhapa was a Tibetan Buddhist scholar and teacher, born in the Tsongkha region of Amdo, Tibet. His birth occurred during a time when Tibetan Buddhism was undergoing significant development, with various schools interpreting Buddhist doctrines differently. Tsongkhapa became a leading figure in Tibetan Buddhist reform, and his teachings laid the groundwork for the Gelug school of Tibetan Buddhism, which later became the most influential in the region. His life's work culminated in a revival of Buddhist monastic discipline and a return to the philosophical roots of Indian Madhyamaka thought.

Tsongkhapa is best known for his emphasis on the integration of Madhyamaka philosophy with rigorous ethical conduct and tantric practice. He followed in the footsteps of earlier Madhyamaka philosophers like Nagarjuna and Chandrakirti, arguing for the importance of understanding the doctrine of emptiness (shunyata), which posits that all phenomena are empty of inherent existence. Tsongkhapa's unique contribution, however, was his insistence that such understanding must be paired with deep meditative practice and ethical discipline. He believed that wisdom, meditation, and ethical conduct were inseparable on the path to enlightenment.

One of Tsongkhapa's most significant philosophical contributions was his interpretation of the two truths doctrine. He taught that while conventional truths describe the way things appear in the world, ultimate truths reveal their lack of inherent existence. However, Tsongkhapa added that conventional truths must still be respected and used skillfully to progress on the path to enlightenment. He argued against nihilism, stating that although phenomena are ultimately empty, they still function within the framework of causality and interdependence in the conventional world.

Tsongkhapa also made significant contributions to Tibetan monasticism. He reformed the monastic system by emphasizing strict adherence to the Vinaya, the monastic code, which he believed had been neglected. His reforms encouraged rigorous philosophical debate and scholasticism, particularly through the establishment of monastic universities like Ganden Monastery. These institutions became the intellectual centers of Tibetan Buddhism, where the study of logic, ethics, and Madhyamaka philosophy flourished under his guidance.

Tsongkhapa's legacy extends beyond his philosophical works, as he is revered as a bodhisattva and a figure of immense spiritual attainment. His teachings on the "Lamrim," or stages of the path to enlightenment, continue to be foundational texts within the Gelug school, and his balanced approach to ethics, philosophy, and meditation has had a lasting impact on Tibetan Buddhist practice and thought.

Nicholas of Cusa (1401 – 1464 CE)

Nicholas of Cusa, born in Kues, Germany, was a cardinal, philosopher, and mathematician whose work laid the foundation for a transition between medieval Scholasticism and Renaissance humanism. He studied canon law at the University of Padua and theology at the University of Cologne, becoming deeply involved in ecclesiastical affairs throughout his life. Nicholas lived during a time when the Catholic Church faced challenges from within and without, including the growing influence of humanism and the aftermath of the Great Schism. His philosophical contributions reflect a synthesis of medieval theological concerns with the emerging emphasis on human reason and individual inquiry that characterized the Renaissance.

One of Nicholas of Cusa's most influential ideas is the concept of docta ignorantia, or "learned ignorance." He argued that human beings, with their limited faculties, cannot fully comprehend the infinite nature of God or the universe. This acknowledgment of the limits of human knowledge, combined with a faith in the power of reason, forms the core of Nicholas' epistemology. He believed that although humans could not attain complete understanding, they could strive toward knowledge through intellectual humility and the recognition of their limitations, influencing later developments in negative theology and mystical traditions.

Nicholas also introduced the idea of the "coincidence of opposites," a metaphysical concept that sought to reconcile apparent contradictions in the nature of reality. He believed that in God, all opposites—such as the finite and infinite, the one and the many—are unified and transcended. For Nicholas, human understanding is constrained by the dualities of earthly existence, but divine reality transcends these contradictions. This concept prefigured later Renaissance explorations of the unity of all things in the divine.

Nicholas of Cusa also made significant contributions to mathematical philosophy. He explored the philosophical implications of infinity, using geometric analogies to illustrate his metaphysical ideas. For example, he compared God to an infinite circle, whose center is everywhere and circumference nowhere, to convey the idea of divine omnipresence and unity. This blending of mathematical reasoning with metaphysical inquiry was innovative for his time and influenced later thinkers such as Giordano Bruno and Leibniz, bridging medieval Scholasticism with Renaissance humanism.

Nicholas of Cusa's influence extended beyond his immediate philosophical contributions. As a Church reformer, he advocated for unity within the Church, calling for the resolution of schisms and the reconciliation of different religious traditions. His emphasis on the limits of human knowledge and his metaphysical explorations of the divine laid the groundwork for later Renaissance inquiries. His works, especially On Learned Ignorance and The Vision of God, continue to be studied for their profound insights and their role in bridging medieval and Renaissance thought.

Marsilio Ficino (1433 – 1499 CE)

Marsilio Ficino, born in Figline Valdarno, Italy, was a philosopher, physician, and priest who played a central role in the revival of Platonic philosophy during the Italian Renaissance. Educated in Florence under the patronage of Cosimo de' Medici, Ficino gained access to the works of Plato and other classical philosophers. Florence, during Ficino's time, was the epicenter of the Renaissance, and his translation of Plato's works into Latin, along with his commentaries, marked the beginning of a new era in Western philosophy. His efforts to reconcile Platonic thought with Christian theology made him one of the most important intellectual figures of the Renaissance.

At the core of Ficino's philosophy is his synthesis of Platonism and Christianity, developed in works such as Theologia Platonica (Platonic Theology). Ficino believed that Plato's philosophy, particularly the idea of a transcendent reality beyond the material world, was compatible with Christian doctrines about God and the soul. He saw Plato as a precursor to Christian revelation and argued that the Platonic tradition could provide a philosophical framework for understanding Christian theology. Ficino's Christian Platonism emphasized the immortality of the soul and the ascent of the soul toward God, drawing on Plato's ideas about the eternal Forms and the relationship between the material and spiritual worlds.

Ficino also developed a metaphysical system that placed the human soul at the center of the universe. He believed that the human soul is a microcosm of the universe, capable of connecting with both the material and spiritual realms. Influenced by Neoplatonic ideas of emanation, Ficino argued that all things emanate from a single divine source and that the soul serves as a link between the material world and the divine. His philosophy of the soul was a central theme in his writings and profoundly influenced Renaissance thinkers seeking to reconcile humanism with spirituality.

Another significant aspect of Ficino's work is his exploration of love, which he saw as a metaphysical force binding all things together, from the material world to the divine. Drawing on Plato's Symposium, Ficino argued that love governs the ascent of the soul toward God and the harmony of the cosmos. His ideas about love influenced Renaissance art and literature, particularly in the works of poets like Dante and Petrarch, who explored similar themes of divine and earthly love.

Ficino's translation and commentary on Plato, along with his development of Christian Platonism, played a crucial role in the intellectual life of the Renaissance. His blending of classical philosophy with Christian theology helped revive Platonic ideas in the West and established him as a key figure in the revival of humanism. Ficino's influence extended beyond philosophy to the arts, where his ideas about the soul, love, and the cosmos resonated with Renaissance artists and writers, laying the foundation for later philosophical developments in the Renaissance and early modern periods.

Pico della Mirandola (1463 – 1494 CE)

Pico della Mirandola, an Italian Renaissance philosopher, was born into nobility in the region of Mirandola, Italy. A prodigy, he began his studies at the age of 14, mastering numerous languages and subjects at universities across Italy and France. He was deeply immersed in the intellectual world of Renaissance humanism, a movement dedicated to reviving classical wisdom and focusing on human potential. Pico is best known for his Oration on the Dignity of Man, a manifesto of Renaissance humanism that reflects his belief in the potential of human beings to achieve divine knowledge and perfection.

Central to Pico's philosophy is the idea of human dignity and the freedom of the individual to shape their own destiny. In the Oration on the Dignity of Man, he argues that humans occupy a unique place in creation because they have free will and the capacity to choose their path in life. While other creatures are bound by their nature, humans can ascend to the level of angels or descend to the level of animals, depending on their choices. This emphasis on free will and self-determination was a radical departure from medieval notions of predestination and hierarchy, aligning with the Renaissance emphasis on individual potential.

Pico's philosophy also embraced syncretism—the attempt to reconcile different philosophical and religious traditions. He believed that the wisdom of ancient philosophers, Christian theology, and Jewish mysticism could be harmonized into a unified system of truth. In his 900 Theses, he sought to demonstrate the compatibility of Platonic, Aristotelian, Christian, and Kabbalistic ideas. This eclectic approach reflects the broader Renaissance project of rediscovering and integrating the wisdom of the past to create a more comprehensive understanding of the world. Pico's syncretism was emblematic of the Renaissance's intellectual curiosity and desire to transcend boundaries between disciplines.

Neoplatonism was another significant influence on Pico's thought, particularly the idea that the human soul could ascend toward God through intellectual and spiritual contemplation. He believed that the highest form of knowledge was mystical, involving a direct experience of the divine. For Pico, philosophy and theology were intertwined paths that led to the same ultimate truth. His vision of human potential as divine and his belief in the unity of truth had a lasting influence on Renaissance thought, particularly through the works of later thinkers like Marsilio Ficino and Giordano Bruno.

Pico's intellectual legacy is closely tied to the broader cultural movements of the Renaissance, particularly its emphasis on humanism, individualism, and the revival of classical learning. His ambitious attempt to synthesize various philosophical and religious traditions into a single system was a hallmark of the Renaissance spirit of inquiry. Though his life was cut short at the age of 31, Pico's writings, particularly the Oration on the Dignity of Man, continue to be studied as foundational texts in the history of Renaissance philosophy.

Niccolò Machiavelli (1469 – 1527 CE)

Niccolò Machiavelli was born in Florence, Italy, during a time of political instability and frequent power struggles between city-states and foreign powers. He served as a diplomat for the Florentine Republic, gaining firsthand experience in the workings of power, both domestic and international. Machiavelli's political career was shaped by the chaotic nature of Italian politics in the late 15th and early 16th centuries, a context that deeply influenced his pragmatic approach to governance. His most famous work, The Prince (1513), is regarded as one of the foundational texts of modern political philosophy.

In The Prince, Machiavelli presents a political philosophy that emphasizes the necessity of maintaining power and securing the stability of the state, even if it requires morally questionable actions. One of his most famous assertions is that it is better for a ruler to be feared than loved, as fear is a more reliable means of maintaining control. Machiavelli's pragmatic approach to politics departs from the idealistic moralism of earlier political philosophers, arguing that rulers must be prepared to do whatever is necessary to preserve their power and protect the state. This "realism" has often been described as a rejection of traditional moral virtues in favor of political efficacy.

Machiavelli's political thought is grounded in his understanding of human nature, which he viewed as fundamentally self-interested and driven by fear and ambition. He argued that rulers must be able to manipulate these tendencies to maintain control and stability. For Machiavelli, political success depends on the ability to adapt to changing circumstances, and a good ruler must be both cunning and ruthless when necessary. This flexibility, along with his dismissal of the idea that politics should be guided by moral ideals, made Machiavelli's ideas highly controversial and influential in shaping modern political thought.

In addition to The Prince, Machiavelli's Discourses on Livy offers a more positive assessment of republicanism and the importance of civic virtue. In this work, Machiavelli praises the Roman Republic's mixed constitution, which balanced the interests of the nobility and the common people. He argues that a well-ordered republic can achieve long-term stability through the active participation of citizens in government. Despite the ruthless pragmatism of The Prince, Machiavelli's Discourses reveal a deeper commitment to republican ideals and the possibility of a political system based on shared power and civic responsibility.

Machiavelli's legacy in political thought has been profound, particularly in his influence on the development of political realism. His emphasis on power, pragmatism, and the realities of human nature set the stage for later political theorists, including Thomas Hobbes and Friedrich Nietzsche. Although often vilified as a cynic or amoral thinker, Machiavelli's works remain central to discussions on the nature of power, governance, and political ethics.

Wang Yangming (1472 – 1529 CE)

Wang Yangming was a prominent Neo-Confucian philosopher during the Ming dynasty in China. He was born into a scholarly family and became a highly respected official, military leader, and philosopher. Wang's intellectual contributions arose during a time when Confucian orthodoxy was dominant, but its rigid interpretations had begun to stifle philosophical creativity. His ideas challenged the prevailing thought of Zhu Xi, the leading figure of Neo-Confucianism, and he developed a new interpretation of Confucian teachings that emphasized the unity of knowledge and action, as well as the innate moral nature of humans. Wang's ability to integrate philosophical insight with practical governance made his ideas particularly influential among scholars and statesmen.

Wang's most significant philosophical contribution is his doctrine of the "unity of knowledge and action" (zhi xing he yi). He argued that knowing what is right and doing what is right are inseparable, as true knowledge comes from acting on one's moral intuitions. For Wang, moral knowledge was not something abstract that one could merely learn through study; it was realized through action. This marked a departure from the Neo-Confucian orthodoxy of Zhu Xi, who emphasized the importance of study and contemplation before moral action could be undertaken.

Another key aspect of Wang's philosophy is his belief in the innate goodness of human nature, building on Mencius's ideas. Wang taught that everyone possesses an inherent moral compass, referred to as the "original mind" (liangzhi), which can guide them in distinguishing right from wrong. However, he also argued that people become deluded by external influences, leading them to act immorally. His solution was to clear the mind of distractions and return to its original, pure state. This internal focus differed from Zhu Xi's more structured, external approach to cultivating virtue through studying the Confucian classics and rituals.

Wang's ideas on self-cultivation also emphasized personal introspection and mindfulness. He believed that individuals must constantly reflect on their thoughts and actions to align themselves with their inherent moral nature. Unlike Zhu Xi, who believed that the investigation of things in the external world was necessary for moral understanding, Wang argued that the investigation should be inward. This made his philosophy more accessible and practical for laypeople, as it allowed for moral development through daily life experiences rather than formal study.

Wang Yangming's impact on Chinese philosophy was profound, and his ideas sparked a major shift in Neo-Confucian thought. His teachings influenced later scholars and political leaders in both China and Japan, particularly in the development of individualistic and reformist ideas. His ability to bridge philosophical insight with real-world application ensured that his philosophy of the unity of knowledge and action remains influential in contemporary discussions on ethics and personal development.

John Calvin (1509 – 1564 CE)

John Calvin was a French theologian and reformer whose work was central to the Protestant Reformation. Born in Noyon, France, Calvin initially trained as a lawyer before turning to theology during a period of religious upheaval. His theological writings, particularly Institutes of the Christian Religion, became foundational texts for Calvinism, a major branch of Protestantism. Calvin spent most of his later life in Geneva, where he implemented a rigorous model of Christian governance that had a lasting impact on the city and beyond. Calvin's theology was shaped by the intellectual and religious conflicts of the Reformation, particularly the challenges posed by Catholicism and other Protestant movements.

At the core of Calvin's theology is the doctrine of predestination, the belief that God has already determined who will be saved (the elect) and who will be damned. Calvin argued that salvation is entirely dependent on God's sovereign will, not on human actions or merits. This idea of unconditional election set Calvinism apart from other branches of Protestantism and emphasized the absolute sovereignty of God in all aspects of life. Calvin believed that humans, due to original sin, are inherently sinful and incapable of earning salvation on their own; only God's grace can save the elect.

Another key aspect of Calvin's theology is his emphasis on the authority of Scripture. He argued that the Bible is the ultimate source of truth and should be the sole guide for Christian faith and practice. Calvin rejected the Catholic Church's reliance on tradition and the authority of the pope, advocating instead for sola scriptura (Scripture alone) as the foundation of religious belief. This focus on Scripture led to a strong emphasis on personal Bible study in the Reformed tradition, encouraging individuals to engage directly with the text without the need for ecclesiastical mediation.

Calvin also introduced a system of church governance known as presbyterianism, which rejected the hierarchical structures of the Catholic Church in favor of a more democratic model. He believed that churches should be governed by elected elders and ministers, who would be accountable to the congregation. This system of governance had a profound influence on the development of Reformed churches in Europe and later on Presbyterianism in Scotland and North America. Calvin's model of church governance reflected his broader theological commitment to the idea of a community of believers who were directly responsible to God and each other.

Calvin's impact on Protestantism and Western Christianity was profound, with his teachings spreading throughout Europe and shaping the development of Reformed theology. His emphasis on predestination, the authority of Scripture, and a rigorous form of church governance laid the foundations for Calvinism and influenced religious, political, and social life in the centuries that followed. Calvin's ideas continue to be influential in both theological and political discussions, particularly in relation to questions of divine sovereignty, individual responsibility, and the role of the church in society.

Michel de Montaigne (1533 – 1592 CE)

Michel de Montaigne was born into a noble family near Bordeaux, France, in 1533. He received a classical education and held various public offices, including serving as mayor of Bordeaux. However, he is best known for his literary and philosophical work, particularly his Essays, which became a foundational text in the development of the modern essay as a literary form. Montaigne lived during a time of religious conflict in France, particularly between Catholics and Protestants during the French Wars of Religion. His writings reflect the turbulent nature of his time, as well as a deep skepticism about human certainty and the capacity for knowledge.

Montaigne's Essays are characterized by their introspective and skeptical approach to philosophy. Drawing from ancient sources such as the Stoics, Epicureans, and Skeptics, Montaigne questioned the reliability of human reason and knowledge. His essay "Of the Inconsistency of Our Actions" reflects his view that human behavior is unpredictable and often contradictory, making it difficult to form clear judgments about people or their actions. Montaigne believed that human beings are limited by their senses and prone to error, and therefore, absolute certainty is impossible. His skepticism was influenced by Pyrrhonian skepticism, which advocates suspending judgment in the face of uncertainty.

In addition to skepticism, Montaigne's philosophy emphasizes self-knowledge and personal introspection. In his essays, Montaigne frequently reflects on his own experiences, thoughts, and emotions, using himself as a case study to explore broader philosophical questions. His essay "Of Experience" showcases this approach, as he discusses his own illnesses and bodily experiences as a way to consider the nature of the self. For Montaigne, philosophy was not about grand, abstract systems but about understanding one's own nature and limitations. His focus on self-reflection influenced later thinkers like René Descartes, who took up the challenge of understanding the self as a fundamental philosophical project.

Montaigne's essays also touch on ethics and the complexity of human morality. Rather than advocating for rigid moral rules, he argued that ethical judgments must be flexible and take into account the diversity of human behavior and the context in which actions occur. In his essay "On Cruelty," for instance, Montaigne examines the ethical ambiguity of acts of violence, suggesting that moral assessments depend on a deeper understanding of the circumstances and motives behind them. His moral relativism and rejection of universal moral laws were groundbreaking in a time when dogmatic moral and religious systems dominated philosophical discourse.

Montaigne's work has had a lasting impact on modern philosophy, particularly in the areas of skepticism, self-reflection, and ethics. His emphasis on the limitations of human knowledge and the importance of introspection laid the groundwork for later existentialist and phenomenological traditions. Montaigne's style—personal, informal, and speculative—opened new possibilities for philosophical writing and made his essays accessible to a wide audience, establishing him as a key figure in both Renaissance humanism and modern philosophy.

Giordano Bruno (1548 – 1600 CE)

Giordano Bruno was born in Nola, near Naples, Italy, in 1548, and became one of the most controversial and influential philosophers of the late Renaissance. Originally a Dominican friar, Bruno's unorthodox views on religion and cosmology led him to flee Italy to avoid persecution by the Catholic Church. He traveled across Europe, engaging with intellectual circles in France, England, and Germany, but his radical ideas eventually led to his arrest by the Roman Inquisition. In 1600, Bruno was burned at the stake for heresy. Bruno's philosophy, particularly his cosmological theories and metaphysical ideas, positioned him as a figure ahead of his time, bridging the gap between the medieval and modern worlds.

One of Bruno's most significant contributions to philosophy was his idea of an infinite universe. Building on the Copernican heliocentric model, Bruno argued that the universe has no center and is boundless, with an infinite number of stars and planets. This radical cosmology challenged the Aristotelian and Ptolemaic views that dominated the intellectual landscape of the time. Bruno also suggested that the stars were suns, each potentially surrounded by planets that could harbor life. His vision of an infinite, dynamic universe was revolutionary and directly opposed the traditional geocentric view endorsed by the Church.

Bruno's metaphysics was heavily influenced by Neoplatonism, particularly the idea of a unified and interconnected reality. He believed in a form of pantheism, where God and the universe were one and the same, and everything in existence was part of a single divine substance. This view contrasted sharply with orthodox Christian theology, which maintained a strict separation between the Creator and creation. Bruno's pantheism was seen as heretical by the Church, as it implied that the divine was immanent in the material world rather than existing beyond it. His belief in the unity of all things and the divinity of nature resonated with later philosophical movements, particularly during the Enlightenment.

Bruno also contributed to epistemology and the philosophy of knowledge by emphasizing the importance of human imagination and intuition in understanding the universe. He rejected the rigid scholasticism of his time, advocating instead for a more dynamic and imaginative approach to knowledge that embraced both reason and mysticism. Bruno believed that through contemplation and intellectual effort, humans could achieve a deeper understanding of the cosmos and their place within it. His blend of mystical and philosophical thought made him a forerunner of later movements that emphasized the integration of reason and spirituality, such as Romanticism.

Bruno's ideas, although suppressed during his lifetime, had a profound influence on later thinkers and on the Scientific Revolution. His vision of an infinite universe and his challenge to established cosmological and theological doctrines paved the way for later developments in astronomy and metaphysics. Bruno's philosophy, which combined scientific speculation with mystical insight, continues to be studied for its innovative approach to the relationship between science, religion, and philosophy.

Francis Bacon (1561 – 1626 CE)

Francis Bacon was born in London to a wealthy and politically influential family, with his father serving as Lord Keeper of the Great Seal. He was educated at Trinity College, Cambridge, and later studied law at Gray's Inn. Bacon held several important political positions throughout his life, including Attorney General and Lord Chancellor, though his political career was marred by charges of corruption. His true legacy lies in his work as a philosopher and advocate for scientific reform. Living during the rise of modern science, Bacon sought to challenge the prevailing scholastic method and replace it with a new approach to knowledge rooted in empirical observation and inductive reasoning.

Bacon's most significant contribution to philosophy was his development of the scientific method, emphasizing experimentation and inductive reasoning as the means to acquire knowledge. In his works Novum Organum and The Advancement of Learning, Bacon criticized the Aristotelian reliance on deductive reasoning and syllogism, which he believed led to erroneous conclusions when applied to the natural world. Instead, he advocated for an empirical approach where knowledge would be built upon careful observation, collection of data, and experimentation.

A key component of Bacon's thought was the idea of "knowledge as power," which reflected his belief that scientific knowledge could be used to improve human life. He believed that by systematically studying nature, humans could harness its forces for practical purposes, thereby achieving mastery over the environment. Bacon saw this as a moral duty, urging society to abandon fruitless speculation in favor of tangible progress. This utilitarian view of knowledge was revolutionary and laid the groundwork for the development of modern science, particularly during the Scientific Revolution.

Bacon also explored the nature of human error, which he attributed to what he called "idols of the mind." These "idols" were inherent biases or cognitive distortions that prevented people from perceiving reality accurately. He categorized them into four types: the Idols of the Tribe (human nature's tendency toward error), the Idols of the Cave (personal biases based on individual experiences), the Idols of the Marketplace (miscommunication through language), and the Idols of the Theater (the influence of philosophical dogma). By identifying and overcoming these obstacles, Bacon believed, individuals could purify their minds and approach the natural world with greater clarity.

Bacon's vision of a collaborative and systematic approach to scientific inquiry had a profound influence on the development of modern science. His emphasis on empirical evidence and the rejection of untested assumptions inspired later scientists, including Isaac Newton and Robert Boyle. Bacon's work helped shift the focus of intellectual inquiry from abstract theorization to practical experimentation, establishing a methodology that still underpins scientific research today. Though his political career ended in disgrace, Bacon's philosophical contributions continue to be celebrated for their foundational role in shaping modern science and rational thought.

Tommaso Campanella (1568 – 1639 CE)

Tommaso Campanella was an Italian philosopher, theologian, and poet born in Stilo, Calabria. He joined the Dominican Order as a young man and became deeply interested in the works of Renaissance thinkers and the reformist ideas of his time. Campanella's life was marked by political and religious conflict, as he was involved in conspiracies against Spanish rule in southern Italy and spent much of his life imprisoned. Despite these hardships, he produced a wide range of writings on philosophy, theology, and political theory, often reflecting a desire for religious and political reform during the height of the Counter-Reformation.

Campanella's most famous work, The City of the Sun, is a utopian vision of an ideal society based on reason, communal ownership, and religious unity. Written while he was in prison, the work describes a society governed by philosopher-priests who rule according to natural law and divine wisdom. In this ideal city, all property is held in common, reflecting Campanella's belief that communal living would eliminate greed and inequality. His vision of a theocratic society, where religious and political authority are united, was deeply influenced by his Catholic faith, while also incorporating elements of Neoplatonism and Renaissance humanism.

Philosophically, Campanella was influenced by naturalism and believed that the natural world was a manifestation of God's will. In his Philosophia Realis, he argued that the universe is a living organism, animated by a divine force that permeates all things. This pantheistic view led him to challenge the mechanistic worldview emerging during his time. He believed that by understanding the divine order in nature, humans could attain greater knowledge and spiritual fulfillment. Campanella also criticized the scholastic tradition for its reliance on Aristotelian logic, advocating for a more intuitive and mystical approach to understanding the world.

Campanella's political philosophy was shaped by his desire for reform. He opposed the oppressive rule of the Spanish monarchy over Italy and advocated for a unified Christian state under the leadership of a philosopher-king. His involvement in anti-Spanish conspiracies led to his imprisonment, where he continued to write and refine his ideas. His vision of a theocratic society, ruled by a divinely inspired leader, was both a critique of contemporary political corruption and an idealistic blueprint for a just and harmonious world, though his political ideas were never realized.

Campanella's intellectual legacy is marked by his efforts to reconcile religion, philosophy, and politics in a unified vision of human society. His work, particularly The City of the Sun, reflects both his mystical religious convictions and his belief in the power of reason to transform society. Despite spending much of his life in prison, Campanella's philosophical writings had a significant impact on the intellectual landscape of the early modern period, influencing both utopian thought and the ongoing dialogue between science, religion, and politics.

Hugo Grotius (1583 – 1645 CE)

Hugo Grotius, born in Delft, Netherlands, was a Dutch jurist, diplomat, and philosopher whose work laid the foundation for international law and the concept of natural rights. A child prodigy, Grotius entered the University of Leiden at age 11 and by his early twenties had already established himself as a brilliant legal scholar. He lived during a time of political and religious upheaval in Europe, including the Eighty Years' War between Spain and the Dutch Republic. Grotius' writings were influenced by the need for legal frameworks that could help resolve conflicts between nations and govern the interactions between states, especially in the context of maritime law.

Grotius' most important work, De Jure Belli ac Pacis (On the Law of War and Peace), published in 1625, is considered one of the foundational texts of modern international law. In this work, Grotius argues for the existence of a universal natural law that applies to all human beings and transcends the laws of individual nations. He believed that natural law was derived from reason and that its principles were self-evident, providing a basis for just conduct in both war and peace. Grotius' conception of natural law laid the groundwork for the development of international legal systems, particularly in relation to the rules of warfare and the rights of nations to defend themselves.

A key aspect of Grotius' philosophy is his emphasis on the moral limits of warfare. He argued that war could be justified only under certain conditions, such as self-defense or the protection of innocent parties, and that even in war, there were rules that should govern the conduct of soldiers and states. This idea of "just war theory" was rooted in earlier Christian and Roman thought, but Grotius expanded and systematized it in a way that had a lasting impact on the development of international norms regarding conflict. His belief that even in times of war, human rights must be respected, contributed to the later formation of the Geneva Conventions.

Grotius also made significant contributions to the philosophy of property and sovereignty. In Mare Liberum (The Free Sea), published in 1609, Grotius argued for the principle of free navigation on the high seas, contending that the sea was international territory and could not be claimed by any one nation. This work had a profound influence on maritime law and the development of the concept of the global commons, which continues to play a role in international law today. His ideas on sovereignty and property, which emphasized the role of reason and justice in the regulation of human affairs, were influential in shaping the Enlightenment's focus on individual rights and the rule of law.

Grotius' legacy in international law, natural rights, and just war theory is enduring. His work provided the intellectual foundations for the development of modern legal systems that regulate relations between states, particularly in terms of war, peace, and trade. Grotius' belief in the universality of natural law and its application to international relations helped to establish a framework for diplomacy and legal order that persists in contemporary discussions of global justice and human rights.

Zera Yacob (1599 – 1692 CE)

Zera Yacob, born in Aksum, Ethiopia, was a philosopher and theologian whose works represent one of the earliest examples of rationalist thought in Africa. Yacob lived during a time of religious conflict between Christianity and Islam in Ethiopia, as well as tension within the Ethiopian Orthodox Church. After fleeing persecution for his religious beliefs, Yacob spent several years in exile, living in a cave near the Tekeze River, where he meditated on the nature of God, morality, and human reason. His major work, Hatata (The Inquiry), reflects his philosophical reflections during this period and is considered a seminal text in Ethiopian philosophy.

At the core of Yacob's philosophy is his belief in the supremacy of reason as the guide to truth. He argued that human beings possess the capacity for rational thought, which allows them to discern moral and religious truths independently of external authority. For Yacob, reason was the faculty given by God to humanity to distinguish between right and wrong, and he emphasized that reason should be used to question inherited traditions and religious practices. This rationalist approach set Yacob apart from many of his contemporaries, as he rejected blind adherence to religious dogma in favor of a more personal and reflective form of faith.

Yacob was also a staunch critic of religious intolerance and sectarianism. He believed that true faith must be universal and based on love, rather than division or conflict. In Hatata, he criticized both the Ethiopian Orthodox Church and Islam for their exclusivity and intolerance of other religions, advocating instead for a more inclusive and compassionate understanding of faith. Yacob's emphasis on religious tolerance and his rejection of dogmatism were influenced by his own experiences of persecution and exile, leading him to develop a philosophy that promoted peace and mutual understanding.

Another important aspect of Yacob's philosophy was his ethical focus on the equality and dignity of all human beings. He argued that since all humans are created by God and endowed with reason, they are inherently equal and deserving of respect. This belief in universal human dignity led Yacob to critique practices such as slavery and social inequality, which he saw as contrary to divine law and reason. His moral philosophy, grounded in both rationalism and his understanding of divine justice, was revolutionary for its time and contributed to the broader tradition of human rights and equality in philosophical discourse.

Zera Yacob's Hatata remains a significant work in African philosophy, representing a unique fusion of rationalism, religious tolerance, and ethical inquiry. His emphasis on reason as the path to truth and his advocacy for human dignity and religious tolerance have left a lasting legacy in Ethiopian thought and beyond, positioning him as one of the most important African philosophers of his era.

John Amos Comenius (1592 – 1670 CE)

John Amos Comenius, born in Moravia (modern-day Czech Republic), was a philosopher, pedagogue, and theologian, often regarded as the father of modern education. Comenius lived during a time of intense religious conflict, particularly the Thirty Years' War, which devastated much of Europe. As a Protestant bishop and member of the Unity of the Brethren, Comenius experienced religious persecution firsthand, leading him to spend much of his life in exile. His ideas on education, religion, and philosophy were shaped by his experiences of displacement and the broader intellectual movements of the time, including the rise of humanism and early modern science.

Comenius' most lasting contribution to philosophy is his work in pedagogy, particularly his emphasis on universal education. He believed that education was a natural right of all human beings, regardless of social class, gender, or religious background. His magnum opus, Didactica Magna (The Great Didactic), laid out his vision for a universal system of education that would provide comprehensive instruction to all people. Comenius advocated for a curriculum that was holistic, encompassing intellectual, moral, and spiritual education, and he emphasized that education should be based on understanding and reasoning rather than rote memorization.

Central to Comenius' educational philosophy was the idea of pansophia, or universal wisdom, which he believed should be the goal of all learning. Education, in his view, should integrate knowledge from different disciplines to create a harmonious and well-rounded individual. Comenius saw this as not only an intellectual endeavor but also a spiritual one, as he believed that understanding the natural world brought humans closer to the divine order. His vision of pansophia was influenced by Renaissance humanism and the scientific revolution, which promoted the study of nature and the search for universal truths.

Comenius also introduced several innovative teaching methods that are still in use today. He advocated for teaching children in their native language rather than Latin, which was the traditional language of instruction. He promoted the use of visual aids and illustrations in education, recognizing that learning is more effective when it engages multiple senses. Comenius was among the first educators to suggest adapting lessons to the developmental stage of the learner, laying the groundwork for what is now called developmental psychology. His belief in early childhood education and lifelong learning contributed significantly to the modernization of educational theory.

In addition to his work in education, Comenius wrote extensively on theology and philosophy. He believed that the religious conflicts of his time stemmed from ignorance and misunderstanding and that education could play a key role in promoting peace and unity among different religious groups. His ecumenical vision, rooted in his Christian faith, held that education and reason could bridge divides between sects and foster a more harmonious and tolerant society. Comenius' philosophy of education and religion was deeply interconnected, both serving the higher goal of human flourishing and spiritual development.

René Descartes (1596 – 1650 CE)

René Descartes was born in La Haye en Touraine, France, and was educated at the Jesuit college of La Flèche before studying law at the University of Poitiers. His early intellectual development was shaped by the Renaissance humanist tradition, though he later rejected the scholastic philosophy that dominated European universities. Descartes lived during a time when the foundations of medieval thought were being challenged by the rise of modern science, and his work reflects the tension between established scholasticism and the new scientific methods emerging in Europe. His philosophical project aimed to provide a secure foundation for knowledge in an era of intellectual uncertainty.

Descartes' most famous philosophical concept is Cogito, ergo sum ("I think, therefore I am"), which emerged from his method of radical doubt. In his Meditations on First Philosophy, Descartes sought to doubt everything that could be questioned in order to discover an indubitable truth. By systematically doubting the reliability of sensory perception and even the existence of the external world, Descartes arrived at the conclusion that the very act of doubting required a thinking subject. The certainty of the existence of the self as a thinking entity became the foundational point of his epistemology, from which other knowledge could be derived.

Building upon this foundation, Descartes introduced his theory of dualism, which posited that the mind and body are two distinct substances. The mind, according to Descartes, is an immaterial, thinking substance, while the body is a material, extended substance governed by the laws of physics. This "Cartesian dualism" established a clear distinction between the realm of thought and the physical world, a view that had profound implications for later discussions on consciousness, identity, and free will. Descartes' belief that the mind and body interact, particularly through the pineal gland, was one of the earliest attempts to explain the relationship between mental and physical processes.

Descartes also made significant contributions to science and mathematics, most notably through his work in analytical geometry, which linked algebra and geometry in a new way. His mechanistic view of the physical universe, articulated in The World and Principles of Philosophy, described the natural world as a vast machine operating according to mathematical laws. In this framework, all physical phenomena could be explained by matter in motion, without the need for teleological explanations. Descartes' mechanistic philosophy influenced the development of modern physics, particularly through the works of Isaac Newton and others who built upon his mathematical models.

In addition to his dualistic metaphysics, Descartes advocated for a methodological skepticism that laid the groundwork for modern scientific inquiry. His emphasis on reason and doubt as tools for acquiring knowledge marked a shift from reliance on tradition and authority. Descartes' ideas helped shape the Enlightenment's emphasis on rationality and empirical investigation, securing his place as one of the foundational figures in both modern philosophy and science.

Thomas Hobbes (1588 – 1679 CE)

Thomas Hobbes was born in Westport, England, and educated at Magdalen Hall, Oxford, where he studied classical philosophy and political theory. His intellectual development was shaped by the political turmoil of the English Civil War, which deeply influenced his views on human nature and government. Hobbes' career as a philosopher took shape against the backdrop of widespread conflict, religious strife, and social unrest. His most famous work, Leviathan (1651), was written in response to the chaos of the civil war and remains one of the most influential texts in the history of political philosophy.

At the heart of Hobbes' philosophy is his materialist conception of human nature. He believed that all human actions could be explained by physical processes, and he viewed humans as fundamentally self-interested creatures motivated by fear, desire, and the instinct for self-preservation. In his view, without the constraints of society and government, human life in the "state of nature" would be "solitary, poor, nasty, brutish, and short." This bleak view of human nature led Hobbes to argue that in the absence of a central authority, individuals would be in a perpetual state of war with one another, driven by competition and mistrust.

Hobbes' solution to the problem of the state of nature was the social contract, a theoretical agreement in which individuals agree to surrender certain freedoms to a sovereign authority in exchange for security and peace. The central idea of Leviathan is that a powerful, absolute sovereign is necessary to maintain order and prevent the return to the state of nature. Unlike later social contract theorists, Hobbes argued that the sovereign's authority must be absolute and indivisible, as any division of power would lead to instability and conflict. This emphasis on absolute authority made Hobbes a defender of monarchy, though his theory can be applied to any form of government capable of maintaining peace.

Hobbes also made important contributions to moral and political theory, particularly through his rejection of natural law theories that posited an intrinsic moral order. For Hobbes, right and wrong are defined by the sovereign, and justice is whatever is decreed by the governing authority. He viewed laws as necessary constructs that arise from the social contract, not from any inherent moral truths. This legal positivism, in which laws are seen as human inventions rather than reflections of a natural moral order, was a significant departure from the traditional views of his time and influenced later developments in political philosophy and jurisprudence.

Hobbes' political philosophy, particularly his emphasis on the necessity of a strong central authority, has had a lasting influence on modern political thought. His ideas laid the groundwork for later discussions of state power, sovereignty, and the nature of political obligation, influencing thinkers like John Locke and Jean-Jacques Rousseau. Despite his defense of absolutism, Hobbes is often credited with helping to articulate the principles of social contract theory, which became central to the development of democratic governance.

Blaise Pascal (1623 – 1662 CE)

Blaise Pascal was born in Clermont-Ferrand, France, and was a polymath who made significant contributions to mathematics, physics, and philosophy. As a child prodigy, Pascal excelled in mathematics and developed important works on probability theory, fluid mechanics, and geometry. He lived during a time of intense religious and scientific debates, which influenced both his scientific discoveries and philosophical reflections. In his later life, Pascal became deeply involved in religious thought, particularly through his association with Jansenism, a movement within Catholicism that emphasized predestination and human depravity. Pascal's philosophical works, especially the Pensées, reflect his attempt to reconcile faith with reason in the face of human limitations.

Pascal's most famous philosophical contribution is his "wager" argument, which he presents in the Pensées. Faced with the question of whether to believe in God, Pascal framed belief as a bet: if one believes in God and God exists, the potential reward (eternal life) is infinite, whereas if one disbelieves and is wrong, the loss (eternal damnation) is equally infinite. Pascal's wager is not intended as a proof of God's existence but as a pragmatic argument showing that belief in God is rational given the potential outcomes, shifting focus from metaphysical proofs to practical consequences.

Pascal was also known for his critique of rationalism, which he believed was limited in addressing the deeper questions of human existence. In the Pensées, he famously remarked that "the heart has its reasons which reason does not know," emphasizing the importance of emotions, intuition, and faith in human life. While reason is valuable in understanding the physical world, Pascal argued, it cannot answer existential and metaphysical questions such as the nature of God and the meaning of life. For Pascal, these limitations should lead individuals to embrace faith as the means of grasping divine truths beyond human understanding.

In addition to his religious philosophy, Pascal made significant contributions to early existentialist thought, particularly in his reflections on the human condition. He emphasized the frailty and insignificance of human beings in the vastness of the universe, highlighting the tension between human aspirations and the harsh realities of existence. This existential dimension of his thought, combined with his religious convictions, makes Pascal a precursor to later existentialist philosophers such as Søren Kierkegaard.

Pascal's contributions to both science and philosophy have had a lasting influence. His work in probability theory and mathematics laid the groundwork for developments in statistics and economics, while his reflections on faith and reason continue to resonate in theological and existential debates. His emphasis on the limits of human reason and the role of faith shaped modern discussions about the relationship between science, religion, and human existence.

Anne Conway (1631 – 1679 CE)

Anne Conway, born Anne Finch, was an English philosopher whose work, though not widely known during her lifetime, has since been recognized for its originality and depth. Raised in a wealthy and intellectually vibrant family, Conway corresponded with prominent philosophers such as Henry More, a leading Cambridge Platonist, and Gottfried Wilhelm Leibniz. Her philosophical ideas were deeply influenced by Platonism, Cartesian dualism, and the emerging mechanistic worldview of the 17th century. Conway's most significant work, The Principles of the Most Ancient and Modern Philosophy, written in the late 1670s, challenges the dominant dualistic and mechanistic philosophies of her time, offering a unique metaphysical system rooted in a monistic understanding of reality.

At the heart of Conway's philosophy is her rejection of Cartesian dualism, the view that mind and body are distinct, fundamentally different substances. Instead, Conway proposed a form of monism, arguing that all substances are variations of the same essence, differing only in their degree of perfection. For Conway, the universe is composed of a hierarchy of beings, with God at the top as the most perfect being, followed by spiritual beings (such as angels and souls), and finally material beings. This hierarchy is not static, however, as beings can evolve and change, moving toward greater perfection. Conway's rejection of dualism and her dynamic view of the universe challenged the rigid categories of Cartesian and scholastic metaphysics.

Conway's metaphysical system also included a strong critique of mechanistic philosophy, which viewed the physical world as a series of inert, machine-like interactions between particles. She argued that matter was not passive or inert but rather infused with life and activity, much like spiritual beings. This view, which closely aligned with Neoplatonism, suggested that the entire universe is interconnected and animated by divine energy. Conway's holistic and vitalistic view of the natural world contrasted sharply with the emerging scientific worldview, which emphasized reductionism and mechanical explanations of natural phenomena.

In addition to her metaphysical views, Conway's philosophy had significant ethical implications. She believed that because all beings are part of the same divine substance, they are interconnected and share a common destiny. This led her to advocate for a more compassionate and egalitarian approach to ethics, one that recognized the inherent worth of all beings, regardless of their position in the hierarchy of existence. Her ethical views, grounded in her metaphysical monism, resonated with later thinkers who emphasized the unity and interconnectedness of life, including those in the Romantic and Transcendentalist movements.

Though Conway's work was largely neglected after her death, it has since been rediscovered by scholars who recognize her contributions to metaphysics and early modern philosophy. Her critique of Cartesian dualism, her dynamic view of the universe, and her ethical vision have earned her a place among the most innovative thinkers of the 17th century, influencing later developments in metaphysical thought and ethical philosophy.

Baruch Spinoza (1632 – 1677 CE)

Blaise Pascal was born in Clermont-Ferrand, France, and was a polymath who made significant contributions to mathematics, physics, and philosophy. As a child prodigy, Pascal excelled in mathematics and developed important works on probability theory, fluid mechanics, and geometry. He lived during a time of intense religious and scientific debates, which influenced both his scientific discoveries and philosophical reflections. In his later life, Pascal became deeply involved in religious thought, particularly through his association with Jansenism, a movement within Catholicism that emphasized predestination and human depravity. Pascal's philosophical works, especially the Pensées, reflect his attempt to reconcile faith with reason in the face of human limitations.

Pascal's most famous philosophical contribution is his "wager" argument, which he presents in the Pensées. Faced with the question of whether to believe in God, Pascal framed belief as a bet: if one believes in God and God exists, the potential reward (eternal life) is infinite, whereas if one disbelieves and is wrong, the loss (eternal damnation) is equally infinite. Pascal's wager is not intended as a proof of God's existence but as a pragmatic argument showing that belief in God is rational given the potential outcomes, shifting focus from metaphysical proofs to practical consequences.

Pascal was also known for his critique of rationalism, which he believed was limited in addressing the deeper questions of human existence. In the Pensées, he famously remarked that "the heart has its reasons which reason does not know," emphasizing the importance of emotions, intuition, and faith in human life. While reason is valuable in understanding the physical world, Pascal argued, it cannot answer existential and metaphysical questions such as the nature of God and the meaning of life. For Pascal, these limitations should lead individuals to embrace faith as the means of grasping divine truths beyond human understanding.

In addition to his religious philosophy, Pascal made significant contributions to early existentialist thought, particularly in his reflections on the human condition. He emphasized the frailty and insignificance of human beings in the vastness of the universe, highlighting the tension between human aspirations and the harsh realities of existence. This existential dimension of his thought, combined with his religious convictions, makes Pascal a precursor to later existentialist philosophers such as Søren Kierkegaard.

Pascal's contributions to both science and philosophy have had a lasting influence. His work in probability theory and mathematics laid the groundwork for developments in statistics and economics, while his reflections on faith and reason continue to resonate in theological and existential debates. His emphasis on the limits of human reason and the role of faith shaped modern discussions about the relationship between science, religion, and human existence.

John Locke (1632 – 1704 CE)

John Locke was born in Wrington, Somerset, England, and became one of the most influential philosophers of the Enlightenment. Educated at Westminster School and Christ Church, Oxford, Locke initially studied medicine but developed a deep interest in philosophy and political theory. Locke's intellectual development took place against the backdrop of the English Civil War, the Glorious Revolution, and the rise of constitutional monarchy in England. His work was shaped by the scientific discoveries of his contemporaries, such as Isaac Newton, and his friendship with political figures like Lord Shaftesbury. Locke's ideas on natural rights, government, and empiricism were revolutionary, influencing not only philosophy but also political developments in England and the American colonies.

Locke is best known for his theory of empiricism, which he developed in An Essay Concerning Human Understanding (1690). In this work, Locke argued that all knowledge originates from sensory experience and that the human mind at birth is a tabula rasa (blank slate), challenging the Cartesian idea of innate knowledge. For Locke, knowledge is built gradually through sensory impressions, which the mind organizes into ideas. He rejected the notion of inherent truths or principles, asserting that all concepts must be derived from experience. Locke's empiricism laid the groundwork for later developments in British empiricism, influencing philosophers like George Berkeley and David Hume.

In political philosophy, Locke's most influential work is Two Treatises of Government (1690), where he articulates his theory of natural rights and the social contract. Locke argued that in a state of nature, all individuals are equal and possess inalienable rights, such as life, liberty, and property. Governments, he proposed, are formed through a social contract to protect these natural rights, and political authority is only legitimate if it is based on the consent of the governed. Locke's defense of individual rights and limited government was a direct challenge to the divine right of kings, which had been the dominant political doctrine in Europe.

Locke also introduced the idea of the right to revolution, stating that if a government fails to protect the natural rights of its citizens, they have the right to overthrow it. This idea profoundly impacted political thought, particularly during the Glorious Revolution in England and later in the American and French Revolutions. His advocacy for religious freedom, expressed in A Letter Concerning Toleration (1689), argued that civil government should not interfere in matters of personal belief, a radical notion for his time.

Locke's philosophy had a far-reaching impact on both the Enlightenment and the development of modern liberalism. His ideas on empiricism influenced epistemology and psychology, while his political theories became foundational to liberal democratic thought. The notion that government exists to protect individual rights and that power derives from the consent of the governed continues to resonate in contemporary political discourse, making Locke a central figure in the history of philosophy and political theory.

Gottfried Wilhelm Leibniz (1646 – 1716 CE)

Gottfried Wilhelm Leibniz was born in Leipzig, Germany, and became one of the most prominent philosophers and mathematicians of the early modern period. Educated at the universities of Leipzig and Altdorf, Leibniz was a polymath with wide-ranging interests in mathematics, philosophy, theology, and law. His philosophical ideas emerged during a time of significant scientific and intellectual development, influenced by thinkers like Descartes and Spinoza, as well as the scientific revolution led by figures like Isaac Newton. Leibniz is best known for his contributions to metaphysics, particularly his concept of monads, and for co-developing calculus independently of Newton.

Leibniz's metaphysical system is articulated most fully in his Monadology (1714), where he introduces the concept of monads, which he described as the fundamental building blocks of reality. Monads are simple, indivisible substances that contain no parts and are not influenced by external forces. Unlike physical matter, monads are metaphysical entities that have internal principles of action and are capable of perception and reflection. Leibniz envisioned the universe as a collection of monads, each reflecting the entire cosmos in its own way, but without interacting with one another in the traditional sense. This metaphysical framework provided an alternative to the mechanistic worldview of Descartes and Spinoza.

One of Leibniz's most famous philosophical principles is the principle of sufficient reason, which holds that nothing happens without a reason. According to this principle, for every event or state of affairs, there must be an explanation as to why it is the case rather than otherwise. This idea underpins Leibniz's belief in a rationally ordered universe, where every occurrence can be understood through logical analysis. Leibniz also developed the principle of pre-established harmony, which suggests that the mind and body, though separate substances, operate in perfect synchronization without direct interaction. This was Leibniz's response to the problem of mind-body interaction, providing an alternative to Cartesian dualism.

Leibniz's optimism about the universe is most famously encapsulated in his claim that we live in "the best of all possible worlds." He argued that God, being omnipotent and benevolent, chose to create the best possible world out of all conceivable worlds, even if this world contains evil. For Leibniz, the existence of evil is a necessary condition for the greater good, a notion that sought to reconcile the problem of evil with the existence of a benevolent God. This idea of the best possible world was later satirized by Voltaire in Candide, but it remains a central element of Leibniz's theodicy and his broader metaphysical system.

Leibniz's contributions to philosophy and mathematics were profound. His development of calculus (independently of Newton) revolutionized mathematics, and his metaphysical ideas influenced subsequent philosophers, including Kant. His work in logic and his idea of a universal language, or characteristica universalis, anticipated later developments in symbolic logic and the philosophy of language. Leibniz's rationalism, optimism, and intricate metaphysical system continue to make him a key figure in early modern philosophy.

Giovanni Battista Vico (1668–1744 CE)

Giovanni Battista Vico was born in Naples in 1668, a city rich with the intellectual currents of the Baroque and Counter-Reformation periods. Vico grew up in a humble family and was self-taught for much of his education after an injury limited his schooling. His intellectual pursuits were influenced by the scholastic tradition, humanism, and the emerging ideas of Enlightenment thinkers. Despite the dominance of Cartesianism in his time, Vico critiqued its emphasis on mathematical reasoning and sought a more comprehensive understanding of human nature and culture. His major work, The New Science (1725), emerged in a context of historical and philosophical debates about the nature of history, knowledge, and progress.

Vico's philosophy is centered on the idea of history as a dynamic and cyclical process governed by divine providence. Rejecting the Cartesian method's reliance on abstract reasoning, he argued for the primacy of verum-factum, the principle that truth is verified through creation or making. According to this, humans can truly understand only what they have made, which means human history and culture, rather than the physical world, are the realms of true knowledge. Vico developed a framework that emphasized how societies evolve through cycles of development, decay, and renewal, illustrating these patterns through his studies of myth, law, and language in ancient civilizations.

Central to Vico's philosophy is his theory of the three ages of history: the Age of Gods, the Age of Heroes, and the Age of Men. In the Age of Gods, societies are governed by religious and divine authority, with myths and rituals dominating cultural life. The Age of Heroes follows, marked by aristocratic rule and the beginnings of law and governance, though justice remains personalized and hierarchical. Finally, the Age of Men is characterized by rationality, equality, and the rule of law. While this stage suggests progress, Vico warned of its dangers: excessive rationality can lead to societal fragmentation and eventual decline, restarting the cycle.

Vico's concept of imaginative universals is a cornerstone of his philosophy. He argued that early humans used myth and metaphor to make sense of the world, a process that shaped the foundations of culture and society. Unlike Enlightenment rationalists, who often dismissed mythology as irrational, Vico saw it as a form of early knowledge. Poetry, religion, and art are thus vital components of human development, encoding collective experiences and shaping the transition from primal to civilized states. This approach offered a radical alternative to the Enlightenment's faith in reason as the sole path to progress.

Despite limited recognition during his lifetime, Vico's ideas influenced later thinkers, including the German historicist tradition and the 20th-century philosophy of history. His critique of universalist and linear narratives of progress resonates with contemporary debates about the complexity of cultures and the role of myth in shaping human understanding. Vico's legacy lies in his pioneering view of history as a human construct that must be understood through its own cultural and imaginative contexts, a perspective that continues to challenge modern assumptions about knowledge and progress.

Giambattista Vico (1668 – 1744 CE)

Giambattista Vico, often referred to as Giovanni Battista Vico, was born in Naples, Italy, and became one of the most original thinkers of the early modern period. He was educated at the University of Naples, where he studied law, philosophy, and rhetoric. Vico spent much of his life as a professor of rhetoric at the University of Naples and as a private tutor. Living during a time when Enlightenment rationalism dominated European intellectual life, Vico developed a philosophy that challenged prevailing Cartesian and empiricist worldviews. His most influential work, The New Science (1725), laid the foundation for modern historical philosophy and the study of culture.

Vico's New Science is centered on his belief that human history follows cyclical patterns rather than linear progression. Rejecting the Cartesian notion that human knowledge is based solely on reason and that history is a mere accumulation of facts, Vico argued that human societies evolve through recurring stages, which he described as the "corsi e ricorsi" (cycles and recurrences) of history. These stages—divine, heroic, and human ages—represent different forms of social and political organization. This cyclical theory of history stood in contrast to the Enlightenment's belief in the steady advancement of reason and progress.

Vico also challenged the Cartesian emphasis on rational knowledge, proposing that understanding human history and culture requires a more holistic approach. He argued that the study of society must include myth, poetry, and language, as these elements reveal the deeper structures of human thought and social organization. Vico believed that humans create their own history and institutions, which they can understand more deeply than the natural world, a product of God. This human-centered approach to knowledge, which Vico called "verum factum" (truth through creation), was revolutionary in emphasizing the role of human agency in shaping history.

In The New Science, Vico introduced the "ideal eternal history," a concept suggesting that all societies pass through the same historical cycles driven by universal laws of human nature. For Vico, this ideal history was a tool for understanding the development of individual societies. His focus on the importance of language, myth, and culture in shaping human consciousness laid the groundwork for later developments in anthropology, sociology, and the philosophy of history. Vico's insights into the social construction of knowledge anticipated ideas later explored in postmodernism and cultural studies.

Though largely ignored during his lifetime, Vico's work was rediscovered in the 19th and 20th centuries and is now recognized as foundational to the philosophy of history and social sciences. His critique of rationalism, emphasis on the importance of culture and myth, and cyclical theory of history have had a lasting impact. Vico's ideas influenced thinkers like James Joyce, Benedetto Croce, and Isaiah Berlin, and remain relevant to contemporary debates about the nature of history and the role of human creativity in shaping the world.

Christian Wolff (1679 – 1754 CE)

Christian Wolff was born in Breslau (modern-day Wrocław, Poland), and became one of the most important philosophers of the German Enlightenment. He studied mathematics and philosophy at the University of Leipzig, where he was heavily influenced by the works of Gottfried Wilhelm Leibniz. Wolff's career was marked by both academic success and political controversy; after being expelled from his position at the University of Halle due to religious and philosophical disputes, he later returned to prominence in Prussian academic life. Wolff is best known for systematizing Leibniz's philosophy and for his role in the development of German rationalism, which greatly influenced later thinkers like Immanuel Kant.

Wolff's philosophy was deeply rooted in Leibniz's ideas, particularly the notion of a rational, ordered universe governed by logical principles. In works such as Philosophia Rationalis and Philosophia Practica, Wolff sought to create a comprehensive system of philosophy encompassing all areas of human knowledge, from metaphysics and logic to ethics and political theory. He believed that reason could uncover the fundamental truths of reality and sought to demonstrate that philosophy could provide a unified, scientific understanding of the world. His goal was to make philosophy as rigorous and systematic as mathematics, applying logical principles to every aspect of human inquiry.

One of Wolff's key contributions to philosophy was his distinction between theoretical and practical philosophy. Theoretical philosophy concerns the study of what is, including metaphysics, logic, and natural philosophy, while practical philosophy deals with what ought to be, including ethics, politics, and law. This division influenced later developments in German philosophy, particularly in Kant's distinction between theoretical and practical reason. Wolff's systematic approach aimed to bring coherence to these fields by showing their interconnection through rational principles.

Wolff's influence extended beyond metaphysics and epistemology into ethics and political philosophy. He developed a rationalist ethics grounded in human perfection, arguing that moral action consists in acting according to reason to perfect oneself and contribute to societal perfection. In his political philosophy, Wolff advocated for a rational state governed by laws promoting the common good, believing rulers should govern based on reason rather than tradition or religious authority. His rationalist approach to ethics and politics laid the groundwork for Enlightenment political theory and the development of natural law in Germany.

Wolff's philosophical system, often referred to as Wolffianism, was highly influential in the German-speaking world during the 18th century. His attempt to create a comprehensive, rationalist system of thought profoundly impacted the development of German philosophy, influencing figures such as Alexander Baumgarten and Immanuel Kant. Although Wolff's reputation declined in the 19th century, his work remains significant for its role in shaping Enlightenment intellectual thought and the development of systematic philosophy in Europe.

George Berkeley (1685 – 1753 CE)

George Berkeley was born in Ireland and became one of the most prominent figures in early modern philosophy, primarily known for his development of idealism. Berkeley studied at Trinity College in Dublin, where his engagement with the works of John Locke and other philosophers deeply influenced his thinking. His early philosophical career was marked by his efforts to challenge and refine the ideas of empiricism and materialism. Berkeley's major works include A Treatise Concerning the Principles of Human Knowledge (1710) and Three Dialogues between Hylas and Philonous (1713), which articulate his philosophical system and critique of contemporary thought.

Berkeley's philosophy is best known for its assertion that material substance does not exist independently of perception. He famously argued that "esse est percipi" (to be is to be perceived), meaning that objects only exist in so far as they are perceived by a mind. This view, known as immaterialism, posits that the only things that exist are minds and their ideas. According to Berkeley, physical objects are collections of ideas that depend entirely on the perception of a perceiving mind. This radical departure from materialism and Cartesian dualism challenged the prevailing notions of substance and existence.

In the context of early 18th-century philosophy, Berkeley's immaterialism was a direct response to the materialist and empiricist philosophies of his time. His work aimed to address what he saw as the shortcomings of Locke's and Newton's theories, particularly the notion of abstract material substance. Berkeley criticized the idea that physical objects have an existence independent of the mind and argued that the reality of the external world is rooted in the perceptions and experiences of conscious beings. His critique extended to the theory of abstract ideas, which he believed were incoherent and unnecessary for understanding experience.

Berkeley's philosophy also includes his theistic perspective, which was integral to his immaterialism. He argued that the continuous existence of objects when not perceived is ensured by the perpetual perception of God. According to Berkeley, God's omnipresence guarantees that objects remain in existence and that the order and regularity of nature are preserved. This view provided Berkeley with a way to reconcile his idealism with a coherent account of the persistence and consistency of the external world.

Throughout his career, Berkeley was engaged in various theological and philosophical controversies. His ideas were both praised and criticized, and his work had a profound impact on the development of later philosophical thought. Berkeley's immaterialism influenced subsequent philosophers, including David Hume, who grappled with the implications of Berkeley's denial of material substance. Berkeley's ideas also anticipated some of the arguments of later idealists and influenced discussions about perception, reality, and the nature of existence.

Montesquieu (1689 – 1755)

Charles-Louis de Secondat, Baron de La Brède et de Montesquieu, commonly known as Montesquieu, was born on January 18, 1689, in Bordeaux, France, into a noble family with a background in law and governance. Educated by Catholic priests and later at the University of Bordeaux, he pursued a career in law before inheriting his title and position as a parlement (court) president in Bordeaux upon his uncle's death. His early experiences in law and governance influenced his ideas on politics, liberty, and law. Montesquieu became a prominent Enlightenment thinker, moving within influential intellectual circles in Paris and Europe. He traveled extensively, observing political systems in different countries, including England, which left a lasting impression on his philosophy.

Montesquieu's most significant work, The Spirit of the Laws (1748), explores the relationship between law, government structure, and the social and environmental conditions of different societies. In this groundbreaking text, he proposed that laws should be adapted to each nation's unique geography, climate, and cultural values, suggesting that no single set of laws could apply universally. This perspective marked a departure from the prevailing view that laws were absolute and static. Instead, Montesquieu emphasized a flexible approach to governance, which accounted for the particular needs of each society. His comparative analysis of monarchies, republics, and despotisms identified principles suited to each form of governance, setting the stage for political sociology.

One of Montesquieu's most influential contributions to political thought was his theory of the separation of powers, which he developed as a safeguard for political liberty. He argued that the powers of government should be divided into three branches—executive, legislative, and judicial—to prevent any one entity from becoming tyrannical. Montesquieu admired the English political system, which he saw as embodying this division of powers, and he believed it was the key to preserving individual freedoms. This idea became a fundamental principle in modern constitutional democracies, notably influencing the framers of the United States Constitution.

Montesquieu also believed that each form of government required distinct guiding principles. He argued that republics should be driven by virtue, monarchies by honor, and despotisms by fear. For Montesquieu, these principles explained the internal logic of each system and helped determine which laws would sustain them. For instance, republics require laws that promote public virtue and equality, while monarchies rely on laws that uphold social distinctions and honor. Montesquieu's insights into the principles of government helped frame political science as a discipline focused on understanding the nature of various political systems and the laws best suited to sustain them.

Montesquieu's legacy lies in his emphasis on political liberty, his analysis of the checks and balances necessary to prevent tyranny, and his pioneering view that law must align with social context. By advocating for government structures that align with the character of the people they serve, he provided an early argument for cultural relativism in political philosophy.

Francis Hutcheson (1694 – 1746 CE)

Francis Hutcheson was a Scottish philosopher known for his contributions to moral philosophy and the development of the Scottish Enlightenment. Born in County Antrim, Ireland, Hutcheson studied at the University of Glasgow, where he was influenced by the intellectual climate of the Scottish Enlightenment and the works of earlier philosophers such as John Locke and George Berkeley. Hutcheson became a prominent figure in moral philosophy with his influential writings, including A System of Moral Philosophy (1755, posthumously) and An Inquiry into the Original of Our Ideas of Beauty and Virtue (1725).

Hutcheson's moral philosophy is particularly notable for his development of the concept of the "moral sense," which he proposed as an innate faculty through which individuals discern moral values. According to Hutcheson, this moral sense enables people to perceive and respond to moral qualities in actions and character. He argued that moral judgments are not solely derived from reason or self-interest but from an innate sense of benevolence and empathy. This idea was a significant departure from the prevailing rationalist theories of morality and laid the groundwork for later ethical theories.

In addition to his work on moral sense, Hutcheson made significant contributions to aesthetics. In An Inquiry into the Original of Our Ideas of Beauty and Virtue, he explored the nature of beauty and virtue, asserting that aesthetic appreciation is guided by a sense of beauty, which is also an innate faculty. Hutcheson's exploration of beauty and virtue emphasized the role of sentiment and emotional responses in shaping human experience and judgment, contrasting with the more rationalist approaches of his contemporaries.

Hutcheson's ideas were influential in shaping the ethical and aesthetic theories of the Enlightenment and had a profound impact on later philosophers such as David Hume and Adam Smith. His emphasis on the moral sense and the role of sentiment in moral judgments contributed to the development of sentimentalism and the broader tradition of moral philosophy that focuses on human emotions and moral intuitions. Hutcheson's work also influenced the development of utilitarian ethics and social philosophy.

Throughout his career, Hutcheson engaged in various philosophical debates and maintained a reputation as a leading figure in the Scottish Enlightenment. His contributions to moral philosophy, aesthetics, and social theory remain relevant in contemporary discussions of ethics, sentiment, and the nature of human values. Hutcheson's emphasis on moral sense and his exploration of beauty and virtue have continued to shape philosophical thought and contribute to ongoing debates about the nature of morality and human experience.

Thomas Reid (1710 – 1796 CE)

Thomas Reid was a Scottish philosopher born in Strachan, Aberdeenshire, and is considered the founder of the Scottish School of Common Sense. Reid's work arose in response to the growing influence of empiricism and skepticism, particularly the works of David Hume. Reid studied at the University of Aberdeen and later became a professor at King's College and the University of Glasgow. His intellectual environment was shaped by the Scottish Enlightenment, a period of intense philosophical and scientific development in Scotland. Reid sought to counter the skepticism of Hume by defending the reliability of common sense and direct perception.

Reid's most significant contribution to philosophy is his theory of common sense realism. In contrast to the skepticism of Hume, Reid argued that humans possess an innate ability to perceive the world as it is. According to Reid, the existence of the external world, other minds, and basic moral principles are self-evident and do not require complex philosophical proof. He believed that skepticism about these matters was the result of misguided philosophical reasoning rather than genuine doubt. Reid's philosophy was a reaction against both the idealism of George Berkeley and the extreme empiricism of Hume.

Central to Reid's philosophy is his theory of perception, which he argued is a direct, immediate experience of the world rather than a construction of ideas or impressions. He rejected the "theory of ideas," which posits that we perceive the world indirectly through mental representations. Instead, Reid claimed that when we perceive an object, we are directly aware of the object itself, not an idea of it. This theory of "direct realism" was revolutionary, as it countered the prevailing belief that human knowledge of the world was always mediated by mental representations, leaving room for doubt about the world's existence.

Reid also made significant contributions to ethics and moral philosophy. He believed that moral principles, like truths about the external world, are self-evident. Reid argued for a form of moral realism, claiming that moral truths exist independently of human perception and that humans have an inherent faculty for perceiving these truths, much like our ability to perceive the physical world. He held that moral judgments are based on common sense and that basic moral principles, such as the wrongness of murder or the importance of justice, do not require complex philosophical justification.

Reid's influence on philosophy was profound, particularly in the English-speaking world. His work provided an important alternative to the skepticism and empiricism that dominated Enlightenment thought, and his common sense realism became a cornerstone of Scottish philosophy. Reid's ideas influenced later philosophers, including those in the American pragmatist tradition, such as Charles Sanders Peirce and William James. Though often overshadowed by Hume, Reid's defense of common sense and direct realism continues to resonate in contemporary discussions of epistemology and philosophy of mind.

David Hume (1711 – 1776 CE)

David Hume, born in Edinburgh, Scotland, was a central figure in the Scottish Enlightenment and one of the most influential philosophers of the 18th century. He studied at the University of Edinburgh and was deeply engaged in the intellectual currents of his time, including empiricism and skepticism. Hume's philosophical writings, including A Treatise of Human Nature (1738–1740) and An Enquiry Concerning Human Understanding (1748), made significant contributions to epistemology, metaphysics, ethics, and philosophy of religion. Beyond his philosophical work, Hume was also a respected historian and essayist, known for his History of England, which was widely read during his lifetime.

Hume's philosophy is characterized by his empirical approach and his skepticism about human knowledge. He famously questioned the notion of causality, arguing that our belief in cause and effect is not based on rational deduction but on habit and custom. According to Hume, we cannot perceive causal connections directly; instead, we infer them based on repeated observations of events occurring together. This challenge to the traditional notion of causality had a profound impact on subsequent philosophical thought and contributed to the development of modern scientific and empirical methods.

In addition to his work on causality, Hume explored the nature of human understanding and the limitations of reason. He argued that human knowledge is confined to experiences and impressions, and that reason alone cannot provide knowledge of metaphysical or theological concepts. Hume's critique of religious belief, particularly in his Dialogues Concerning Natural Religion (1779), questioned the rational basis of religious faith and contributed to the rise of secularism and naturalism in philosophical and theological discourse.

Hume also made important contributions to moral philosophy. He proposed that moral judgments are based on sentiment rather than reason, asserting that our feelings of approval or disapproval determine our sense of moral values. In his A Treatise of Human Nature, Hume argued that moral distinctions arise from human emotions and social interactions rather than from objective moral truths. This perspective laid the foundation for later developments in moral psychology and ethics, including the work of sentimentalists and utilitarians.

Despite his skepticism and critique of established doctrines, Hume's work had a lasting influence on the development of modern philosophy. His empiricism and naturalism laid the groundwork for later philosophers such as Immanuel Kant, who engaged with Hume's ideas in formulating his own critical philosophy. Hume's exploration of human nature, causality, and morality continues to be relevant in contemporary philosophical discussions and debates, reflecting his enduring impact on the field.

Jean-Jacques Rousseau (1712 – 1778 CE)

Jean-Jacques Rousseau was born in Geneva in 1712, a city-state with a strong tradition of civic participation and philosophical thought. His early life was marked by hardship; after his mother's death and his father's subsequent abandonment, Rousseau was raised by relatives and had a fragmented education. Despite these challenges, he eventually moved to Paris, where he engaged with the intellectual circles of the Enlightenment. Rousseau's early works, including his Discourse on the Arts and Sciences (1750) and Discourse on the Origin and Basis of Inequality Among Men (1755), established him as a radical thinker who critiqued the societal values of his time.

Rousseau's philosophy was deeply concerned with the concept of human nature and the corrupting influence of society. In his seminal work The Social Contract (1762), he argued that the development of civilization had led to inequality and moral decay. Rousseau proposed a revolutionary idea: that political legitimacy arises from a social contract agreed upon by free and equal individuals. He introduced the notion of the "general will," a collective desire that represents the true interest of the people, and argued that this general will should guide the government. His call for direct democracy and the sovereignty of the people was groundbreaking and influenced the French Revolution.

In Emile, or On Education (1762), Rousseau explored the nature of education and its role in personal development. He advocated for a form of education that focused on the natural development of children, arguing that education should be aligned with the child's inherent interests and abilities rather than imposed through rigid curricula. Rousseau's educational philosophy emphasized the importance of experiential learning and the development of moral character, marking a departure from traditional educational methods of his time.

Rousseau's personal life was as turbulent as his intellectual career. He faced significant opposition from the authorities due to his controversial ideas, and his personal relationships, including those with fellow intellectuals like Voltaire, were often fraught with conflict. His later years were marked by periods of self-imposed exile and isolation, during which he continued to write and reflect on his ideas. Despite his contentious relationships and personal struggles, Rousseau's influence on political theory, education, and romanticism remains profound.

Rousseau's legacy is evident in the various social and political movements that drew inspiration from his ideas. His emphasis on the inherent goodness of humanity and his critique of social inequality contributed to the development of modern democratic and educational theories. Rousseau's work laid the groundwork for later philosophical and political developments, including the theories of Karl Marx and the educational reforms of the 19th and 20th centuries.

Denis Diderot (1713 – 1784 CE)

Denis Diderot was born in Langres, France, in 1713, into a family of modest means. He pursued a career in philosophy and literature, and his early work focused on the nature of knowledge and the limitations of human understanding. Diderot is best known for his role as the chief editor of the Encyclopédie, a monumental work that aimed to compile and disseminate human knowledge across various disciplines. His efforts in the Encyclopédie reflected his commitment to the Enlightenment ideals of reason, science, and secularism. This ambitious project involved collaboration with leading thinkers of the time, including Voltaire and Rousseau, highlighting Diderot's central role in the intellectual network of the Enlightenment.

Diderot's philosophical contributions were diverse and often radical. His work in the Encyclopédie was a collective effort to challenge traditional religious and political authorities by promoting scientific knowledge and rational thought. Diderot used the Encyclopédie to critique established institutions and advocate for a more empirical approach to understanding the world. His writings in the Encyclopédie often questioned the legitimacy of religious dogma and explored the implications of scientific discoveries. The project faced significant resistance from church and state authorities, but Diderot persevered, believing that knowledge should be accessible to all as a means of social progress.

In addition to his editorial work, Diderot wrote several influential philosophical and literary works, including Jacques the Fatalist and Rameau's Nephew. In Jacques the Fatalist, Diderot explored themes of determinism and free will, questioning the nature of human agency and the role of fate in shaping our lives. In Rameau's Nephew, he presented a dialogue that critiqued contemporary social and moral values, reflecting his skepticism towards societal norms and the hypocrisy of the bourgeoisie. Both works showcased Diderot's skill in blending philosophical inquiry with literary creativity, making complex ideas accessible and engaging for his readers.

Diderot's intellectual contributions were also marked by his engagement with various philosophical movements, including materialism and atheism. His philosophical works often challenged the status quo and sought to promote a more secular and scientific understanding of human existence. He developed ideas on the interconnectedness of life and matter, emphasizing the dynamic nature of the universe, which influenced later developments in biology and natural philosophy. Despite facing censorship and opposition from religious and political authorities, Diderot remained a staunch advocate for Enlightenment ideals throughout his life.

Diderot's impact on the Enlightenment and modern thought is significant. His efforts in compiling the Encyclopédie were instrumental in shaping the intellectual landscape of the 18th century, and his writings continue to be studied for their insights into the philosophical and social issues of his time. His dedication to the dissemination of knowledge and his critiques of authoritarianism and dogma helped lay the groundwork for modern secular and democratic principles. Diderot's legacy is evident in the continued relevance of his ideas and his role in advancing the principles of reason, empiricism, and secularism in Western thought.

Baron d'Holbach (1723 – 1789 CE)

Baron Paul-Henri Thiry d'Holbach was a French-German philosopher, writer, and prominent figure of the French Enlightenment. Born in Edesheim, Germany, d'Holbach later moved to Paris, where he became an influential member of the intellectual circles of the time. His home became a renowned salon where thinkers like Denis Diderot, Jean-Jacques Rousseau, and Voltaire gathered to discuss philosophy, science, and politics. D'Holbach was known for his materialist and atheist views, which he expressed in numerous works, often published anonymously due to their controversial nature. His intellectual development occurred during the Enlightenment, a period characterized by a shift away from religious authority and toward reason, science, and individual rights.

D'Holbach's most significant work is The System of Nature (1770), which presents a thorough critique of religion and a defense of atheism and materialism. In this work, d'Holbach argues that the universe operates according to natural laws, with no need for a divine creator. He denies the existence of the soul, free will, and any supernatural phenomena, asserting that human beings are entirely products of nature and governed by physical laws. D'Holbach's materialism was radical for his time, as he rejected the existence of God and asserted that human thought and consciousness were purely material processes.

A key element of d'Holbach's philosophy is his critique of religion, particularly Christianity, which he saw as a source of ignorance, fear, and oppression. He describes religion as a human invention designed to control people by exploiting their fear of death and the unknown. D'Holbach believed that moral behavior does not require belief in God and that human happiness could be achieved through reason, knowledge, and a just society. His call for a secular morality based on human nature and reason was a bold challenge to the religious orthodoxy of his time.

D'Holbach was also a fierce critic of the political and social structures of the ancien régime, particularly the monarchy and the Church's influence over the state. He advocated for a society based on reason, freedom, and equality, arguing that the institutions of his time perpetuated inequality and injustice. Influenced by the broader Enlightenment critique of absolute monarchy and hereditary privilege, he emphasized that scientific and educational progress was essential to creating a more rational society.

Though his atheism and materialism made d'Holbach a controversial figure during his life, his ideas contributed to the intellectual foundations of modern secularism and scientific naturalism. His rejection of religious authority and advocacy for a society based on reason and nature influenced later thinkers such as Karl Marx and Friedrich Nietzsche. D'Holbach's work remains significant for its bold critique of religion and its defense of a materialist worldview, reflecting the broader currents of Enlightenment thought that sought to liberate humanity from superstition and tyranny.

Adam Smith (1723 – 1790 CE)

Adam Smith, born in 1723 in Kirkcaldy, Scotland, was a key figure in the Scottish Enlightenment, a period characterized by significant intellectual and cultural development. Smith studied at the University of Glasgow and later at Balliol College, Oxford, where he honed his interests in moral philosophy and economics. His academic career included a position as a professor at the University of Glasgow, where he delivered influential lectures on moral philosophy. Smith's contributions, particularly through his works The Theory of Moral Sentiments (1759) and An Inquiry into the Nature and Causes of the Wealth of Nations (1776), established him as a foundational thinker in both economics and ethics.

In The Theory of Moral Sentiments, Smith explored the nature of human morality and the role of sympathy in ethical behavior. He introduced the concept of the "impartial spectator," an internalized moral agent that helps individuals assess their actions from a neutral standpoint. Smith argued that moral judgments stem from the capacity for empathy and the desire for social approval. This work laid the philosophical groundwork for his later economic theories by emphasizing the role of human emotions and social interactions in shaping moral judgments.

Smith's seminal work, The Wealth of Nations, revolutionized economic thought with its analysis of market mechanisms and economic principles. In this book, he introduced the concept of the "invisible hand," which describes how individuals pursuing their self-interest unintentionally contribute to the public good. Smith argued that free markets, driven by competition and limited government intervention, lead to economic prosperity and efficient resource allocation. His insights into labor, capital, and trade provided a comprehensive framework for understanding economic growth and the dynamics of market economies.

Smith's ideas had a profound impact on economic theory and policy, influencing the development of classical economics and shaping the principles of free-market capitalism. His advocacy for economic freedom, competition, and limited government intervention helped to shape modern economic thought and policy. The enduring relevance of his ideas is evident in contemporary discussions on market economies and the role of government in economic regulation.

Adam Smith's legacy extends beyond economics into moral philosophy, where his exploration of human behavior and ethics continues to be influential. His work on the interplay between self-interest and social welfare, as well as his examination of moral sentiments, remains a cornerstone of economic and ethical theory. Smith's contributions to the Enlightenment and his impact on subsequent philosophical and economic thought underscore his significance as a foundational figure in Western intellectual history.

Immanuel Kant (1724 – 1804 CE)

Immanuel Kant, born in 1724 in Königsberg (now Kaliningrad, Russia), is considered one of the most influential philosophers in Western history. Educated at the University of Königsberg, Kant's work encompasses a wide range of philosophical disciplines, including metaphysics, epistemology, ethics, and aesthetics. Known for his systematic and rigorous approach, Kant sought to reconcile the rationalist and empiricist traditions that dominated 18th-century philosophy. His critical philosophy, particularly articulated in his major works—Critique of Pure Reason (1781), Critique of Practical Reason (1788), and Critique of Judgment (1790)—aims to address fundamental questions about human knowledge, morality, and the nature of reality.

In Critique of Pure Reason, Kant explores the nature and limits of human understanding. He introduces the concept of transcendental idealism, which posits that while we can know phenomena (things as they appear to us), we cannot access things in themselves (noumena). Kant argues that our knowledge is shaped by the cognitive structures and categories of our mind, which impose order on our sensory experiences. This work marks a significant departure from previous metaphysical and epistemological theories, emphasizing the active role of the mind in constructing knowledge.

In Critique of Practical Reason, Kant shifts focus to moral philosophy, introducing the idea of the categorical imperative. This principle asserts that actions should be guided by maxims that can be universally applied, regardless of personal desires or consequences. Kant's deontological ethics emphasizes the importance of duty, autonomy, and rationality in moral decision-making. His approach contrasts with consequentialist theories by prioritizing the inherent moral value of actions and adherence to moral law. Kant also argued that freedom, as the ability to act according to moral law, is a fundamental aspect of human dignity.

Critique of Judgment extends Kant's philosophical project to aesthetics and teleology. In this work, he examines the nature of aesthetic experience and the concept of beauty, arguing that aesthetic judgments involve a harmonious interplay between imagination and understanding. Kant also explores teleological concepts, considering how humans impose purpose and design on the natural world. This work contributes to discussions on the nature of art, beauty, and the role of human cognition in interpreting nature.

Kant's philosophical contributions have had a profound and lasting impact on subsequent thought, influencing fields such as German Idealism, existentialism, and contemporary ethics. His critical method and ideas about knowledge, morality, and aesthetics continue to shape philosophical discourse. Kant's work remains central to discussions on the nature of human understanding and the principles governing moral and aesthetic judgments, making him a cornerstone of modern philosophy.

Moses Mendelssohn (1729 – 1786 CE)

Moses Mendelssohn was a German-Jewish philosopher and a key figure in the Haskalah, or Jewish Enlightenment. Born in Dessau, Germany, Mendelssohn came from a modest background and received a traditional Jewish education. However, he also taught himself German, Latin, and philosophy, quickly gaining recognition for his intellectual capabilities. Moving to Berlin in 1743, Mendelssohn became involved with the leading intellectual circles of the time, befriending figures like Gotthold Ephraim Lessing. His philosophy, which attempted to reconcile Jewish faith with Enlightenment values, placed him at the center of both Jewish and European intellectual life during a period when reason, individual rights, and secularism were challenging traditional societal norms.

Mendelssohn's most significant philosophical work, Jerusalem, or on Religious Power and Judaism (1783), argues for the separation of church and state and defends the compatibility of Judaism with Enlightenment principles. He believed that religion should be a private matter and that the state should not interfere in religious affairs. At the same time, he upheld the importance of religion in providing moral guidance. Mendelssohn asserted that Judaism, with its emphasis on ethical laws rather than dogma, was uniquely suited to coexist with Enlightenment ideals. His defense of Judaism as a rational, tolerant faith challenged stereotypes of Jewish inferiority and helped pave the way for Jewish emancipation in Europe.

One of the central tenets of Mendelssohn's philosophy was his belief in the harmony between faith and reason. Unlike some Enlightenment thinkers who saw religion as irrational or outdated, Mendelssohn maintained that reason and religious faith could complement each other. He argued that while reason could uncover moral truths, religious traditions provided ethical frameworks that reinforced these truths. Mendelssohn, influenced by Leibniz and Christian Wolff, believed that reason and revelation were not mutually exclusive but could work together to promote the common good.

Mendelssohn also made significant contributions to aesthetics and the philosophy of art. In his Letters on the Feelings (1755), Mendelssohn developed a theory of aesthetics that emphasized the role of emotional response in the appreciation of art. He argued that beauty arises from the harmonious interplay of form and content and that art's ability to evoke emotional reactions was central to its value. This view challenged more rigid, formalist approaches to aesthetics and contributed to a broader appreciation of art's emotional and subjective dimensions.

Mendelssohn's legacy lies in his efforts to bridge the gap between Jewish religious life and the European Enlightenment. He championed the idea that Jews could remain true to their religious traditions while participating fully in secular society. His commitment to religious tolerance, defense of reason and faith, and contributions to the philosophy of art made him a key figure in Jewish and European intellectual history, laying the foundation for the modernization of Jewish thought.

Gotthold Ephraim Lessing (1729 – 1781 CE)

Gotthold Ephraim Lessing was a German philosopher, playwright, and critic who played a central role in the German Enlightenment. Born in Kamenz, Saxony, Lessing was raised in a religious household, his father being a Lutheran pastor. He studied theology at the University of Leipzig but soon shifted his focus to literature and philosophy. Lessing's intellectual development took place in a period marked by intense philosophical debates about reason, religion, and freedom of thought. His wide-ranging work, encompassing drama, theology, and aesthetics, reflected the Enlightenment's commitment to reason and individual freedom, and he became a prominent advocate for religious tolerance and intellectual liberty.

Lessing's most enduring philosophical contribution is his defense of religious tolerance, expressed most famously in his play Nathan the Wise (1779). Set during the Crusades, the play centers on the Jewish merchant Nathan, whose wisdom and humanity bridge the religious divide between Jews, Christians, and Muslims. The central parable of the three rings symbolizes the equality of the three Abrahamic religions, suggesting that no single religion holds the exclusive truth. Lessing's advocacy for tolerance directly challenged the religious conflicts and dogmatism of his time, making the play a celebrated work for its message of peaceful coexistence and respect for diverse beliefs.

In addition to his contributions to religious philosophy, Lessing made significant strides in the philosophy of aesthetics. His treatise Laocoön: An Essay on the Limits of Painting and Poetry (1766) explores the differences between the visual and literary arts. Lessing argues that each art form operates according to its own principles: painting conveys beauty through space and visual composition, while poetry unfolds over time and captures action and emotion. This distinction between spatial and temporal arts was groundbreaking, influencing future discussions on aesthetics and art criticism and laying the foundation for later developments in art theory.

Lessing also explored the nature of religion and history in his work The Education of the Human Race (1780). In this text, he presents the idea that humanity's understanding of religious truths evolves over time, with each religious tradition contributing to the moral progress of humankind. He viewed Judaism, Christianity, and other religions as stages in this development, each providing valuable lessons for advancing ethical understanding. This progressive view of religion and history, aligned with Enlightenment ideals, also challenged conventional religious authority by suggesting that dogma was subject to reinterpretation.

The "Fragment Controversy" (Fragmentenstreit), which erupted when Lessing published the critical writings of Hermann Samuel Reimarus, further highlighted his commitment to intellectual freedom. Reimarus questioned the historical basis of Christianity, and Lessing defended the right to question religious doctrine without undermining its moral teachings. He argued that religious truth should rest on ethical and philosophical insights rather than historical facts, cementing his legacy as a thinker who championed the autonomy of reason and the moral development of humanity.

Edmund Burke (1729 – 1797 CE)

Edmund Burke was an Irish statesman and political philosopher, known for his influential role in shaping modern conservatism. Born in Dublin, he studied at Trinity College before moving to London to pursue a career in law, which eventually led him into politics. Burke was elected to the British Parliament in 1765, where he gained prominence through his support of the American Revolution and opposition to British imperialism. However, he is most famous for his opposition to the French Revolution, which he believed posed a serious threat to societal order. His work, particularly Reflections on the Revolution in France (1790), became a cornerstone of conservative thought.

Burke's philosophy revolves around the defense of tradition and established institutions. He believed that society is an intricate system of interconnected customs, values, and institutions that have evolved over centuries. This heritage, according to Burke, should not be hastily dismantled by revolutionary change. For him, societal stability depended on the preservation of these traditions, which he saw as a form of accumulated wisdom passed down through generations. This cautious approach to change contrasted sharply with the revolutionary ideals of equality and liberty that were being promoted in France during his time.

A key element of Burke's thought is his critique of abstract, utopian ideals. He argued that political systems should be grounded in practical experience rather than theoretical principles. In Reflections on the Revolution in France, Burke warned that attempting to impose radical changes based on abstract ideals, such as those of the French Revolution, would inevitably lead to chaos and tyranny. He believed that humans are too fallible and society too complex for such drastic alterations to be successful. Burke advocated for gradual, organic reform that respected the historical and cultural foundations of society.

Burke also placed a strong emphasis on the importance of hierarchy and authority in maintaining social order. He viewed human nature as inherently flawed, which necessitated the existence of strong institutions to curb selfish tendencies. While he recognized that reform was sometimes necessary, Burke insisted that it should be done with great caution and respect for the established order. This view positioned him as a critic of both radical revolutionaries and overly zealous reformers who sought to reshape society too quickly.

Although Burke is often associated with conservatism, his views were not entirely reactionary. He supported the grievances of the American colonists against British oppression and advocated for greater rights for Catholics in Ireland. His willingness to support certain reforms demonstrates that his conservatism was not a blanket rejection of change but a call for thoughtful, measured progress that preserved the essential structures of society. Burke's legacy continues to influence conservative thought today, particularly in debates about the role of tradition and the risks of radical change.

Thomas Paine (1737 – 1809 CE)

Thomas Paine was an English-born political activist and philosopher who became one of the most influential figures in the American and French revolutions. Born in Thetford, England, Paine emigrated to the American colonies in 1774, just as tensions between the colonies and Britain were escalating. His pamphlet Common Sense (1776) is widely credited with inspiring the American colonists to seek independence from Britain. Paine's writings, which combined clear, accessible prose with powerful arguments for democracy and human rights, played a key role in shaping the political landscape of the late 18th century. His ability to communicate complex ideas in a way that resonated with ordinary citizens made his work a cornerstone of revolutionary thought.

Paine's philosophy was rooted in the Enlightenment ideals of individual rights and reason. He believed that all men were born equal and possessed certain inalienable rights, including the rights to life, liberty, and property. According to Paine, the primary role of government was to protect these natural rights. If a government failed in this duty, it was the right of the people to overthrow it and establish a new government that would uphold their liberties. This radical belief in the sovereignty of the people was central to his arguments in Common Sense and The Rights of Man (1791).

One of Paine's most significant contributions to political thought was his advocacy for republicanism. He rejected monarchy and hereditary privilege, arguing that these systems were inherently corrupt and oppressive. In The Rights of Man, Paine defended the French Revolution and the establishment of a republic in France, seeing it as a necessary step toward securing human rights and equality. Paine believed that true political legitimacy could only be derived from the consent of the governed, not from the divine right of kings or aristocratic inheritance.

In addition to his political ideas, Paine was a strong advocate for religious freedom and the separation of church and state. His work The Age of Reason (1794) criticized organized religion, particularly Christianity, for its role in supporting authoritarian regimes and suppressing free thought. Paine identified as a deist, believing in a rational God who created the universe but did not interfere in human affairs. He argued that religious institutions should have no role in government and that individuals should be free to worship (or not) as they saw fit.

Paine's legacy as a radical thinker made him both celebrated and vilified in his time. While he was hailed as a hero in revolutionary America and France, his outspoken criticism of religion alienated many, particularly in England, where he was branded a traitor. Nevertheless, Paine's unwavering commitment to the principles of liberty, equality, and reason has ensured his place as one of the most influential political philosophers of the Enlightenment.

Johann Gottfried Herder (1744 – 1803 CE)

Johann Gottfried Herder was a German philosopher, theologian, and literary critic who played a pivotal role in the development of German Romanticism and modern nationalism. Born in Mohrungen, Prussia, Herder initially trained as a theologian before becoming a key figure in the intellectual life of 18th-century Germany. His work was influenced by the philosophical currents of his time, particularly the ideas of Immanuel Kant and the Enlightenment, but he ultimately rejected the Enlightenment's emphasis on universal reason, advocating instead for a more historically grounded and culturally specific understanding of human experience.

Herder is best known for his theory of cultural relativism, which argued that each nation or people has its own unique culture and spirit, or Volksgeist, that cannot be judged by external standards. He believed that each culture developed its own values, traditions, and language in response to its historical and geographical context, and that these should be respected as expressions of a people's identity. This view was a departure from the universalist ideals of the Enlightenment, which sought to apply reason and science to all aspects of human life, often disregarding the particularities of different cultures.

Herder's theory of language was central to his philosophy. He argued that language is not merely a tool for communication but a fundamental aspect of human thought and identity. Each language, according to Herder, shapes the way its speakers perceive the world and expresses the unique spirit of the people who speak it. This idea had a profound influence on later thinkers, including Wilhelm von Humboldt and Martin Heidegger, and contributed to the development of linguistic relativity—the notion that the structure of a language affects its speakers' worldview.

In contrast to the Enlightenment's linear view of history as a progression toward greater rationality and enlightenment, Herder saw history as a more complex and dynamic process. He believed that each historical period and culture contributed to the richness of human experience and that no single culture or era could claim superiority over another. This pluralistic view of history emphasized the diversity of human achievement and rejected the idea of a universal standard by which all societies should be measured.

Herder's ideas on culture and language also had a significant impact on the development of nationalism in the 19th century. By emphasizing the importance of national identity and the unique character of each people, Herder helped lay the intellectual foundations for the rise of nationalist movements in Europe. However, his vision of nationalism was more cultural than political, focusing on the preservation of cultural diversity rather than the dominance of one nation over others.

Mary Wollstonecraft (1759 – 1797 CE)

Mary Wollstonecraft was an English writer and philosopher who became a pioneer of women's rights during the late 18th century. Born in London to a financially unstable and often abusive family, Wollstonecraft was largely self-educated, a circumstance that shaped her deep belief in the transformative power of education. Throughout her early life, Wollstonecraft worked as a governess and teacher, gaining firsthand experience of the limited opportunities available to women. She rose to prominence with the publication of her seminal work, A Vindication of the Rights of Woman (1792), which argued for the intellectual and social equality of women. Her ideas developed in the context of the Enlightenment, an era that championed reason and individual rights but excluded women from its vision of progress.

In A Vindication of the Rights of Woman, Wollstonecraft argued that women were not naturally inferior to men but had been made so by their lack of access to education. She believed the social system confined women to domestic roles, denying them the opportunity to develop their intellectual capacities and contribute to society as equals. Wollstonecraft's argument was revolutionary, as she insisted that women, like men, should be educated to develop their reason and moral judgment. Her work challenged the conventional wisdom that women were best suited to be passive companions to men, suggesting instead that they should be independent individuals capable of participating in public life.

Wollstonecraft's critique extended to marriage and the domestic sphere. She argued that marriage, as it was commonly practiced, reduced women to subservient roles, treating them as property rather than partners. She called for a reformation of marriage, envisioning it as a relationship based on mutual respect and equality, where both partners could grow intellectually and emotionally. Her groundbreaking ideas on marriage and women's roles proposed a society where women were not merely defined by their relationships to men.

While Wollstonecraft is best known for her feminist writings, her philosophy also encompassed broader social and political critiques. Influenced by the revolutionary ideas of the time, particularly those of the American and French revolutions, she criticized thinkers such as Jean-Jacques Rousseau for excluding women from Enlightenment ideals of liberty and equality. Wollstonecraft believed that a just society could not exist if half the population remained oppressed and denied their rights.

Despite the radical nature of her ideas, Wollstonecraft's personal life was often subject to public scrutiny and controversy. Her relationships with Gilbert Imlay and later marriage to the philosopher William Godwin were widely criticized. Nevertheless, Wollstonecraft's legacy as a trailblazer in feminist thought has endured. Her advocacy for education, equal rights, and the reformation of societal structures laid the groundwork for later feminist movements and continues to inspire debates about gender equality and women's rights today.

Friedrich Schiller (1759 – 1805 CE)

Friedrich Schiller was a German poet, philosopher, and playwright, whose works contributed significantly to the development of German Idealism and Romanticism. Born in Marbach, Württemberg, Schiller originally studied medicine and served as a military doctor before turning to literature and philosophy. His early works, particularly the play The Robbers (1781), brought him immediate fame, though they also led to conflict with the authorities due to their revolutionary themes. Schiller's philosophy evolved during a period of intense intellectual and political change in Europe, shaped by the Enlightenment, the French Revolution, and Germany's burgeoning Romantic movement.

Schiller's philosophical ideas are closely linked to his work in aesthetics, where he explored the relationship between beauty, morality, and freedom. In his Letters on the Aesthetic Education of Man (1794), Schiller argued that beauty serves as a bridge between the sensuous and rational aspects of human nature. He believed that aesthetic experience allows individuals to reconcile their physical desires with their higher moral capacities, leading to personal and social harmony. Schiller's concept of the "play drive" (Spieltrieb) was central to this theory, suggesting that humans achieve their fullest potential through a balance between reason and emotion, facilitated by art and beauty.

One of Schiller's major contributions to philosophy was his theory of freedom, developed in response to the political upheavals of his time, particularly the French Revolution. While initially sympathetic to the revolution's ideals of liberty and equality, Schiller became increasingly disillusioned by its violent excesses. In his writings, he distinguished between physical freedom, often pursued through political revolution, and moral freedom, which is attained through self-cultivation and aesthetic education. Schiller believed that true freedom could not be imposed by external force but had to be achieved internally through the development of virtue and reason.

Schiller's exploration of freedom also intersected with his ideas about the state and society. He was skeptical of both absolute monarchy and radical democracy, fearing that both systems could lead to tyranny if not tempered by moral and aesthetic considerations. For Schiller, art and culture played a vital role in educating citizens to become virtuous and self-regulating individuals capable of participating in a just society. His ideal was a society driven not solely by material needs or political power but by a higher sense of moral and aesthetic purpose.

Schiller remained committed to the idea that art and philosophy had the power to transform society. His plays, poems, and essays sought to inspire individuals to strive for personal and collective improvement. Schiller's vision of aesthetic education as a means of achieving moral and political freedom influenced later thinkers, including his close friend and collaborator Johann Wolfgang von Goethe. His legacy as a poet-philosopher who bridged the worlds of art, politics, and philosophy continues to resonate, particularly in discussions about the role of culture in shaping ethical and democratic societies.

Friedrich Schleiermacher (1768 – 1834 CE)

Friedrich Schleiermacher was a German theologian, philosopher, and biblical scholar, often regarded as the father of modern Protestant theology. Born in Breslau, Prussia, Schleiermacher was educated in a Moravian Brethren community, which had a lasting influence on his religious thought. However, he eventually distanced himself from their strict orthodoxy, pursuing a broader intellectual journey that led him to study theology at the University of Halle. His career unfolded during a time of intense intellectual and political transformation in Europe, with the Enlightenment, Romanticism, and German Idealism all shaping his thought. Schleiermacher is best known for his efforts to reconcile Enlightenment rationalism with Christian faith.

Schleiermacher's central philosophical contribution lies in his development of a new understanding of religion, which he outlined in On Religion: Speeches to Its Cultured Despisers (1799). He rejected the idea that religion was primarily about doctrine or ethical behavior, instead arguing that its essence was rooted in a feeling of absolute dependence on the divine. For Schleiermacher, religion was not a system of beliefs or moral codes but an immediate, intuitive experience of the infinite. This concept of religious feeling distinguished him from the rationalist approaches to religion that were dominant in his time and set the stage for modern liberal theology.

Schleiermacher also made significant contributions to hermeneutics, the theory and methodology of interpretation. His work in this field aimed to provide a framework for understanding texts, particularly the Bible, in a way that took into account both the historical context and the subjective experience of the interpreter. He developed what is known as the "hermeneutic circle," the idea that understanding a text involves a continuous interplay between grasping the whole and understanding its parts. This approach to interpretation became influential not only in theology but also in the broader fields of literary theory and philosophy.

In addition to his work on religion and hermeneutics, Schleiermacher engaged with the major philosophical movements of his time, particularly German Idealism. He was in dialogue with figures like Immanuel Kant and Johann Gottlieb Fichte, though he maintained a critical distance from their more speculative approaches to philosophy. Schleiermacher's thought was shaped by his belief that human existence is fundamentally relational, grounded in both individual consciousness and communal life. This relational view of human nature informed his theology, where he emphasized the importance of community in the experience of faith.

Schleiermacher's legacy is particularly significant in the development of modern Christian thought. His emphasis on the subjective and experiential dimensions of religion laid the groundwork for existential and liberal theology in the 20th century. Moreover, his approach to biblical interpretation influenced later theological and philosophical debates about the role of history, culture, and personal experience in understanding religious texts. Although controversial in his own time, Schleiermacher's efforts to reconcile faith with modern intellectual life continue to resonate in contemporary theology.

Georg Wilhelm Friedrich Hegel (1770 – 1831 CE)

Georg Wilhelm Friedrich Hegel was a German philosopher whose work has had a profound influence on a wide range of fields, including philosophy, political theory, and history. Born in Stuttgart, Hegel studied theology at the University of Tübingen but soon shifted his focus to philosophy. He became a central figure in German Idealism, alongside contemporaries such as Johann Gottlieb Fichte and Friedrich Schelling. Hegel's philosophy developed during a time of revolutionary change in Europe, including the French Revolution and the Napoleonic Wars, which deeply impacted his thinking about history, politics, and human development.

Hegel is perhaps best known for his dialectical method, a process of development where ideas (thesis) encounter their opposites (antithesis), leading to a higher synthesis. This dialectical progression, Hegel argued, is the engine of history and human thought. His major work, Phenomenology of Spirit (1807), outlines this process as it unfolds in human consciousness, moving from individual sensation to self-awareness and, ultimately, to absolute knowledge. Hegel's dialectical method was revolutionary in that it suggested history and human experience were not static but dynamic, always evolving through contradiction and resolution.

Another key aspect of Hegel's philosophy is his concept of "absolute idealism." He argued that reality is not made up of discrete, independent entities but is a single, interconnected whole—what he called the "Absolute." For Hegel, the world is a manifestation of spirit or mind (Geist), and everything that exists is an expression of this universal consciousness. Individual consciousness and self-awareness, therefore, are moments in the larger development of the Absolute. This idea contrasted sharply with Kant's critical philosophy, which separated the knowing subject from the external world of objects.

Hegel also made significant contributions to political philosophy, particularly in his work Philosophy of Right (1821). He argued that the state is the realization of ethical life (Sittlichkeit), where individual freedom is actualized through participation in the institutions of civil society and the state. Hegel saw the state not as a coercive power but as the embodiment of freedom, where individuals find their highest fulfillment. His political philosophy was influential in both conservative and progressive circles, providing a theoretical foundation for later debates on democracy, nationalism, and the role of the state.

Hegel's influence on later thinkers is difficult to overstate. His ideas shaped the development of existentialism, Marxism, and phenomenology, with figures like Karl Marx, Friedrich Nietzsche, and Jean-Paul Sartre engaging deeply with his work. While Hegel's dense and complex writings have often been criticized for their opacity, his vision of history, reality, and freedom continues to inspire philosophical inquiry across a range of disciplines.

Arthur Schopenhauer (1788 – 1860 CE)

Arthur Schopenhauer was a German philosopher known for his pessimistic philosophy, which challenged the dominant optimism of his time. Born in Danzig, Schopenhauer was deeply influenced by both Western philosophy, particularly Immanuel Kant, and Eastern thought, especially Buddhism and Hinduism. He studied philosophy at the University of Göttingen and later at the University of Berlin, where he developed his major philosophical work, The World as Will and Representation (1818). Schopenhauer's thought emerged in the context of German Idealism, but he rejected the idealism of figures like Hegel, offering instead a more grounded and existential approach to human suffering.

Schopenhauer's central philosophical concept is the "will," which he described as the irrational, blind force that drives all existence. He argued that the will is the underlying reality of the world, manifesting itself in everything from human desires to the laws of nature. Unlike thinkers who viewed human reason as the defining characteristic of life, Schopenhauer believed that reason was secondary to the will, which he saw as the root cause of all suffering. For Schopenhauer, human existence was marked by a constant striving and desire, which could never be fully satisfied, leading to perpetual dissatisfaction and suffering.

This pessimistic view of life led Schopenhauer to advocate for asceticism and the denial of the will as a path to relief from suffering. He believed that by suppressing our desires and detaching ourselves from the material world, individuals could achieve a state of tranquility and peace. Schopenhauer found inspiration for this idea in Eastern philosophies, particularly Buddhism's emphasis on the cessation of desire as the key to overcoming suffering. In this sense, Schopenhauer's philosophy represented a radical departure from the dominant Western emphasis on progress and fulfillment.

Schopenhauer's aesthetic theory was also central to his philosophy. He argued that art, particularly music, offers a unique escape from the suffering caused by the will. Through aesthetic contemplation, individuals can temporarily transcend their desires and experience a state of pure, disinterested awareness. For Schopenhauer, great art reveals the underlying truths of existence and provides a brief respite from the suffering inherent in life. Music, in particular, was seen as the highest form of art because it directly expresses the will itself, without the mediation of concepts or representations.

Although Schopenhauer's pessimism made him unpopular during his lifetime, his influence grew significantly after his death. His ideas influenced a wide range of later thinkers, including Friedrich Nietzsche, Sigmund Freud, and Thomas Mann, as well as artists and composers like Richard Wagner. Schopenhauer's emphasis on the irrational aspects of human nature and his critique of optimism laid the groundwork for existentialism and psychoanalysis, making him a pivotal figure in the history of Western thought.

William Whewell (1794 – 1866 CE)

William Whewell was an English polymath, philosopher, and historian of science, known for his contributions to the philosophy of science and for coining several scientific terms still in use today, such as "scientist" and "physicist." Born in Lancaster, Whewell excelled academically, studying at Trinity College, Cambridge, where he eventually became a professor and later the Master of the college. Whewell's intellectual career spanned a wide range of disciplines, including mathematics, geology, theology, and philosophy, reflecting the breadth of scientific inquiry during the 19th century. His philosophical work developed in the context of the scientific revolution and the growing specialization of scientific disciplines.

Whewell is best known for his theory of "inductive reasoning," which he outlined in his two-volume work The Philosophy of the Inductive Sciences (1840). He believed that scientific knowledge progresses through a process of induction, where general principles are derived from specific observations. However, unlike the empirical approach of thinkers such as John Stuart Mill, Whewell argued that scientific discovery also involves a creative act of forming hypotheses, which are then tested against empirical data. He described this as a "colligation of facts," where seemingly disparate pieces of information are brought together under a unifying theory.

Whewell's view of science emphasized the role of both observation and theory in the advancement of scientific knowledge. He believed that while empirical data was essential, the creative formulation of hypotheses played an equally crucial role. This idea stood in contrast to the purely inductive methods advocated by some of his contemporaries, who emphasized data collection without fully appreciating the theoretical insights necessary for scientific progress. Whewell's balanced view of observation and theory helped lay the groundwork for the modern understanding of scientific methodology.

In addition to his work on the philosophy of science, Whewell made significant contributions to the history of science. His book History of the Inductive Sciences (1837) traced the development of various scientific disciplines from antiquity to the 19th century. Whewell was one of the first thinkers to approach the history of science as a philosophical endeavor, aiming to show how scientific ideas evolved over time and how they were shaped by broader intellectual currents. His work in this field helped establish the history of science as a distinct academic discipline and influenced later historians such as Thomas Kuhn.

Whewell's influence extended beyond the philosophy and history of science. He was a theologian who sought to reconcile scientific discovery with religious belief, arguing that science and faith were complementary rather than antagonistic. Whewell's writings on natural theology, particularly his work Astronomy and General Physics Considered with Reference to Natural Theology (1833), were part of the Bridgewater Treatises, a series of works that aimed to demonstrate the harmony between science and Christianity. His belief in the unity of knowledge, encompassing both science and religion, reflected the intellectual spirit of his time, which sought to integrate diverse fields of inquiry.

Auguste Comte (1798 – 1857 CE)

Auguste Comte was a French philosopher and sociologist, best known as the founder of positivism and one of the key figures in the development of sociology as an academic discipline. Born in Montpellier, Comte was educated in mathematics and science before becoming involved in the intellectual and political movements of post-revolutionary France. He worked as a secretary to the utopian socialist Claude Henri de Rouvroy, Comte de Saint-Simon, whose ideas influenced his early thinking. However, Comte later broke away from Saint-Simon's influence and developed his own philosophy, which sought to create a systematic approach to understanding human society through scientific principles.

Comte's most important philosophical contribution was his theory of positivism, which he outlined in his Course of Positive Philosophy (1830–1842). He argued that human thought progresses through three stages: the theological stage, in which natural phenomena are explained by reference to gods or supernatural forces; the metaphysical stage, where abstract principles are used to explain the world; and finally, the positive stage, where scientific observation and empirical methods become the foundation for understanding reality. In the positive stage, Comte believed, society could achieve progress and order by relying on science rather than superstition or metaphysics.

Positivism was not just a philosophy of science for Comte—it was a social and political vision as well. He believed that society should be organized on scientific principles, with sociologists acting as the "priests" of a new secular order. Comte envisioned a hierarchical society where the intellectual elite would guide the masses, using their knowledge of social laws to create a stable and harmonious social order. His vision of a technocratic society, governed by experts in science and sociology, was a reaction to the instability and chaos he saw in post-revolutionary France.

Comte also made significant contributions to the field of sociology, which he coined as a term. He saw sociology as the highest and most complex of the sciences, because it dealt with the most advanced phenomena—human societies. His System of Positive Polity (1851–1854) proposed a detailed plan for reorganizing society according to positivist principles, emphasizing the need for social cohesion and moral regeneration. Although some of Comte's more authoritarian ideas, such as his concept of a "Religion of Humanity," were criticized, his insistence on the scientific study of society laid the foundation for modern sociology.

Comte's influence extended well beyond his lifetime. His ideas about the stages of human thought, the application of science to social problems, and the importance of sociology as a discipline influenced later thinkers such as Émile Durkheim and Karl Marx. While his vision of a positivist society was never fully realized, Comte's work remains a foundational text in both sociology and the philosophy of science.

Ralph Waldo Emerson (1803 – 1882 CE)

Ralph Waldo Emerson was an American essayist, philosopher, and poet, who became a central figure in the Transcendentalist movement of the early 19th century. Born in Boston, Massachusetts, Emerson attended Harvard Divinity School and became a Unitarian minister before resigning his position due to personal doubts about traditional Christian doctrines. His departure from conventional religion marked the beginning of his journey toward developing a new philosophical outlook, influenced by Romanticism, Eastern religions, and the emerging philosophy of individualism in the United States. The intellectual climate of post-Revolutionary America, with its growing emphasis on self-reliance and democratic ideals, provided a fertile ground for Emerson's thought.

Emerson's philosophy revolved around the concept of Transcendentalism, which asserted that individuals could access higher truths directly through intuition and spiritual experiences, without relying on organized religion or empirical observation. In his famous essay Nature (1836), Emerson argued that the natural world was a reflection of the divine, and that by contemplating nature, individuals could achieve a deeper understanding of themselves and the universe. He believed that each person possesses an inner spirit that connects them to the universal "Oversoul," a concept that emphasized the unity of all existence and the interconnectedness of humanity with nature.

One of Emerson's most influential ideas was his advocacy for self-reliance and individualism. In his essay Self-Reliance (1841), he emphasized the importance of trusting oneself and rejecting societal conformity. Emerson argued that people should not be afraid to think and act independently, as true genius comes from within, not from external approval. This philosophy was not only a critique of institutionalized religion and rigid social structures but also a celebration of the creative potential of the individual. Emerson's call for self-reliance resonated deeply in a rapidly industrializing America, where individuals were seeking new forms of personal and intellectual freedom.

Emerson's views on social reform were also significant, though somewhat more complex. He was an abolitionist and supported the cause of freeing enslaved African Americans, yet his philosophy of individualism sometimes led to a reluctance to engage directly in political activism. He believed that true social change would come from personal transformation rather than from collective action. However, his influence on later reform movements, including civil rights and women's rights, was profound, as his ideas about the inherent worth and dignity of every person inspired generations of activists and thinkers.

Despite criticisms that his philosophy was overly idealistic, Emerson's ideas had a lasting impact on American thought and culture. His work laid the foundation for future philosophical movements, including pragmatism and existentialism, and his emphasis on individuality and spiritual experience continues to resonate in modern discussions about personal freedom and the role of the individual in society.

Ludwig Feuerbach (1804 – 1872 CE)

Ludwig Feuerbach was a German philosopher and anthropologist, best known for his critique of religion and his influence on later thinkers like Karl Marx and Friedrich Engels. Born in Landshut, Bavaria, Feuerbach studied theology and philosophy at the University of Heidelberg, where he initially followed the ideas of Georg Wilhelm Friedrich Hegel. However, Feuerbach later broke with Hegelian idealism, developing a materialist approach that would underpin much of his philosophical work. His critique of religion emerged during a time of increasing skepticism toward traditional Christian doctrines in the wake of the Enlightenment and the rise of historical-critical methods of biblical interpretation.

Feuerbach's most famous work, The Essence of Christianity (1841), marked a radical departure from Hegelian philosophy. In this text, he argued that religion is essentially a projection of human nature. According to Feuerbach, the attributes humans ascribe to God—such as wisdom, power, and love—are actually idealized versions of human qualities. Thus, religion is not the revelation of divine truths but the externalization of human desires and fears. Feuerbach's materialist view suggested that understanding humanity, rather than metaphysical speculation, should be the focus of philosophical inquiry. His critique of religion laid the foundation for subsequent materialist and atheist thought in the 19th century.

Central to Feuerbach's philosophy is the idea that human beings are the measure of all things. He argued that the essence of Christianity and other religions is not found in their doctrines but in their human content—the ways in which they reflect human needs and aspirations. For Feuerbach, the study of religion was essentially the study of anthropology, as religious beliefs and practices provided insight into the nature of human existence. By reducing theology to anthropology, Feuerbach shifted the focus of philosophical inquiry from the divine to the human, anticipating the secular humanism that would dominate much of modern philosophy.

Feuerbach's materialism also extended to his understanding of consciousness and the self. He rejected the Hegelian notion that human consciousness was a reflection of the Absolute Spirit, arguing instead that consciousness arises from physical and social conditions. In this sense, Feuerbach's materialism was a precursor to the historical materialism of Marx, who took Feuerbach's ideas further by applying them to social and economic structures. Although Feuerbach did not develop a fully-fledged theory of society, his focus on human needs and material conditions influenced the development of Marxist thought.

Despite being overshadowed by thinkers like Marx and Engels, Feuerbach's work remains significant for its bold critique of religious belief and its emphasis on human-centered philosophy. His ideas contributed to the broader 19th-century movement away from metaphysical speculation and toward a more grounded, materialist understanding of human nature and society. Today, Feuerbach is remembered as a key figure in the transition from German Idealism to modern materialism and humanism.

Alexis de Tocqueville (1805 – 1859 CE)

Alexis de Tocqueville was a French political thinker and historian, renowned for his analysis of democracy and its effects on society. Born into an aristocratic family in Paris, Tocqueville studied law and began a career in politics, though he is best remembered for his travels in the United States and his subsequent work, Democracy in America (1835, 1840). Tocqueville visited the U.S. in 1831, ostensibly to study the prison system, but his observations expanded into a comprehensive examination of American democracy. His work developed during a time of political transformation in Europe, where monarchies were being challenged by rising democratic and republican movements.

In Democracy in America, Tocqueville provided a detailed account of how democracy functioned in the United States, particularly in contrast to the aristocratic systems of Europe. He admired the political equality and civic engagement that characterized American society, yet he was also cautious about the potential dangers of democracy. Tocqueville warned of the "tyranny of the majority," where the desires of the majority could override the rights of minorities, leading to a form of democratic despotism. He believed that while democracy promoted political freedom, it also carried the risk of conformity and the suppression of individual thought.

Tocqueville's analysis of American society also emphasized the importance of civil institutions and associations in maintaining democracy. He argued that the strength of American democracy lay not just in its formal political institutions but in its vibrant civil society, where citizens actively participated in a wide range of voluntary associations. These associations, according to Tocqueville, helped to counterbalance the individualism and isolation that could arise in a democratic society, fostering a sense of shared responsibility and collective action.

Tocqueville's broader political philosophy was shaped by his concern for liberty and his belief in the need to balance freedom with social order. He was wary of both revolutionary movements, which he believed could lead to chaos, and rigid authoritarian regimes, which stifled freedom. His vision of democracy was one where individual liberty was protected through a combination of strong institutions, civic participation, and a moral sense of responsibility. Tocqueville's observations of American democracy were deeply influential, not just in Europe but around the world, as his work became a foundational text in the study of democratic governance.

Tocqueville's legacy extends beyond his analysis of American democracy. His reflections on the relationship between equality, freedom, and civic engagement have influenced generations of political theorists, sociologists, and historians. Tocqueville remains a central figure in discussions about the strengths and weaknesses of democratic systems, particularly in an era where democracy continues to face challenges from both authoritarianism and internal divisions.

Max Stirner (1806 – 1856 CE)

Max Stirner, born Johann Kaspar Schmidt, was a German philosopher best known for his radical individualist philosophy, which is laid out in his major work, The Ego and Its Own (1844). Stirner was born in Bayreuth, Bavaria, and studied philosophy at the University of Berlin, where he was influenced by the Young Hegelians, a group of intellectuals who critiqued the work of Hegel. However, Stirner soon diverged from the idealism of Hegel and the political radicalism of the Young Hegelians, developing a philosophy that emphasized extreme individualism and a rejection of all forms of authority and collective identity.

At the heart of Stirner's philosophy is the concept of the "ego," which he defined as the unique, self-interested individual who exists independently of all social, religious, and moral constraints. In The Ego and Its Own, Stirner argued that all abstract ideas, such as religion, morality, and even the state, are mere illusions that serve to oppress the individual. For Stirner, these concepts are "spooks" that haunt human consciousness, preventing individuals from achieving true freedom. He claimed that individuals should reject these external authorities and live according to their own desires and interests, free from any obligation to society or others.

Stirner's rejection of all forms of external authority extended to his critique of political movements, including socialism and communism, which were gaining popularity in his time. He argued that these ideologies merely replaced one form of domination with another, as they still imposed collective goals and identities on individuals. Stirner believed that true freedom could only be achieved through a radical form of individualism, where each person acted purely in their own interest, unconstrained by any external forces. This radical rejection of all forms of collectivism set Stirner apart from other political philosophers of his time.

Stirner's ideas had a significant, though often underappreciated, influence on later philosophical movements, particularly existentialism and anarchism. His emphasis on individual autonomy and the rejection of external authority resonated with later thinkers like Friedrich Nietzsche, who similarly critiqued traditional values and embraced individual will. Stirner's work also influenced anarchist thought, particularly in its rejection of the state and its emphasis on personal liberty. Although Stirner was largely ignored during his lifetime, his ideas experienced a revival in the 20th century, particularly in discussions of individualism and anti-authoritarianism.

Despite the controversial nature of his philosophy, Stirner's radical individualism remains a provocative challenge to more conventional theories of society, politics, and morality. His insistence on the primacy of the individual and the rejection of all external constraints continues to inspire debates about the limits of personal freedom and the role of social institutions in shaping human behavior.

John Stuart Mill (1806 – 1873 CE)

John Stuart Mill was an English philosopher, political economist, and social reformer, who is best known for his contributions to utilitarianism and his defense of individual liberty. Born in London, Mill was educated by his father, James Mill, who was a follower of the philosopher Jeremy Bentham. Mill was subjected to an intense and rigorous education from an early age, mastering Greek, Latin, and mathematics before he was ten. His intellectual development took place in the context of the early 19th century, a time of rapid industrialization, political reform, and philosophical debate about the nature of liberty and democracy. This unique upbringing shaped Mill into one of the most precocious and influential thinkers of his era, deeply committed to advancing knowledge and social progress.

Mill's philosophy is most closely associated with utilitarianism, a moral theory that he inherited from Bentham. In his seminal work Utilitarianism (1863), Mill argued that the rightness or wrongness of actions should be judged by their consequences, specifically by the extent to which they promote happiness or pleasure. However, Mill refined Bentham's utilitarianism by distinguishing between higher and lower pleasures, emphasizing that intellectual and moral pleasures are superior to purely physical ones. For Mill, the goal of ethics was not merely to maximize pleasure but to cultivate human flourishing and moral development.

In addition to his work on ethics, Mill made significant contributions to political philosophy, particularly in his defense of individual liberty. His essay On Liberty (1859) is a cornerstone of liberal political thought, in which he argued that individuals should be free to act as they wish, so long as their actions do not harm others. Mill was a strong advocate for free speech, believing that the free exchange of ideas was essential for intellectual and social progress. He also emphasized the importance of individuality, arguing that society should not impose conformity on its citizens but should allow for diverse ways of life and thought.

Mill was also deeply concerned with issues of social justice and political reform. He was a vocal advocate for women's rights, publishing The Subjection of Women (1869), where he argued for gender equality and women's suffrage. He believed that the emancipation of women was essential for the moral and intellectual progress of society. Mill was also an early proponent of political and economic reforms aimed at alleviating poverty and reducing inequality, supporting the extension of the franchise and advocating for progressive taxation.

Mill's intellectual legacy is vast, influencing a wide range of fields, including ethics, political theory, economics, and social reform. His defense of liberty, equality, and individual rights has made him one of the most important figures in the history of liberal thought, and his works continue to be foundational texts in discussions of democracy, ethics, and human rights.

Charles Darwin (1809 – 1882 CE)

Charles Darwin was an English naturalist and biologist, best known for his groundbreaking work on the theory of evolution by natural selection. Born in Shrewsbury, England, Darwin was initially sent to study medicine at the University of Edinburgh but later switched to theology at Cambridge. His true passion, however, was the study of nature. In 1831, he embarked on a five-year voyage aboard the HMS Beagle, during which he collected a wealth of specimens and observations that would later form the foundation of his theory. His work took place during a period of scientific exploration and challenge to established religious views about the origins of life.

Darwin's theory of evolution, as articulated in his 1859 book On the Origin of Species, was based on the idea that species evolve over time through a process of natural selection. In this process, individuals within a species vary in their traits, and those traits that provide a reproductive or survival advantage become more common in subsequent generations. Darwin's insights were radical because they provided a naturalistic explanation for the diversity of life, challenging the dominant religious view that species were created in their present form by a divine creator. His theory suggested that all species, including humans, share common ancestry.

Central to Darwin's philosophy was the notion of gradualism, the idea that evolutionary changes occur slowly over long periods of time. This contrasted with earlier theories that suggested sudden, large-scale transformations in species. Darwin's emphasis on slow, incremental change reflected the influence of geologist Charles Lyell, whose work on uniformitarianism posited that the Earth's features were shaped by continuous processes over vast time scales. Darwin applied this principle to biology, arguing that even complex organisms could evolve through the accumulation of small, advantageous variations.

Darwin also grappled with the implications of his theory for human beings. In his later work, The Descent of Man (1871), he applied the theory of evolution to humans, arguing that human beings were not separate from the natural world but were subject to the same evolutionary forces as other animals. He proposed that traits such as intelligence and morality evolved through natural selection, thus offering a biological explanation for behaviors previously attributed to divine intervention or human uniqueness. This extension of evolutionary theory to humans was met with both fascination and controversy, as it challenged deeply held views about human exceptionalism.

Although Darwin's ideas were initially controversial, they gradually gained acceptance and revolutionized the biological sciences. His work laid the foundation for modern evolutionary biology, influencing not only scientists but also philosophers, theologians, and social theorists. The implications of his theory extended beyond biology, shaping debates about human nature, ethics, and society. Darwin's legacy remains profound, as his theory of evolution continues to be a cornerstone of modern science.

Søren Kierkegaard (1813 – 1855 CE)

Søren Kierkegaard was a Danish philosopher and theologian, widely regarded as the father of existentialism. Born in Copenhagen, Kierkegaard was raised in a devout Lutheran family and initially studied theology at the University of Copenhagen. However, he became increasingly critical of institutionalized Christianity and developed a highly individualistic philosophy focused on the nature of faith, existence, and the self. Kierkegaard's work emerged during a time of growing secularism in Europe, as well as a reaction against the dominant Hegelian philosophy, which emphasized abstract systems of thought over individual experience.

Kierkegaard's philosophy centered on the concept of individual existence and the subjective nature of human experience. He believed that philosophy should not be concerned with abstract, universal truths but with the lived experiences of individuals. For Kierkegaard, existence was characterized by anxiety, uncertainty, and choice, as individuals are constantly confronted with decisions that shape their identity and relationship with the world. This emphasis on personal experience and choice made Kierkegaard a precursor to existentialist thinkers such as Jean-Paul Sartre and Martin Heidegger.

A key theme in Kierkegaard's work is the "leap of faith," which refers to the existential decision to believe in God despite the absence of objective evidence. In works like Fear and Trembling (1843), Kierkegaard explored the story of Abraham's willingness to sacrifice his son Isaac as an example of the paradoxes of faith. He argued that true faith requires a leap beyond reason and ethics, a personal commitment to something that cannot be rationally justified. This radical view of faith was a critique of both rationalist philosophy and the complacency of institutionalized religion, which Kierkegaard saw as detached from authentic religious experience.

Kierkegaard also introduced the concept of "the stages of life," which he described in works like Either/Or (1843) and Stages on Life's Way (1845). He proposed that individuals progress through three stages of existence: the aesthetic, the ethical, and the religious. The aesthetic stage is characterized by a pursuit of pleasure and avoidance of responsibility, while the ethical stage involves a commitment to moral duty and social norms. The religious stage, however, represents the highest form of existence, where the individual transcends both pleasure and ethics in a personal relationship with God. Kierkegaard believed that only by reaching the religious stage could one achieve true freedom and authenticity.

Kierkegaard's influence on philosophy and theology has been profound, particularly in the 20th century. His exploration of existential themes such as anxiety, despair, and the search for meaning resonated with later existentialist and phenomenological thinkers. Although his ideas were largely ignored during his lifetime, Kierkegaard is now regarded as one of the most important philosophers of modernity, whose work continues to inspire debates about faith, individuality, and the human condition.

Henry David Thoreau (1817 – 1862 CE)

Henry David Thoreau was an American philosopher, naturalist, and writer, best known for his reflections on nature and his advocacy for civil disobedience. Born in Concord, Massachusetts, Thoreau was part of the Transcendentalist movement, which emphasized the inherent goodness of people and nature. He was a close associate of Ralph Waldo Emerson, whose ideas about self-reliance and individualism deeply influenced Thoreau's own thought. Thoreau's philosophy developed in the context of 19th-century American transcendentalism and a growing concern for social justice, particularly in response to slavery and the Mexican-American War.

Thoreau's most famous work, Walden (1854), is a reflection on simple living and self-sufficiency, based on his two-year experiment living in a cabin near Walden Pond. In Walden, Thoreau explored the idea that modern society, with its materialism and focus on progress, alienates individuals from nature and their true selves. He advocated for a return to a simpler, more deliberate way of life, where individuals could cultivate a deeper connection with nature and themselves. Thoreau's philosophy of nature was not just about physical wilderness but also about spiritual renewal, as he saw nature as a source of moral and intellectual inspiration.

Another central aspect of Thoreau's philosophy was his belief in civil disobedience as a moral duty in the face of unjust laws. In his essay Civil Disobedience (1849), Thoreau argued that individuals should not blindly follow government authority when it conflicts with their conscience. He famously refused to pay taxes in protest against slavery and the Mexican-American War, spending a night in jail as a result. Thoreau's act of resistance was grounded in his belief that justice and morality transcended legal and political systems. He encouraged individuals to follow their conscience, even if it meant breaking the law, a stance that would later influence figures like Mahatma Gandhi and Martin Luther King Jr.

Thoreau's individualism was deeply tied to his understanding of self-reliance and personal responsibility. He believed that each person had the capacity to live a meaningful, independent life, free from the constraints of social conventions and materialism. His philosophy was not only a critique of industrial society but also a call for individuals to cultivate their inner resources and live authentically. Thoreau's rejection of consumerism and his advocacy for simple living remain relevant in contemporary discussions about sustainability and environmentalism.

Though Thoreau was relatively unknown during his lifetime, his influence grew significantly after his death. His writings on nature, civil disobedience, and individualism have inspired generations of thinkers, activists, and environmentalists. Today, Thoreau is remembered as one of the key figures in American philosophical and literary traditions, whose ideas continue to challenge and inspire those seeking a deeper connection to nature and social justice.

Karl Marx (1818 – 1883 CE)

Karl Marx was a German philosopher, economist, and revolutionary socialist whose ideas became foundational for modern communism. Born in Trier, Germany, Marx studied law and philosophy at the University of Bonn and later in Berlin, where he was influenced by thinkers like Georg Wilhelm Friedrich Hegel. Marx's ideas were shaped by the Industrial Revolution and the social inequalities it produced, as well as by his collaboration with Friedrich Engels. Together, they sought to explain the exploitation of the working class and offer a vision of a future society free from class struggle. Marx's works, such as The Communist Manifesto (1848) and Das Kapital (1867), remain central to Marxist philosophy and socialist thought.

Marx's philosophy is best understood through his theory of historical materialism, which posits that the economic base of society—the mode of production—determines its political and ideological superstructure. He argued that history is driven by class conflict, as different classes struggle over control of the means of production. Marx identified two key classes in capitalist society: the bourgeoisie (capitalist class), who own the means of production, and the proletariat (working class), who sell their labor. According to Marx, the inherent contradictions within capitalism, particularly the exploitation of labor by the bourgeoisie, would lead to a proletarian revolution and the eventual establishment of a classless, communist society.

Central to Marx's critique of capitalism is the concept of alienation. He argued that under capitalism, workers are alienated from the products of their labor, the process of production, their fellow workers, and their own human potential. In a capitalist system, the products workers create are owned by capitalists, who profit from them, while workers receive only a fraction of the value they generate. This separation from the fruits of their labor, according to Marx, dehumanizes workers and reduces them to mere instruments of production, preventing them from realizing their full creative and social capacities.

Marx also developed a theory of surplus value, which explains how capitalists profit from the exploitation of labor. In Das Kapital, Marx argued that workers produce more value than they receive in wages, and this surplus value is appropriated by capitalists as profit. This exploitation, Marx believed, was the engine of capitalist accumulation, but it also created tensions between the bourgeoisie and the proletariat. Marx predicted that as capitalism developed, these contradictions would become increasingly untenable, leading to crises and, ultimately, to the overthrow of the capitalist system by the working class.

While Marx's ideas were controversial during his lifetime, they gained significant influence in the 20th century, particularly through the Russian Revolution and the spread of communist ideologies. His analysis of capitalism, class struggle, and historical development continues to shape political thought and activism. Marx's vision of a classless, stateless society remains a powerful ideal for those seeking to address inequality, exploitation, and social injustice in the modern world.

Friedrich Engels (1820 – 1895 CE)

Friedrich Engels was a German philosopher, social scientist, and political activist, best known for his close collaboration with Karl Marx and his contributions to the development of Marxist theory. Born in Barmen, Prussia, Engels came from a wealthy industrialist family, but he became deeply critical of the capitalist system after witnessing the exploitation of workers in his father's textile mills. Engels' experiences in industrial England, where he lived for several years, provided much of the material for his influential work The Condition of the Working Class in England (1845). His partnership with Marx began in the 1840s and lasted until Marx's death in 1883, after which Engels played a crucial role in editing and publishing Marx's unfinished works.

Engels shared Marx's belief in historical materialism, which posits that the economic structure of society determines its social and political institutions. Together, they developed the theory of class struggle, arguing that throughout history, society has been divided into classes based on their relationship to the means of production. In the capitalist system, Engels and Marx identified the bourgeoisie (owners of capital) and the proletariat (working class) as the primary antagonistic classes. They predicted that the contradictions of capitalism—particularly the exploitation of labor—would lead to the overthrow of the bourgeoisie and the establishment of a communist society.

One of Engels' key contributions to Marxist theory was his analysis of the family, private property, and the state in his work The Origin of the Family, Private Property and the State (1884). Engels argued that the institution of the family, particularly in its patriarchal form, developed alongside private property as a means of controlling inheritance and maintaining class divisions. He believed that the subjugation of women in the family mirrored the exploitation of the working class in the capitalist economy. Engels suggested that the abolition of private property and the establishment of a classless society would lead to the liberation of women and the dissolution of the traditional family structure.

Engels also played a key role in articulating dialectical materialism, building on Marx's historical materialism and incorporating Hegel's dialectical method. This approach viewed societal development as a process of contradictions and resolutions, with each stage of history containing the seeds of its own destruction. Engels applied this method to natural science in works like Dialectics of Nature (1883), arguing that dialectical laws governed both social life and the natural world.

After Marx's death, Engels safeguarded Marx's legacy by editing the second and third volumes of Das Kapital and spreading Marxist theory through his writings and political activity. His contributions to Marxist thought, particularly in the areas of gender, family, and dialectical materialism, remain influential in contemporary Marxist and feminist theory. The intellectual partnership between Marx and Engels significantly shaped the trajectory of socialist and communist movements around the world.

Herbert Spencer (1820 – 1903 CE)

Fyodor Dostoevsky was born on November 11, 1821, in Moscow, Russia, to a middle-class family. His early life was marked by hardship and loss, as his mother died when he was 15, and his father, a strict doctor, was allegedly murdered by serfs. Dostoevsky attended the St. Petersburg Academy of Military Engineering but was more drawn to literature than his military studies. His first novel, Poor Folk (1846), earned him acclaim and entry into St. Petersburg's literary circles. However, his involvement with radical intellectuals led to his arrest in 1849 and a sentence of four years of hard labor in Siberia, an experience that profoundly shaped his worldview and deepened his Christian faith.

Dostoevsky's time in Siberia fundamentally transformed his views on morality, faith, and human nature. He witnessed the brutality of the prison camp but also saw resilience and compassion among his fellow prisoners. This experience led him to see suffering as a path to self-knowledge and spiritual growth. His empathy for the marginalized became a recurring theme in his work, manifesting in characters who wrestle with guilt, redemption, and despair. His prison years also cemented his distrust of radical ideologies and moral absolutism, positioning him against nihilism and in favor of a spiritually grounded worldview.

In works like Crime and Punishment (1866), Dostoevsky explored the psychology of crime and morality. The novel follows Raskolnikov, a student who believes he is justified in committing murder to fulfill his intellectual vision of justice. Raskolnikov's descent into guilt and suffering illustrates Dostoevsky's skepticism toward ideologies that justify cruelty for the sake of ideals. Dostoevsky emphasized the moral complexity of human beings and the spiritual consequences of immoral acts, suggesting that personal salvation lies in humility, empathy, and acknowledgment of one's failings.

In The Brothers Karamazov (1880), his final novel, Dostoevsky examined faith, doubt, and moral responsibility. The "Grand Inquisitor" chapter presents a parable questioning free will and divine justice in a world of suffering. Through the contrasting beliefs of the Karamazov brothers, Dostoevsky delves into themes of divine justice and human agency. Ivan's atheism and Alyosha's faith reflect Dostoevsky's own philosophical struggles, highlighting the paradoxes of faith and the need for a leap of faith to reconcile life's ambiguities.

Dostoevsky's critique of rationalism and nihilism is central to Demons (1872), which addresses the radical movements in Russia. He viewed these ideologies as promoting violence and moral decay under the guise of progress. In Demons, he illustrates the chaos that arises when spiritual and moral values are rejected in favor of ideological pursuits. For Dostoevsky, true freedom lay not in rejecting God but in embracing humility, compassion, and communal responsibility. His work endures for its profound philosophical insights into faith, morality, and the redemptive power of suffering.

Wilhelm Wundt (1832 – 1920 CE)

Wilhelm Wundt was a German psychologist, philosopher, and physiologist, widely regarded as the father of modern experimental psychology. Born in Neckarau, Germany, Wundt initially studied medicine before turning to psychology and philosophy, becoming a professor at the University of Leipzig. His work marked the transition of psychology from a branch of philosophy to a scientific discipline based on empirical research. Wundt's contributions to psychology were shaped by the intellectual environment of 19th-century Germany, where positivism, experimental science, and the study of human consciousness were gaining prominence. He is best known for establishing the first psychological laboratory in 1879, laying the foundation for psychology as an experimental science.

Wundt's central philosophical contribution was his theory of "voluntarism," which emphasized the role of will and volition in human experience. In contrast to earlier mechanistic models of the mind, Wundt argued that human consciousness was not merely the passive reception of sensory stimuli but an active process of organizing and interpreting experience. His work in Principles of Physiological Psychology (1874) sought to investigate the structure of conscious experience through systematic observation and experimentation. Wundt believed that by analyzing sensations, perceptions, and emotions, psychologists could uncover the basic elements of the mind and how they combine to form complex mental processes.

In addition to his focus on the individual mind, Wundt also explored the relationship between psychology and culture, developing what he called "Völkerpsychologie" (cultural psychology). He argued that higher mental functions, such as language, art, religion, and social institutions, could not be fully understood through laboratory experiments alone but required a broader, cultural-historical approach. Wundt's work in cultural psychology aimed to understand how human cognition and behavior are shaped by social and historical contexts, contributing to the development of the social sciences.

Wundt's methodology was grounded in introspection, the careful observation and reporting of one's own conscious experience. While introspection had been used in philosophy for centuries, Wundt sought to formalize it as a scientific method, with rigorous controls and careful attention to the conditions under which mental phenomena occurred. He believed that psychology should be concerned with immediate experience, rather than abstract metaphysical speculation. This empirical approach to psychology set Wundt apart from earlier philosophers of mind, such as Immanuel Kant, who had doubted the possibility of psychology as a science.

Although Wundt's introspective method later fell out of favor with the rise of behaviorism and cognitive psychology, his contributions to the development of psychology as an experimental discipline remain foundational. His emphasis on empirical research, the structure of consciousness, and the role of culture in shaping mental life influenced subsequent generations of psychologists and philosophers, solidifying his legacy as a pioneering figure in modern psychology.

Wilhelm Dilthey (1833 – 1911 CE)

Wilhelm Dilthey was a German philosopher, historian, and psychologist, best known for his contributions to hermeneutics and the philosophy of the human sciences. Born in Biebrich, Germany, Dilthey initially studied theology before turning to philosophy and history, where he developed a keen interest in understanding human experience and culture. His work emerged in response to the growing dominance of natural sciences in the 19th century, as he sought to establish a distinct methodology for the human sciences (Geisteswissenschaften), which he believed required different methods from the natural sciences. Dilthey's intellectual project was shaped by his engagement with thinkers like Immanuel Kant, Johann Gottfried Herder, and Friedrich Schleiermacher.

Dilthey's most significant philosophical contribution was his development of a hermeneutic approach to the human sciences, which emphasized the importance of understanding subjective human experience. In contrast to the natural sciences, which seek to explain phenomena through causal relationships, Dilthey argued that the human sciences should aim to understand the meaning of human actions, beliefs, and cultural products. His concept of "Verstehen" (understanding) became central to his philosophy, as he believed that understanding human life required an interpretive approach that took into account historical context, individual experience, and cultural meanings.

Dilthey's philosophy of history was also a key element of his thought. He rejected the positivist idea that history could be understood through objective, scientific laws, arguing instead that history is a product of human consciousness and meaning-making. In his work Introduction to the Human Sciences (1883), Dilthey proposed that historians and philosophers should focus on interpreting the lived experiences of individuals and societies, rather than attempting to derive universal historical laws. This approach to history emphasized the uniqueness of human experience and the need for a pluralistic understanding of historical events.

In addition to his work on hermeneutics and history, Dilthey made important contributions to the philosophy of psychology. He was critical of the mechanistic models of psychology that were popular in the late 19th century, which treated human consciousness as a series of causal processes. Instead, Dilthey argued for a descriptive psychology that focused on understanding the lived experiences of individuals. He believed that psychology should be concerned with describing the inner world of human beings, including emotions, motivations, and values, rather than reducing them to physiological or mechanistic explanations.

Dilthey's legacy lies in his emphasis on the interpretive nature of the human sciences and his critique of positivism. His ideas influenced later thinkers in hermeneutics, such as Martin Heidegger and Hans-Georg Gadamer, and played a crucial role in the development of phenomenology and existentialism. Although Dilthey's work was not widely appreciated during his lifetime, his contributions to the philosophy of history, psychology, and the human sciences have had a lasting impact on the study of human experience and culture.

Henry Sidgwick (1838 – 1900 CE)

Henry Sidgwick was an English philosopher, ethicist, and economist whose contributions to utilitarianism and moral philosophy made him one of the most important thinkers of the 19th century. Born in Skipton, Yorkshire, Sidgwick was educated at Rugby School and then Cambridge University, where he became a prominent academic figure. Initially influenced by John Stuart Mill and other utilitarians, he sought to refine and expand upon their theories during a time of significant social and political change in Britain. His most famous work, The Methods of Ethics (1874), remains a central text in modern ethical theory.

Sidgwick's philosophy revolved around utilitarianism, the moral theory that actions are right if they promote the greatest happiness for the greatest number. In The Methods of Ethics, he identified three main approaches to moral philosophy: intuitionism, which holds that moral truths are self-evident; egoism, which advocates acting in one's self-interest; and utilitarianism, which prioritizes societal well-being. Sidgwick aimed to reconcile these methods and ultimately defended utilitarianism as the most rational and comprehensive moral system, addressing its complexities and potential conflicts.

A central problem Sidgwick confronted was the "dualism of practical reason," the tension between self-interest and the greater good. He acknowledged that individuals often face situations where their personal interests conflict with the utilitarian imperative to maximize happiness for all. While he argued that utilitarianism provides a rational framework for moral decision-making, he admitted that it does not always align with self-interest, leaving this dualism unresolved. This enduring conflict remains a central challenge in utilitarian ethics and continues to shape debates in moral philosophy.

In addition to ethics, Sidgwick made contributions to political philosophy, particularly in his discussions of justice and the state's role in promoting welfare. He advocated for social reforms, including expanded education and women's rights, playing a key role in founding Newnham College at Cambridge to provide higher education for women. Although his views on women's political rights were occasionally tempered by the conservatism of his time, he was a strong supporter of their broader social advancement.

Sidgwick's influence extended to economics and education, contributing to debates on taxation, wealth distribution, and the state's role in managing the economy. His philosophical rigor and engagement with moral theory complexities earned him widespread respect among contemporaries, laying the groundwork for later developments in ethics and social theory. Today, he is remembered as one of the most thoughtful utilitarian thinkers, whose work on reconciling self-interest with the common good continues to resonate in philosophical discussions.

Charles Sanders Peirce (1839 – 1914 CE)

Charles Sanders Peirce was an American philosopher, logician, and scientist, often considered the father of pragmatism and one of the most significant figures in the history of American philosophy. Born in Cambridge, Massachusetts, Peirce was educated at Harvard and began his career in science, working for the U.S. Coast and Geodetic Survey. His philosophical work developed in the intellectual context of the late 19th century, a time when American thought was increasingly influenced by scientific discoveries and a growing interest in the philosophy of knowledge. Peirce's contributions to philosophy, especially his work in semiotics, logic, and the philosophy of science, continue to have a profound impact.

Peirce's central philosophical contribution was his development of pragmatism, a theory of meaning and truth that emphasized the practical consequences of ideas. In his famous "pragmatic maxim," Peirce argued that the meaning of a concept lies in its observable effects and that beliefs should be judged by their practical consequences. For Peirce, truth was not an absolute or fixed entity but something that emerged over time through inquiry and experience. This approach to philosophy was grounded in the scientific method, which Peirce believed was the best way to achieve reliable knowledge. His pragmatism was less concerned with abstract metaphysical speculation and more focused on the application of ideas to real-world problems.

Peirce's work in logic was also highly influential. He made significant contributions to formal logic, including the development of a system of symbolic logic that anticipated later advances in mathematical logic. Peirce was a pioneer in the study of semiotics, the theory of signs, which became a central aspect of his philosophy. He argued that all thought is mediated by signs and that understanding the nature of signs was essential to understanding human cognition and communication. Peirce's triadic model of the sign—consisting of the sign itself, the object it represents, and the interpretant (the understanding of the sign)—remains a foundational concept in the field of semiotics.

In addition to his work on pragmatism and semiotics, Peirce developed a theory of inquiry that emphasized the importance of fallibilism, the idea that all knowledge is provisional and subject to revision. He argued that scientific inquiry is a self-correcting process, where hypotheses are tested and revised based on experience and evidence. This commitment to fallibilism was central to Peirce's philosophy, as he believed that certainty in knowledge could never be fully achieved but that inquiry could progressively lead to more accurate and reliable beliefs.

Peirce's influence on American philosophy and beyond has been profound, particularly in the development of pragmatism, which was later expanded by thinkers like William James and John Dewey. His contributions to logic, semiotics, and the philosophy of science have had a lasting impact, shaping fields as diverse as linguistics, communication theory, and cognitive science. Although Peirce's work was not widely recognized during his lifetime, he is now regarded as one of the most original and important philosophers of the modern era.

William James (1842 – 1910 CE)

William James was an American philosopher and psychologist, widely regarded as one of the most influential thinkers of the 19th and early 20th centuries. Born into an intellectual family in New York, James was educated in both the United States and Europe. He studied medicine at Harvard University but became increasingly interested in psychology and philosophy, eventually joining the Harvard faculty, where he taught for many years. James's intellectual development was shaped by his exposure to diverse philosophical traditions, including empiricism, pragmatism, and transcendentalism, with his most significant contributions lying in the fields of pragmatism, psychology, and the philosophy of religion.

James is best known for developing the philosophical doctrine of pragmatism, articulated in works like Pragmatism: A New Name for Some Old Ways of Thinking (1907). Pragmatism, for James, was a method of resolving philosophical disputes by evaluating ideas based on their practical consequences. He argued that truth is not an abstract property but something verified through its usefulness and effectiveness in real-world situations. This approach contrasted with traditional philosophies seeking absolute, immutable truths, offering a flexible and dynamic way of thinking about truth that adapted to the complexities of human experience.

James's contributions to psychology are equally significant, particularly his work on consciousness and emotion. In The Principles of Psychology (1890), James introduced his theory of the "stream of consciousness," arguing that human thought is continuous and ever-flowing rather than segmented into discrete ideas or perceptions. This idea profoundly influenced psychology and literature, impacting thinkers like John Dewey and writers such as Virginia Woolf. James also co-developed the James-Lange theory of emotion, proposing that emotions result from physiological reactions to stimuli, a view that marked a major departure from traditional theories of emotion.

Another major area of James's work was his exploration of religious experience. In The Varieties of Religious Experience (1902), James adopted an empirical approach to religion, focusing on the personal and psychological aspects of faith rather than institutional doctrines. He argued that religious experiences, even if subjective, had real effects on individuals' lives and could provide profound insights into human nature. His focus on mystical experiences and altered states of consciousness laid the groundwork for later studies in psychology and the sociology of religion.

James's pragmatic philosophy became a cornerstone of American thought, influencing figures like John Dewey and Richard Rorty. His work helped establish psychology as a scientific discipline, while his ideas about religious experience continue to shape debates in philosophy and psychology. His legacy is that of a thinker who bridged multiple disciplines, creating a philosophy deeply rooted in the practical concerns of human life.

Friedrich Nietzsche (1844 – 1900 CE)

Friedrich Nietzsche was a German philosopher, cultural critic, and philologist, whose work profoundly influenced Western thought, particularly existentialism and postmodernism. Born in Röcken, Prussia, Nietzsche was educated in classical philology and became a professor at the University of Basel at a young age. However, health issues forced him to retire early, and he devoted the remainder of his life to writing. Nietzsche's philosophy developed in reaction to the intellectual and cultural trends of his time, including German Idealism, Christianity, and the growing influence of scientific rationalism. His works, such as Thus Spoke Zarathustra (1883–1885) and Beyond Good and Evil (1886), challenged conventional morality and questioned the foundations of Western thought.

Central to Nietzsche's philosophy is the concept of the "will to power," which he described as the fundamental driving force behind human behavior and the development of culture. For Nietzsche, the will to power was not just a desire for domination over others but a more general striving for achievement, creativity, and self-overcoming. He believed that all life is characterized by this drive, and that it manifests in various forms, from individual ambition to artistic creation. Nietzsche's emphasis on the will to power reflected his broader critique of traditional morality, which he saw as repressive and life-denying.

One of Nietzsche's most famous ideas is the notion of the "Übermensch" or "Overman," introduced in Thus Spoke Zarathustra. The Übermensch represents an ideal of human existence, a figure who transcends conventional values and creates new ones based on their own will. Nietzsche saw the Übermensch as the antithesis of the "last man," a complacent, mediocre figure who seeks only comfort and security. For Nietzsche, the Übermensch embodies the possibility of human greatness, achieved through self-overcoming and the rejection of moral norms imposed by society and religion.

Nietzsche's critique of Christianity is another central element of his philosophy. He famously declared "God is dead," not to suggest a literal death, but to indicate the decline of traditional religious authority in the modern world. Nietzsche believed that Christianity, with its emphasis on humility, self-sacrifice, and pity, had weakened Western civilization by promoting a "slave morality" that discouraged strength, vitality, and individual excellence. He argued that the decline of religious belief created an existential vacuum, and he urged humanity to confront the consequences of this loss of meaning by creating new values grounded in the will to power.

Nietzsche's ideas were often misunderstood and misappropriated during his lifetime and after, particularly by nationalist and fascist movements. However, his philosophy of existential freedom, individualism, and the critique of conventional morality has had a lasting impact on 20th-century philosophy. His work influenced existentialist thinkers like Jean-Paul Sartre, Martin Heidegger, and Albert Camus, and continues to be studied and debated across a wide range of disciplines, from ethics to literature and cultural theory.

Gottlob Frege (1848 – 1925 CE)

Gottlob Frege was a German philosopher, logician, and mathematician, considered one of the founders of modern analytic philosophy. Born in Wismar, Germany, Frege studied mathematics and physics at the University of Jena and the University of Göttingen, where he developed his interest in logic and the foundations of mathematics. His work emerged during a period of rapid development in the mathematical sciences, and Frege's contributions were crucial in shaping the direction of both mathematical logic and the philosophy of language. His most influential works include Begriffsschrift (1879) and The Foundations of Arithmetic (1884), which revolutionized the study of logic and the philosophy of mathematics.

Frege's most significant contribution to philosophy was his development of predicate logic, which extended the capabilities of traditional Aristotelian logic. In Begriffsschrift (Concept-Script), Frege introduced a formal system that allowed for the precise analysis of mathematical statements and reasoning. This system laid the foundation for modern symbolic logic and enabled the formalization of arguments involving multiple variables, something not possible with traditional logic. Frege's work in this area had a profound influence on later philosophers and logicians, including Bertrand Russell and Ludwig Wittgenstein, who built upon his ideas to develop the field of analytic philosophy.

Frege also made important contributions to the philosophy of language, particularly through his distinction between "sense" (Sinn) and "reference" (Bedeutung). In his essay "On Sense and Reference" (1892), Frege argued that words and phrases have both a sense, which is the mode of presentation of an object, and a reference, which is the actual object itself. This distinction was groundbreaking in its implications for understanding meaning, as it allowed philosophers to analyze how language relates to the world in a more nuanced way. Frege's theory of meaning influenced many subsequent philosophers, including Russell and Wittgenstein, and remains central to debates in the philosophy of language today.

Another major aspect of Frege's philosophy was his work on the foundations of arithmetic. In The Foundations of Arithmetic, Frege sought to demonstrate that arithmetic could be derived from logic alone, a position known as logicism. He argued that numbers and mathematical truths were not empirical objects but logical entities that could be understood through formal logical systems. Although Frege's logicist program was later challenged by developments in set theory and paradoxes discovered by Russell, his work laid the groundwork for later studies in the philosophy of mathematics and the development of formal systems.

Frege's influence on 20th-century philosophy is profound, particularly in the areas of logic, the philosophy of language, and the philosophy of mathematics. Although his work was not widely recognized during his lifetime, it became central to the analytic tradition, influencing figures such as Russell, Wittgenstein, and the logical positivists. Frege's pioneering ideas continue to shape contemporary debates in philosophy, particularly in discussions of meaning, reference, and the nature of mathematical truth.

Vladimir Solovyov (1853 – 1900 CE)

Vladimir Solovyov was a Russian philosopher, theologian, and poet, often regarded as one of the most influential figures in Russian religious philosophy. Born in Moscow, Solovyov was the son of a prominent historian and grew up in an intellectually vibrant environment. He studied philosophy and theology at Moscow University and later at the University of St. Petersburg, where he engaged deeply with Western European philosophical traditions, particularly the works of Plato, Kant, and Hegel. Solovyov's thought developed in the context of a Russia grappling with modernization, religious revival, and political unrest, as he sought to reconcile Christian theology with philosophical idealism, synthesizing faith, knowledge, and social progress.

Solovyov's philosophy centered on the concept of "Godmanhood" (Bogochelovechestvo), which he understood as the ultimate goal of human history—the unity of humanity with the divine. This idea, rooted in his Christian faith and devotion to Eastern Orthodoxy, drew upon the mystical tradition of theosis, or divinization. Solovyov believed that through moral and spiritual development, humanity could evolve toward perfect unity with God. His vision of Godmanhood was not only metaphysical but also social and political, as he argued that this divine union would bring about universal harmony, justice, and peace.

A central element of Solovyov's thought was his critique of materialism and positivism, which he saw as inadequate explanations of the human condition. In works such as The Crisis of Western Philosophy (1874), he rejected the materialist and empiricist approaches dominant in European thought, arguing that they neglected the spiritual and transcendent dimensions of existence. Solovyov sought to reintroduce metaphysical and theological considerations into philosophy, proposing a form of "integral knowledge" that would encompass both empirical science and spiritual wisdom. For Solovyov, this synthesis was essential to understanding the full scope of reality and human potential.

Solovyov was a staunch advocate of Christian universalism, which he articulated in The Meaning of Love (1892). He believed that true love, grounded in the divine, could unify humanity and overcome divisions based on nationality, race, and class. His vision of love extended beyond personal relationships to social and political life, arguing that a society based on Christian love would embody justice and mutual respect. Solovyov's ideas on love and unity influenced later Russian religious thinkers, such as Sergei Bulgakov and Nikolai Berdyaev, and contributed to the development of Russian Christian socialism.

Despite his idealism, Solovyov engaged deeply with the political and social issues of his time. He supported the idea of a Christian state but criticized the Russian Empire's failure to fulfill its spiritual mission. While advocating for church and state cooperation to promote moral development, he opposed authoritarianism and championed greater freedom and social justice. His work remains a key part of the Russian intellectual tradition, influencing both religious and secular thinkers in Russia and beyond.

Josiah Royce (1855 – 1916 CE)

Josiah Royce was an American philosopher, often regarded as one of the most important figures in the development of American idealism. Born in Grass Valley, California, Royce grew up during a period of rapid expansion and change in the United States. He studied philosophy at the University of California, Berkeley, and later pursued graduate studies in Germany, where he encountered the works of Immanuel Kant, G.W.F. Hegel, and other German idealists. Royce's intellectual career unfolded during a time when pragmatism, particularly the work of William James and Charles Sanders Peirce, was gaining prominence in American philosophy, but he developed his own system of idealism, focusing on community, loyalty, and the absolute.

Central to Royce's philosophy was his concept of loyalty, explored in The Philosophy of Loyalty (1908). Royce defined loyalty as the willing and practical devotion of an individual to a cause greater than oneself. He argued that loyalty is the foundation of moral life, connecting individuals to their communities and providing a sense of purpose and meaning. For Royce, loyalty was not blind allegiance but a rational commitment to causes that promote the well-being of others and contribute to the larger social good. He believed a life guided by loyalty could transcend selfishness and foster deeper connections between individuals and society.

Royce also developed the idea of the "Beloved Community," which he described as the ultimate goal of human moral and social development. Rooted in his Christian idealism and influenced by the social gospel movement, Royce envisioned this community as a spiritual and moral union of individuals bound by loyalty and mutual recognition of each other's worth. He believed that through loyalty to just causes and the pursuit of truth, humanity could progress toward this ideal, overcoming divisions and achieving a higher form of social cooperation and understanding.

In addition to his ethical philosophy, Royce made significant contributions to metaphysics and epistemology. As a proponent of absolute idealism, Royce argued that reality is fundamentally mental or spiritual in nature, with the absolute being a unified, all-encompassing mind or spirit that gives meaning to all individual experiences. He believed that human knowledge is grounded in this absolute, as individual minds participate in a larger, shared reality. Royce's idealism contrasted with pragmatism by emphasizing the unity and coherence of truth over the practical consequences of beliefs.

Royce's work had a lasting impact on American philosophy, particularly in ethics, metaphysics, and the philosophy of religion. His ideas about loyalty and community influenced later thinkers, including Martin Luther King Jr., who drew on Royce's concept of the Beloved Community in his vision of social justice and nonviolent activism. Although overshadowed by the rise of pragmatism and analytic philosophy in the 20th century, Royce's contributions to moral philosophy and social theory remain relevant and are still studied today.

Georg Simmel (1858 – 1918 CE)

Georg Simmel was a German sociologist, philosopher, and cultural critic, widely regarded as one of the founders of sociology as an academic discipline. Born in Berlin, Simmel studied philosophy and history at the University of Berlin, where he later taught as a lecturer. His intellectual career unfolded during a time of significant social and cultural change in Europe, including the rapid urbanization and industrialization of cities like Berlin. Simmel's work was shaped by his engagement with both German idealism and the emerging social sciences, and he is best known for his pioneering contributions to social theory and his analysis of modernity and culture.

Simmel's philosophy focused on the dynamics of social interaction and the structures that shape individual and collective life. In his major work The Philosophy of Money (1900), Simmel explored how economic exchange affects social relationships and individual identity in modern capitalist societies. He argued that money, as an abstract and impersonal medium of exchange, transforms human relationships by reducing them to calculations of value and utility. This process of abstraction, according to Simmel, leads to alienation in modern life, as individuals become increasingly disconnected from meaningful personal relationships.

Another key aspect of Simmel's philosophy is his theory of social forms. He argued that social life is structured by recurring patterns of interaction, which he called "forms," such as domination, cooperation, conflict, and exchange. These forms provide the framework through which individuals engage with one another, shaping their experiences and relationships. Simmel was particularly interested in the dual nature of social interactions, where individuals are both autonomous and interdependent, asserting their individuality while conforming to social norms. His analysis of social forms laid the foundation for later developments in sociology, especially in the study of group dynamics and social structures.

Simmel also made significant contributions to the philosophy of culture, particularly in his analysis of modernity. He argued that modern urban life, with its constant stimulation and diversity of experiences, creates both opportunities and challenges for individuals. While the modern city offers greater freedom and individuality through exposure to diverse ideas and opportunities, it also fosters a sense of alienation and fragmentation. Simmel's concept of the "blasé attitude" described the emotional detachment individuals develop as a defense mechanism against the overwhelming stimuli of urban life.

Simmel's interdisciplinary approach, blending sociology, philosophy, and cultural criticism, had a profound influence on later thinkers, including Max Weber, Walter Benjamin, and Theodor Adorno. His insights into social interaction, culture, and modernity remain relevant to contemporary discussions of urban life, consumer culture, and the impact of capitalism on human relationships. While sometimes overshadowed by more systematic thinkers like Weber and Durkheim, Simmel's innovative approach to understanding social life continues to inspire sociologists and philosophers alike.

Edmund Husserl (1859 – 1938 CE)

Edmund Husserl was a German philosopher and the founder of phenomenology, a philosophical method focused on the structures of consciousness and the direct experience of phenomena. Born in Prossnitz, Moravia (now the Czech Republic), Husserl initially studied mathematics at the University of Vienna and later in Berlin under Karl Weierstrass. His interest in philosophy grew after studying under Franz Brentano, who introduced him to the concepts of intentionality and descriptive psychology. Husserl's work arose in a period of philosophical transition, as traditional metaphysical systems were being questioned, and scientific rigor was increasingly applied to the humanities.

Husserl's central contribution to philosophy was his method of phenomenology, which sought to describe the structures of experience as they appear to consciousness, free from presuppositions. His seminal work, Logical Investigations (1900-1901), marked a departure from both empiricism and idealism by emphasizing the role of consciousness in constituting the meaning of objects. He introduced the concept of intentionality, the idea that consciousness is always directed toward something—it is never empty or passive. This insight became the cornerstone of phenomenology, highlighting that all mental acts are about objects or states of affairs, whether real or imagined.

One of Husserl's key philosophical techniques was "epoché," or phenomenological reduction, which involved "bracketing" or suspending judgments about the existence of the external world to focus solely on the structures of consciousness. By putting aside concerns about whether objects exist independently, Husserl aimed to examine how things appear in pure experience. This method allowed him to explore the ways in which phenomena are constituted in consciousness, leading to a deeper understanding of perception, time, and the self. His later work, Ideas Pertaining to a Pure Phenomenology and to a Phenomenological Philosophy (1913), expanded on these themes and laid the foundation for later phenomenologists like Martin Heidegger and Maurice Merleau-Ponty.

Husserl also made significant contributions to the philosophy of time and intersubjectivity. He argued that our experience of time is structured by a flow of retention (the immediate past), protention (the anticipated future), and the living present. In his later work, The Crisis of European Sciences and Transcendental Phenomenology (1936), Husserl addressed the problem of intersubjectivity, or how individuals can share a common world of experience. He sought to show that the objective world is constituted through shared acts of consciousness, thus providing a foundation for the sciences and human understanding.

Husserl's influence on 20th-century philosophy was profound, particularly in the development of existentialism, hermeneutics, and deconstruction. Although his work was later critiqued and reinterpreted by his students, including Heidegger, his phenomenological method remains a pivotal contribution to modern thought. Husserl's emphasis on the lived experience of consciousness continues to inform contemporary discussions in philosophy of mind, cognitive science, and the human sciences.

Henri Bergson (1859 – 1941 CE)

Henri Bergson was a French philosopher, renowned for his exploration of time, memory, and free will. Born in Paris to a Polish Jewish family, Bergson studied at the École Normale Supérieure and later became a professor at the Collège de France. His philosophical work emerged during a period of significant scientific and intellectual change in Europe, as Darwin's theory of evolution, advances in psychology, and the mechanistic worldview of the late 19th century challenged traditional metaphysical concepts. Bergson's thought offered an alternative to the dominant scientific materialism of his time, advocating for a more fluid and dynamic understanding of life and consciousness.

Bergson's philosophy is best known for its critique of static, mechanistic approaches to time and reality, which he argued failed to capture the richness of lived experience. In his early work, Time and Free Will (1889), Bergson introduced the concept of "duration" (la durée), a qualitative experience of time that contrasts with the quantitative, spatialized time of physics. He argued that real time is a continuous flow in which past, present, and future interpenetrate, rather than a series of discrete, measurable moments. This view of time as fluid underpinned his arguments for free will, as he believed that human actions arise from the dynamic unfolding of consciousness rather than deterministic processes.

Bergson's critique of mechanistic thought extended to his analysis of life and evolution. In Creative Evolution (1907), he challenged the Darwinian view that life could be fully explained by natural selection and adaptation. Instead, Bergson posited the existence of an "élan vital," or vital force, which drives the creative and unpredictable development of life. This force, according to Bergson, is not reducible to mechanical or biological explanations but is a manifestation of life's intrinsic creativity and spontaneity. His concept of élan vital influenced later vitalist and process philosophies, as well as thinkers in fields such as biology, psychology, and theology.

Another important aspect of Bergson's philosophy is his theory of memory, which he explored in Matter and Memory (1896). Bergson argued that memory is not merely a reproduction of past events but an active process that shapes our perception of the present. He distinguished between two forms of memory: "habit-memory," tied to bodily actions, and "pure memory," which preserves the past and informs conscious awareness. Bergson's insights into memory and perception had a significant impact on later phenomenological and existential philosophers, particularly Maurice Merleau-Ponty.

Bergson's influence on 20th-century thought was extensive, though his reputation declined somewhat later in his life. He won the Nobel Prize in Literature in 1927 for his ability to synthesize philosophy with vivid, poetic language. While his vitalism was overshadowed by developments in biology and philosophy, Bergson's explorations of time, creativity, and consciousness remain an important part of the history of modern philosophy.

John Dewey (1859 – 1952 CE)

John Dewey was an American philosopher, psychologist, and educational reformer, best known as one of the leading figures of pragmatism and progressive education. Born in Burlington, Vermont, Dewey was educated at the University of Vermont and Johns Hopkins University, where he studied philosophy under George Sylvester Morris and psychology with G. Stanley Hall. Dewey's career unfolded during a time of rapid industrialization and social change in the United States, and his work was deeply influenced by the democratic ideals of the time and Darwinian evolutionary theory. His philosophy sought to bridge the gap between abstract theory and practical experience, making him one of the most influential public intellectuals of the 20th century.

Dewey's pragmatism was rooted in the idea that knowledge and truth are not fixed or absolute but are instead products of active inquiry and experimentation. In works like The Quest for Certainty (1929) and Experience and Nature (1925), Dewey argued that human thought arises from the interaction between individuals and their environments and must be tested through practical consequences. He rejected traditional dualisms, such as mind versus body or theory versus practice, in favor of a more holistic understanding of human experience. For Dewey, knowledge was always in the process of being shaped and reshaped through ongoing inquiry.

One of Dewey's most significant contributions was his theory of education, which emphasized learning through experience rather than rote memorization or passive absorption of information. In his seminal work Democracy and Education (1916), Dewey argued that education should be a process of active engagement, where students learn by doing and solving real-world problems. He believed that schools should function as miniature democracies, fostering skills and habits necessary for participation in civic life. Dewey's progressive educational philosophy promoted reforms that stressed critical thinking, creativity, and social responsibility.

Dewey's commitment to democracy extended beyond the classroom and into his political philosophy. He believed that democracy was not just a form of government but a way of life requiring constant participation and deliberation. In works like The Public and Its Problems (1927), Dewey argued that a healthy democracy depends on an informed and engaged citizenry and criticized how industrial society often alienated individuals from meaningful political involvement. For Dewey, philosophy's role was to help people think critically about collective challenges, fostering a more participatory society.

Dewey's influence on American philosophy and education was immense, and his ideas continue to resonate in discussions of democracy, ethics, and learning. Although his pragmatism was criticized by some for its perceived lack of metaphysical rigor, Dewey's emphasis on the practical application of ideas and his vision of education as a tool for social progress left a lasting legacy. Today, his work remains a cornerstone of progressive education and continues to inspire debates about the role of philosophy in public life.

Jane Addams (1860 – 1935 CE)

Jane Addams was an American social reformer, philosopher, and activist, best known for her pioneering work in social work and her advocacy for women's rights and world peace. Born in Cedarville, Illinois, Addams was educated at Rockford Female Seminary and briefly attended medical school before her health prevented her from completing her studies. Inspired by a visit to Toynbee Hall in London, a settlement house aimed at addressing urban poverty, Addams co-founded Hull House in Chicago in 1889, which became the model for social work in the United States. Her philosophy developed during a period of rapid industrialization, urbanization, and social inequality in the U.S., as she sought to bridge the gap between philosophy and social activism.

Addams's philosophy was deeply rooted in pragmatism, drawing on the works of John Dewey and William James, as well as her own experiences as a social reformer. She believed in the importance of "sympathetic knowledge," which involved engaging with people's lived experiences to better understand and address social problems. Addams rejected abstract theories of justice and morality in favor of practical solutions grounded in everyday life. Her work at Hull House emphasized community engagement, education, and direct service as means to foster social change. Addams viewed social work not as charity but as democracy in action, where citizens collaborate to improve their collective well-being.

Central to Addams's thought was the concept of social democracy, which she viewed as essential to achieving both political and social justice. She argued that democracy was not just a political system but a way of life requiring active participation from all members of society, particularly those marginalized by poverty, gender, or race. Addams believed that social reform could only be achieved through collective action and championed the idea that education and economic opportunity should be accessible to all citizens. Her vision of democracy extended beyond formal political institutions to include a moral responsibility for one another.

Addams was also a staunch advocate for women's rights and played a key role in the women's suffrage movement. She believed that women's experiences as caregivers and community organizers uniquely qualified them to contribute to social reform and civic life. Addams argued that women's suffrage was not only a matter of equality but also a way to bring about reforms benefiting children, workers, and the poor. Her philosophy called for a redefinition of women's roles in society and an acknowledgment of their contributions to public life.

Throughout her life, Addams was a vocal advocate for peace and internationalism, earning the Nobel Peace Prize in 1931. She opposed militarism and argued that war undermined democratic values of cooperation and shared responsibility. Her pacifism was grounded in her broader philosophy of social ethics, which emphasized the interconnectedness of all people and the need for collective action to achieve justice and peace. Addams's legacy as a philosopher, social worker, and activist continues to influence debates about democracy, social justice, and the role of women in public life.

Rabindranath Tagore (1861 – 1941 CE)

Rabindranath Tagore was a Bengali poet, philosopher, and polymath, renowned for his contributions to literature, music, and education, as well as his role in shaping modern Indian thought. Born into a prominent family in Calcutta, Tagore was educated both in India and England, where he studied law but ultimately devoted himself to writing and philosophy. Tagore's intellectual development took place during the height of British colonial rule in India, and his work sought to reconcile Eastern and Western philosophical traditions. In 1913, he became the first non-European to win the Nobel Prize in Literature, gaining international recognition for his contributions.

Tagore's philosophy was rooted in the Vedantic tradition of Indian thought, which emphasizes the unity of all existence and the interconnectedness of the individual with the divine. He adapted these ideas to address the political and social challenges of modernity, particularly the struggle for Indian independence. In works such as Gitanjali (1910) and The Religion of Man (1931), Tagore expressed a vision of spiritual humanism, where personal freedom and self-realization were intimately connected with the well-being of society. He believed that true freedom came not from political independence alone but from spiritual liberation and the realization of one's higher self.

Tagore's educational philosophy was deeply influenced by his belief in creativity, self-expression, and harmony with nature. He founded the school Visva-Bharati in 1901, which later became a university, with the goal of fostering a holistic education that integrated the arts, sciences, and spiritual growth. Rejecting the rigid, rote-learning model of British colonial education, he advocated for a system that nurtured creativity and encouraged social responsibility. His educational reforms emphasized learning through experience, engagement with the natural world, and a deep respect for cultural diversity.

A key element of Tagore's philosophy was his critique of nationalism. Although he supported Indian independence from British rule, he was critical of the aggressive nationalism developing both in India and abroad. In works such as Nationalism (1917), Tagore warned against blind patriotism and the glorification of the nation-state, arguing that such attitudes could lead to violence and oppression. He advocated for a cosmopolitan vision of the world, where individuals and nations would recognize their shared humanity and work together for the common good.

Tagore's influence extended far beyond India, as he engaged with intellectuals and leaders worldwide, including figures like Albert Einstein and Mahatma Gandhi. His philosophy of universal humanism and his commitment to cultural and spiritual renewal resonated with movements for decolonization and global peace. Today, Tagore is remembered not only for his literary genius but also for his profound contributions to philosophy, education, and social reform, which continue to inspire efforts toward a more just and harmonious world.

Alfred North Whitehead (1861 – 1947 CE)

Alfred North Whitehead was an English mathematician and philosopher born in Ramsgate, England. Initially, he made significant contributions to mathematics, particularly in logic and algebra, and co-authored Principia Mathematica with Bertrand Russell, which became a foundational text in mathematical logic. Whitehead later shifted towards philosophy, especially metaphysics, and spent his later years as a professor at Harvard University. His philosophical work emerged during a time of rapid scientific and philosophical change, particularly with the development of quantum physics and relativity, which influenced his ideas. Whitehead's ability to synthesize scientific advancements with profound metaphysical questions positioned him as a bridge between the sciences and the humanities.

Whitehead is best known for his development of process philosophy, which emphasizes becoming and change over static being. He argued that reality is not composed of material objects but of processes and events. This idea contrasts with the traditional metaphysical view that sees reality as composed of discrete, unchanging entities. In his work Process and Reality, Whitehead introduced the idea of "actual occasions," the fundamental units of reality, which are dynamic and interconnected. This view of reality as a network of events that influence one another revolutionized metaphysical thinking.

A key concept in Whitehead's philosophy is the "philosophy of organism." In this framework, he viewed the universe as an interconnected web of processes where each part affects the whole. This organic view rejects the mechanistic model of the universe prevalent in earlier scientific thought. Instead, Whitehead emphasized the interdependence of all entities and processes, arguing that no event exists in isolation. This interconnectedness extends to human experience and consciousness, where individuals are part of the broader process of reality. Whitehead's holistic approach resonated with thinkers seeking alternatives to reductionist perspectives.

Whitehead's philosophy also challenged traditional views on time and space. He argued that time is not a linear, absolute framework within which events occur, but rather a feature of the relationships between events themselves. This perspective aligns with developments in modern physics, particularly Einstein's theory of relativity, which also views time and space as relational rather than absolute. Whitehead's ideas influenced later thinkers in fields ranging from theology to ecology, making him a pivotal figure in 20th-century philosophy.

Despite his complex and sometimes difficult-to-interpret ideas, Whitehead's influence extended across disciplines. His process philosophy laid the groundwork for process theology, environmental philosophy, and even influenced contemporary physics. By integrating scientific developments with metaphysical inquiry, Whitehead created a philosophical framework that continues to inspire debate and exploration in various fields of thought.

George Santayana (1863 – 1952 CE)

George Santayana was a Spanish-American philosopher, poet, and cultural critic, best known for his contributions to naturalism, aesthetics, and the philosophy of religion. Born in Madrid, Spain, Santayana moved to the United States as a child and later studied at Harvard University, where he earned his Ph.D. and became a prominent figure in American philosophy. Although Santayana was closely associated with the American pragmatists, such as William James and John Dewey, his work often diverged from theirs in important ways. His philosophy arose during a time of intellectual tension between scientific naturalism and religious belief, seeking to bridge these realms through a focus on human experience.

Santayana's naturalism was central to his philosophy, particularly his understanding of the human condition. He rejected supernatural explanations of existence and argued that human beings are fundamentally part of the natural world, governed by the same physical laws as everything else. In works like The Life of Reason (1905–1906), Santayana emphasized that reason and imagination are products of natural evolution and that human culture, art, and ethics arise from our biological and social needs. While he saw reason as a tool for navigating the world, he believed much of human experience—including art and religion—could not be fully captured by rational thought.

A significant aspect of Santayana's philosophy was his distinction between "essence" and "existence." He argued that essence refers to the abstract, timeless qualities of things, while existence is the contingent, concrete reality we experience. Santayana believed that humans have a unique capacity to recognize essences, which allows us to create art, philosophy, and religion as ways of contemplating these ideal forms. However, he cautioned against confusing essence with reality, emphasizing that human life is ultimately finite and material. This tension between idealism and materialism informed his critiques of both religious dogmatism and scientific reductionism.

Santayana's views on religion were nuanced. Although he was an atheist and critical of organized religion, he admired the symbolic and cultural value of religious practices. In The Sense of Beauty (1896) and Interpretations of Poetry and Religion (1900), he argued that religion, like art, expresses humanity's deepest emotions and desires, even if it does not correspond to literal truth. For Santayana, religion was a product of the human imagination, offering a way to grapple with existential questions and the mysteries of life. His famous saying, "Those who cannot remember the past are condemned to repeat it," reflects his belief in the importance of historical awareness.

Santayana's influence on American and European thought was considerable, particularly in the areas of aesthetics, cultural criticism, and the philosophy of history. His skepticism of both scientific positivism and religious orthodoxy made him a distinctive voice in early 20th-century philosophy. Although he spent much of his later life in Europe, where he wrote extensively on political and cultural issues, his contributions to naturalism, the philosophy of art, and the critique of modernity remain vital elements of his legacy.

Max Weber (1864 – 1920 CE)

Max Weber was a German sociologist, historian, and political economist, considered one of the founding figures of modern sociology. Born in Erfurt, Germany, Weber grew up in an intellectual household and studied law and economics at the University of Heidelberg. His work emerged during a period of rapid industrialization and social change in Germany, where debates about capitalism, religion, and political authority were central. Influenced by Karl Marx and Émile Durkheim, Weber developed his own distinct approach to understanding society, particularly through the study of religion, authority, and rationalization.

Weber's most famous work, The Protestant Ethic and the Spirit of Capitalism (1905), explored the relationship between religion and economic behavior. He argued that the asceticism and work ethic promoted by Protestantism, particularly Calvinism, played a significant role in the development of modern capitalism. The belief in predestination and the search for signs of salvation led Calvinists to emphasize hard work, discipline, and frugality, fostering a "spirit of capitalism" that encouraged wealth accumulation and investment. Unlike Marx, who saw economic forces as the primary drivers of social change, Weber believed cultural and religious factors could also shape economic systems.

A central theme in Weber's sociology was his theory of rationalization, the process by which traditional ways of thinking and acting are replaced by more calculated, efficient, and impersonal forms of organization. In his work Economy and Society (1922), Weber examined how modern societies increasingly rely on bureaucratic institutions, characterized by hierarchies, rules, and specialization. While bureaucracies brought efficiency, Weber warned of the "iron cage" of rationalization, where individuals become trapped in rigid systems that limit freedom and creativity, seeing this as a defining feature of modernity.

Weber also made significant contributions to political sociology through his analysis of authority and legitimacy. He identified three sources of authority: traditional, charismatic, and legal-rational. Traditional authority is rooted in long-standing customs, charismatic authority arises from leaders who inspire loyalty, and legal-rational authority is based on formal rules and laws. Weber argued that modern societies increasingly rely on legal-rational authority through bureaucratic systems, while charismatic leaders emerge during crises to instigate change.

Weber's work profoundly impacted sociology and political science, influencing thinkers like Jürgen Habermas and Michel Foucault. His insights into the relationships between religion, economics, and politics continue to shape discussions on modernity, authority, and social organization. Though Weber's vision of the "iron cage" was pessimistic, his foundational contributions remain essential for understanding how societies function and evolve.

Mahatma Gandhi (1869 – 1948 CE)

Mahatma Gandhi, born Mohandas Karamchand Gandhi, was an Indian lawyer, anti-colonial nationalist, and political ethicist whose philosophy of nonviolent resistance (Satyagraha) played a pivotal role in India's struggle for independence from British rule. Gandhi was born in Porbandar, Gujarat, and educated in law at University College London. After practicing law in South Africa, where he experienced racial discrimination, Gandhi became deeply involved in political activism, advocating for the rights of the Indian community. His experiences in South Africa, along with his study of religious texts such as the Bhagavad Gita, Christian teachings, and the works of Leo Tolstoy, shaped his unique approach to ethics and politics.

Gandhi's philosophy of Satyagraha, or "truth-force," was central to his approach to political struggle. He believed that nonviolent resistance, grounded in the pursuit of truth and moral principles, was the most effective way to combat injustice. For Gandhi, Satyagraha was not merely a political tactic but a way of life that required self-discipline, courage, and a commitment to nonviolence in thought, word, and deed. His campaigns of civil disobedience, including the Salt March of 1930, demonstrated how peaceful protest could undermine oppressive regimes and inspire mass movements for social change. Gandhi's belief in the power of nonviolence influenced later leaders like Martin Luther King Jr. and Nelson Mandela.

Gandhi's concept of Ahimsa (nonviolence) was deeply rooted in Hindu, Jain, and Buddhist traditions, but he expanded its application to the political realm. For Gandhi, nonviolence was not just the absence of physical violence but also the rejection of all forms of harm, including psychological and structural violence. He argued that individuals and nations should resolve conflicts through dialogue, empathy, and moral persuasion rather than through force. His commitment to nonviolence extended to his vision of a just society, which he called "Sarvodaya"—the welfare of all. This vision emphasized self-reliance, decentralization, and community-based economies, which Gandhi believed would promote equality and harmony.

A significant aspect of Gandhi's philosophy was his critique of modern industrial civilization, which he saw as materialistic, dehumanizing, and environmentally destructive. In his book Hind Swaraj (1909), Gandhi called for a return to a simpler, more self-sufficient way of life, where individuals would live in harmony with nature and each other. He advocated for the revival of village industries and crafts, such as hand-spinning, as a means of promoting economic independence and resisting the exploitative forces of colonialism. Gandhi's emphasis on sustainability, simplicity, and localism has continued to resonate in contemporary debates about environmentalism and development.

Gandhi's influence extended far beyond India, shaping global movements for civil rights and social justice. His life and philosophy continue to inspire those who seek nonviolent solutions to oppression and inequality. Though Gandhi's ideas have been critiqued for their idealism and lack of practical applicability in all contexts, his emphasis on ethics, nonviolence, and the dignity of the individual remains a powerful legacy in the history of political thought.

D.T. Suzuki (1870 – 1966 CE)

D.T. Suzuki, born in Kanazawa, Japan, was a highly influential scholar and philosopher who played a critical role in introducing Zen Buddhism to the Western world. He studied under the Zen master Shaku Soen and was deeply influenced by the Rinzai school of Zen. Suzuki's work came at a time when Japan was opening up to Western influences, and he saw an opportunity to share Zen philosophy with Western audiences. His translations, writings, and lectures on Zen Buddhism brought Eastern philosophy into dialogue with Western thought, creating a bridge between the two traditions. Suzuki's efforts reflected his belief that the spiritual insights of Zen could address the deeper existential questions of a rapidly modernizing and globalizing world.

Suzuki's interpretation of Zen was heavily shaped by his background in Rinzai Zen, which emphasizes direct experience and sudden enlightenment (kensho) through meditation and koan practice. He viewed Zen as a way to access the intuitive and non-rational aspects of the mind, bypassing the analytical tendencies of Western philosophy. In his many books, including Essays in Zen Buddhism and Zen and Japanese Culture, Suzuki argued that Zen was not merely a religious practice but a way of life, a means to realize one's true nature in everyday activities.

A significant element of Suzuki's philosophy was his interpretation of the concept of "satori," or enlightenment. He emphasized that satori was not an intellectual understanding but a direct, experiential insight into the nature of reality. According to Suzuki, this experience transcended dualistic distinctions between subject and object, allowing the practitioner to see the world in a new, holistic way. He saw this as the essence of Zen, which could not be captured in words but only experienced through practice. His explanations of satori sought to demystify the concept for Western audiences while preserving its profound spiritual significance.

Suzuki also explored the relationship between Zen and Western philosophy, particularly in his dialogue with figures like Carl Jung and Martin Heidegger. He believed that Zen could offer a remedy to the existential crises of modern Western thought by providing an alternative to the Cartesian dualism that separates mind and body. Suzuki's ideas resonated with existentialist philosophers and psychologists, who were grappling with questions of meaning, authenticity, and self-realization in an increasingly fragmented world. His ability to articulate Zen concepts in ways that aligned with contemporary Western intellectual concerns was key to his influence.

D.T. Suzuki's impact on the global understanding of Zen cannot be overstated. His writings and teachings helped shape the modern Western perception of Zen as a philosophy of direct experience and spiritual liberation. Through his work, Suzuki helped to popularize Zen Buddhism beyond Japan, making it accessible to a broad audience of spiritual seekers, intellectuals, and philosophers around the world. His legacy continues to inspire those seeking deeper connections between Eastern and Western traditions.

Nishida Kitaro (1870 – 1945 CE)

Nishida Kitaro was a Japanese philosopher and the founder of the Kyoto School of philosophy, which sought to blend Eastern and Western thought. Born in Ishikawa Prefecture, Nishida studied at Tokyo Imperial University, where he was deeply influenced by Western philosophy, particularly the works of Immanuel Kant, Georg Wilhelm Friedrich Hegel, and William James. His philosophical project was also shaped by traditional Japanese and Buddhist thought, especially Zen Buddhism. Nishida's philosophy arose during a time when Japan was undergoing rapid modernization, as intellectuals grappled with reconciling their cultural heritage with Western scientific and philosophical ideas.

Nishida's primary philosophical contribution was his development of a concept he called "pure experience," first introduced in his seminal work An Inquiry into the Good (1911). Pure experience refers to a state of consciousness where there is no distinction between subject and object, thought and action. For Nishida, this immediate, pre-reflective experience is the foundation of all knowledge and existence. He argued that our ordinary experience, in which we separate ourselves from the world and categorize our perceptions, distorts the true unity of reality. This idea of non-dualistic experience is heavily influenced by Zen Buddhism, which emphasizes direct, unmediated awareness.

Building on his idea of pure experience, Nishida developed a broader philosophical system known as "Basho," or the logic of place. In contrast to Western metaphysics, which focuses on being and substance, Nishida's Basho theory emphasized relationality and context. He argued that all things exist in a dynamic network of relationships, where each thing's meaning and identity are shaped by its place within this whole. This "place" is not a physical location but a metaphysical ground that allows for the emergence of phenomena. Nishida's concept of Basho critiques the dualisms of Western thought, such as subject-object and self-other distinctions.

Nishida sought to reconcile his Buddhist-influenced metaphysics with Western logic and ethics. He developed a unique form of dialectical thinking that borrowed from Hegel's dialectic but adapted it to his non-dualistic framework. In works such as The Self-Identity of Absolute Contradiction (1939), Nishida argued that the self and the world are not separate entities but expressions of a deeper, contradictory unity. This unity is not static but unfolds through self-negation and realization. By combining Buddhist emptiness with the dynamic processes of Western dialectics, Nishida addressed the spiritual and intellectual challenges of his time.

Nishida's influence on Japanese philosophy and culture was profound, laying the foundation for the Kyoto School, which included thinkers like Tanabe Hajime and Nishitani Keiji. His efforts to integrate Eastern and Western thought continue to be studied by philosophers engaged in cross-cultural dialogue and comparative philosophy. Nishida's focus on the experiential and relational nature of reality remains relevant in contemporary discussions about consciousness, identity, and the philosophy of mind.

Bertrand Russell (1872 – 1970 CE)

Bertrand Russell was a British philosopher, logician, and social critic, widely regarded as one of the founders of analytic philosophy. Born into an aristocratic family in Wales, Russell was educated at Trinity College, Cambridge, where he studied mathematics and philosophy. His intellectual career spanned much of the 20th century, a period marked by significant social, political, and scientific changes. Russell's early work focused on logic and mathematics, making him a central figure in symbolic logic and the philosophy of language, while his later writings expanded into broader areas such as social and political theory, nuclear disarmament, and education reform.

One of Russell's most important contributions to philosophy was his development of logicism, the view that mathematics can be reduced to logical principles. In collaboration with Alfred North Whitehead, Russell co-authored Principia Mathematica (1910–1913), a groundbreaking work in mathematical logic that aimed to derive all mathematical truths from a small set of logical axioms. Although later developments in logic, such as Gödel's incompleteness theorems, challenged the feasibility of Russell's project, Principia Mathematica remains a landmark in the history of logic and an influential attempt to clarify the foundations of knowledge.

In addition to his work in logic, Russell made significant contributions to the philosophy of language, particularly with his theory of descriptions. In his influential paper "On Denoting" (1905), Russell introduced the distinction between "definite descriptions" and "indefinite descriptions." He argued that philosophical puzzles could often be resolved by analyzing language more precisely, breaking down complex propositions into their logical components. This approach became a cornerstone of analytic philosophy, influencing later figures such as Ludwig Wittgenstein and the logical positivists.

Russell also addressed questions about knowledge and the limits of certainty. In The Problems of Philosophy (1912), he defended a form of empiricism, arguing that knowledge is grounded in sensory experience while also encompassing abstract concepts like numbers and logical truths. He developed the distinction between "knowledge by acquaintance" (direct, immediate knowledge) and "knowledge by description" (indirect knowledge through descriptions), a framework that became central to later debates in epistemology.

In addition to his philosophical work, Russell was an advocate for social and political causes, including pacifism, civil liberties, and education reform. His activism, particularly his opposition to World War I and criticism of nuclear weapons, made him a prominent public intellectual. Russell's commitment to reason, scientific inquiry, and social justice continues to influence contemporary discussions in logic, philosophy of language, and political theory.

G. E. Moore (1873 – 1958 CE)

G. E. Moore was an English philosopher and a central figure in the development of analytic philosophy, known for his defense of common sense and his contributions to ethics. Born in London, Moore studied at Trinity College, Cambridge, where he became a lifelong friend and intellectual collaborator of Bertrand Russell. Moore's work emerged during a period when British philosophy was transitioning from the dominance of idealism, associated with figures like F. H. Bradley, to a new focus on language, logic, and ordinary experience. Moore played a crucial role in this shift, rejecting the abstract metaphysical systems of idealism in favor of a more grounded approach to philosophy.

Moore's most famous contribution to philosophy is his defense of common sense, which he outlined in works like A Defence of Common Sense (1925) and Proof of an External World (1939). He argued that certain basic beliefs—such as the existence of physical objects, the reality of other minds, and the passage of time—are self-evident and need no further philosophical justification. Moore believed that any philosophical system that denied these common-sense beliefs was inherently flawed, as it contradicted the most fundamental aspects of our experience. His defense of common sense was a reaction against both skepticism and idealism, which he saw as undermining our ordinary understanding of the world.

In ethics, Moore is best known for his development of the "open question argument" and his critique of ethical naturalism. In his seminal work Principia Ethica (1903), Moore argued that attempts to define "good" in terms of natural properties, such as pleasure or desire, are misguided. He introduced the concept of the "naturalistic fallacy," which occurs when one equates a moral property with a natural property. According to Moore, "good" is a simple, indefinable quality that cannot be reduced to any other term or concept. This view became a cornerstone of what is now known as non-naturalistic moral realism, which holds that moral truths exist independently of natural facts.

Moore also formulated the "open question argument," which challenges the idea that moral terms can be defined in naturalistic terms. He argued that for any proposed definition of "good," it is always an open question whether the definition is accurate, suggesting that moral properties cannot be reduced to natural properties. This argument had a profound impact on 20th-century ethics, shaping debates about moral realism, emotivism, and the nature of ethical language. Although Moore's views were later challenged by philosophers such as A. J. Ayer and R. M. Hare, his work in ethics remains influential.

Moore's philosophy had a significant influence on later analytic philosophers, particularly in his emphasis on clarity, precision, and logical analysis. His rejection of metaphysical speculation and his focus on ordinary experience helped shape the trajectory of analytic philosophy in the 20th century. Moore's commitment to common sense and his rigorous approach to ethical theory continue to be studied and debated by contemporary philosophers, and his work remains a foundational part of the analytic tradition.

Ernst Cassirer (1874 – 1945 CE)

Ernst Cassirer was a German philosopher and historian of ideas, best known for his work in the philosophy of symbolic forms and his contributions to the neo-Kantian tradition. Born in Breslau (now Wrocław, Poland), Cassirer studied under the neo-Kantian philosopher Hermann Cohen at the University of Marburg, where he became associated with the Marburg School of neo-Kantianism. His work emerged during a time when early 20th-century intellectual movements grappled with the implications of modern science, art, and culture for philosophical thought. Cassirer's philosophy focused on understanding how human beings create meaning through symbols, language, and culture.

Cassirer's major philosophical project was the development of a theory of symbolic forms, which he outlined in his three-volume work The Philosophy of Symbolic Forms (1923–1929). He argued that human beings do not experience reality directly but through symbolic systems, such as language, myth, art, and science, which mediate our understanding of the world. Each symbolic form represents a different way of organizing and interpreting experience, and together they form the foundation of human culture. Cassirer's philosophy expanded the traditional neo-Kantian focus on scientific knowledge to include the full range of human cultural expression.

Cassirer's philosophy of symbolic forms was influenced by Kant's theory of knowledge and perception, but he extended these ideas to emphasize the active role of culture in shaping human understanding. For Cassirer, the mind constructs reality through symbolic forms, rather than passively receiving sensory information. This allowed him to explore how different cultures and historical periods interpret the world, from mythological thinking to modern scientific rationality. His work bridged the neo-Kantian tradition with a broader study of cultural and historical diversity.

In addition to symbolic forms, Cassirer contributed to the philosophy of science and the history of ideas. In The Problem of Knowledge (1906), he examined the evolution of scientific concepts from the Renaissance to the 19th century, demonstrating how scientific knowledge develops through changes in symbolic frameworks. He also analyzed the Enlightenment's cultural and philosophical transformation in The Philosophy of the Enlightenment (1932), emphasizing its role in reshaping European thought and society.

Cassirer fled Nazi Germany in 1933, continuing to write and teach in exile, notably producing works such as An Essay on Man (1944), where he further developed his ideas on human culture. His influence on 20th-century thought was profound, particularly in philosophy, anthropology, and cultural studies. Cassirer's insights into the role of symbols in human life remain relevant to contemporary discussions on language, meaning, and cultural identity.

Max Scheler (1874 – 1928 CE)

Max Scheler was a German philosopher who made significant contributions to phenomenology, ethics, and philosophical anthropology. Born in Munich, Scheler studied at the universities of Berlin and Jena, where he was influenced by both neo-Kantianism and the phenomenological method developed by Edmund Husserl. Scheler's intellectual context was shaped by early 20th-century debates about value, emotion, and the human condition. Although he initially worked closely with Husserl, Scheler eventually diverged from Husserl's approach, focusing more on values, emotions, and the human spirit. His philosophical work addressed topics such as love, morality, and the human person, making him a key figure in early 20th-century European philosophy.

One of Scheler's most important contributions was his phenomenological theory of values. In works like Formalism in Ethics and Non-Formal Ethics of Values (1913–1916), Scheler argued that values are objective qualities directly perceived through emotional experience. He believed that values exist independently of human preferences or cultural norms and are ranked hierarchically, from lower values like pleasure and utility to higher ones like justice and holiness. Unlike traditional ethical systems that emphasize reason or duty, Scheler highlighted emotional intuition as essential for perceiving and responding to values.

Scheler's theory of love is another key aspect of his philosophy. He viewed love as a fundamental act that reveals higher values and fosters connection to the divine. For Scheler, love is not merely an emotional attachment but an intentional act that opens individuals to the value of others and the world around them. He contrasted this with "ressentiment," a moral degradation where envy and resentment drive individuals to reject higher values and focus on negativity. This emphasis on love as a path to transcend selfishness and ressentiment was central to his moral philosophy and vision of human flourishing.

In addition to ethics, Scheler contributed to philosophical anthropology by examining what it means to be human. In The Human Place in the Cosmos (1928), he argued that humans transcend their biological nature through spirit and culture. He saw human beings as uniquely capable of love, creativity, and self-transcendence, rejecting materialist accounts of human nature prevalent in the early 20th century. This view underscored the spiritual and cultural dimensions of human existence.

Scheler's influence extended beyond his lifetime, shaping existentialism, phenomenology, and Catholic philosophy. His ideas about values, emotions, and the human spirit resonated with thinkers like Martin Heidegger and Jean-Paul Sartre. Despite his relatively short life, Scheler's work remains relevant in contemporary discussions of ethics and the complexities of human existence.

Ramana Maharshi (1879 – 1950 CE)

Ramana Maharshi, born Venkataraman Iyer in Tamil Nadu, India, was a spiritual teacher and mystic who became one of the most revered figures in modern Indian spirituality. Raised in a traditional Hindu family, Maharshi experienced a profound spiritual awakening at the age of 16, when he had a near-death experience that led him to realize the true nature of the self as beyond the body and mind. Following this experience, he left his family and moved to the holy mountain of Arunachala, where he lived as a renunciant, practicing intense meditation and self-inquiry. His teachings arose in the context of Advaita Vedanta, a non-dualistic school of Hindu philosophy that emphasizes the oneness of the individual self (Atman) with the ultimate reality (Brahman).

Central to Ramana Maharshi's teachings was the practice of Atma Vichara, or self-inquiry. He taught that the true nature of the self is pure awareness and that the mind's identification with the body and ego creates the illusion of separation from the divine. To dissolve this illusion, Maharshi encouraged his followers to constantly ask the question, "Who am I?" This inquiry was not intended to yield intellectual answers but to lead practitioners into a direct, experiential understanding of their true nature, which transcends the limitations of thought and individuality. Maharshi believed that through this practice, individuals could attain liberation (moksha) and realize their unity with Brahman.

Maharshi's philosophy was deeply rooted in Advaita Vedanta, but his approach was uniquely simple and accessible. Unlike many traditional teachers, Maharshi did not emphasize complex rituals, scriptures, or intellectual study. Instead, he focused on the direct experience of self-realization through inner silence and contemplation. He believed that the mind's incessant activity was the main obstacle to spiritual awakening, and his teachings encouraged a stilling of the mind to allow the deeper awareness of the self to emerge. His emphasis on direct experience over theoretical knowledge made his teachings accessible to people from various backgrounds, both in India and abroad.

Ramana Maharshi's influence extended far beyond the Indian subcontinent. His teachings attracted a wide range of seekers, including Western philosophers, scholars, and spiritual practitioners, who came to Arunachala to learn from him. Maharshi's emphasis on self-inquiry resonated with individuals seeking a path to self-realization that bypassed the need for external authority or religious dogma. His teachings have had a lasting impact on global spirituality, influencing movements such as Neo-Advaita and contemporary non-dualism, as well as inspiring countless individuals in their spiritual journeys.

Although Maharshi himself lived a simple and ascetic life, his legacy continues to thrive through the many ashrams, books, and spiritual communities that follow his teachings. His message of inner stillness, self-inquiry, and the realization of oneness remains a powerful and accessible path for those seeking to understand the nature of the self and to attain spiritual liberation.

Pierre Teilhard de Chardin (1881 – 1955 CE)

Pierre Teilhard de Chardin was a French Jesuit priest, paleontologist, and philosopher, whose work sought to reconcile Christian theology with the discoveries of modern science, particularly evolution. Born in the Auvergne region of France, Teilhard de Chardin joined the Jesuit order and pursued a career in both theology and science, earning a doctorate in paleontology. His intellectual development took place during a period of intense scientific advancement, particularly in the fields of geology and evolutionary biology, which were challenging traditional religious views of creation. Teilhard's work was an effort to harmonize these new scientific insights with his Christian faith, leading him to develop a unique vision of the universe's spiritual and evolutionary progress.

Teilhard's most famous concept was the "Omega Point," a term he used to describe the ultimate goal of evolution. He believed that evolution was not a random process but one guided by a divine force that aimed to bring all creation into union with God. For Teilhard, the universe was moving toward increasing complexity and consciousness, and human beings, with their capacity for self-awareness and reflection, represented the leading edge of this evolutionary process. The Omega Point, in Teilhard's vision, was the culmination of this evolution, where all consciousness would merge into a final, divine unity with God, completing the process of cosmic evolution.

Central to Teilhard's thought was the idea of noogenesis, the evolution of consciousness. He argued that evolution was not only a physical process but also a mental and spiritual one, where the development of higher forms of life was paralleled by the growth of consciousness and intelligence. Teilhard saw human beings as playing a crucial role in this process, as their capacity for thought, creativity, and love enabled them to participate consciously in the divine plan. He believed that the future of humanity lay in a collective spiritual awakening, where individuals would recognize their interconnectedness and work toward the common goal of realizing the Omega Point.

Teilhard's vision of evolution was also deeply ecological, as he saw all life as part of a single, interconnected whole. He believed that human beings had a moral and spiritual responsibility to care for the planet and to contribute to the evolutionary process by fostering cooperation, love, and unity. His ideas anticipated many of the concerns of modern environmentalism, as well as contemporary movements toward global unity and interfaith dialogue. Teilhard's work bridged the gap between science and spirituality, offering a vision of evolution that was not merely biological but deeply infused with spiritual meaning.

Although Teilhard's ideas were controversial during his lifetime, particularly within the Catholic Church, his work has since gained widespread recognition and appreciation. His writings, particularly The Phenomenon of Man (1955), continue to inspire discussions about the relationship between science, religion, and the future of humanity. Teilhard's synthesis of evolution and spirituality remains a profound contribution to 20th-century thought, influencing fields as diverse as theology, ecology, and philosophy.

Karl Jaspers (1883 – 1969 CE)

Karl Jaspers was a German-Swiss psychiatrist and philosopher, best known for his contributions to existentialism and his work on the philosophy of history and theology. Born in Oldenburg, Germany, Jaspers initially pursued a career in medicine, specializing in psychiatry, before turning to philosophy. His early work in psychiatry, particularly General Psychopathology (1913), laid the foundation for his later philosophical explorations of human existence. Jaspers' intellectual development took place during a time of significant political and social upheaval in Europe, including the aftermath of World War I and the rise of totalitarian regimes.

Jaspers is widely regarded as one of the founders of existential philosophy, although he preferred the term "philosophy of existence." In works such as Philosophy (1932) and Reason and Existenz (1935), Jaspers argued that human beings are defined by their capacity for transcendence and their ability to confront the limits of reason and knowledge. For Jaspers, authentic human existence arises from encounters with "boundary situations"—moments of crisis, death, guilt, or conflict that force individuals to confront their limitations. These situations reveal the finitude of human existence and open the possibility for transcending the mundane world through acts of faith or philosophical reflection.

A key element of Jaspers' philosophy is his distinction between "Existenz" and "Dasein." While Dasein refers to the ordinary, everyday existence of individuals, Existenz represents a higher, more authentic mode of being in which individuals become aware of their freedom and transcendence. Jaspers believed philosophy could guide individuals toward this deeper understanding, enabling them to confront life's uncertainties with courage. Philosophy, in his view, could not provide definitive answers but could help individuals navigate the complexities of existence through dialogue and reflection.

Jaspers also made significant contributions to the philosophy of history, particularly through his concept of the "Axial Age." In The Origin and Goal of History (1949), Jaspers argued that between 800 and 200 BCE, spiritual and philosophical movements across different cultures—Confucianism and Daoism in China, Buddhism in India, and Greek philosophy in the West—emerged simultaneously. He believed this period marked a turning point in human history, representing the emergence of critical thought and the beginnings of a universal human consciousness.

Jaspers' work on existentialism, transcendence, and the philosophy of history profoundly influenced thinkers like Jean-Paul Sartre and Hannah Arendt. His emphasis on the limitations of human knowledge and the importance of individual freedom resonated with those grappling with 20th-century crises, including authoritarianism and the Holocaust. Despite his opposition to totalitarianism, Jaspers maintained a belief in the possibility of human freedom and transcendence, making his work an enduring contribution to existential philosophy and political thought.

Georg Lukács (1885 – 1971 CE)

Georg Lukács was a Hungarian Marxist philosopher, literary critic, and political theorist, widely regarded as one of the most influential Marxist thinkers of the 20th century. Born in Budapest to a wealthy Jewish family, Lukács initially studied literature and philosophy at the universities of Berlin and Heidelberg. His early intellectual development was influenced by German idealism, particularly the works of Hegel, as well as by the existentialism of Søren Kierkegaard. After witnessing the social and political upheavals of World War I and the Russian Revolution, Lukács embraced Marxism and became an active participant in revolutionary politics, engaging deeply with Hegelian dialectics and Marxist theory.

Lukács' most famous work, History and Class Consciousness (1923), represents a landmark contribution to Marxist philosophy. In this collection of essays, Lukács developed a theory of "class consciousness," arguing that the proletariat possesses a unique capacity to grasp the totality of social relations under capitalism. He claimed that the proletariat's awareness of its exploitation allows it to see through the "reification" of capitalist society, where social relations are treated as commodities and people are reduced to objects. Lukács' focus on consciousness and ideology marked a significant departure from deterministic interpretations of Marxism, emphasizing the active role of human agency in historical change.

Lukács also made significant contributions to literary theory and aesthetics, particularly through his concept of "realism." In works such as The Historical Novel (1937), Lukács argued that realist literature, particularly the works of authors like Balzac and Tolstoy, provides a more accurate reflection of social reality than modernist or avant-garde literature. He believed that realism, by portraying the contradictions of society and the development of characters within historical processes, could reveal the underlying structures of capitalism and help readers develop a critical consciousness. This contrasted sharply with modernist aesthetics, which Lukács saw as alienating and disconnected from material conditions.

Lukács' concept of "reification," borrowed from Marx's theory of commodity fetishism, was central to his critique of capitalism. He argued that in capitalist societies, social relations are increasingly mediated by commodities, leading to the objectification and alienation of human beings. Reification, for Lukács, was not just an economic phenomenon but also a cultural and psychological one, affecting how people think and interact with each other. Overcoming reification, he believed, required a revolutionary transformation of society in which human beings could regain control over their social and economic lives.

Despite his early revolutionary fervor, Lukács' later years were marked by a more cautious approach to Marxism, particularly in light of the failures of Stalinism and the repressive policies of Eastern European communist regimes. His commitment to Marxist theory remained steadfast, but he sought to reconcile Marxist analysis with humanism and democratic values. Lukács' work on class consciousness, reification, and realism continues to influence contemporary debates in critical theory, literary studies, and political philosophy.

Paul Tillich (1886 – 1965 CE)

Paul Tillich was a German-American theologian and philosopher, known for his contributions to existential theology and his attempts to reconcile Christianity with modern existentialist thought. Born in Starzeddel, Germany, Tillich studied theology and philosophy at the universities of Berlin, Tübingen, and Halle. He was profoundly shaped by the intellectual climate of early 20th-century Europe, particularly the existentialist philosophy of thinkers like Martin Heidegger and the challenges posed to traditional religion by modern science and secularism. After being dismissed from his academic position in Germany due to his opposition to the Nazi regime, Tillich emigrated to the United States, where he became a prominent professor at Union Theological Seminary and Harvard University.

Tillich's theology is best known for its concept of "the courage to be," which he developed in The Courage to Be (1952). In this work, Tillich explored the existential anxiety that arises from the human confrontation with non-being, or the possibility of meaninglessness and death. He argued that modern individuals, living in an age of scientific rationalism and secularism, face a deep sense of existential dread, as traditional religious frameworks no longer provide answers to questions of meaning and purpose. However, Tillich believed that this anxiety could be overcome through the "courage to be," which involves accepting the limits of human existence and finding ultimate meaning in one's relationship with the divine.

A central aspect of Tillich's theology was his reinterpretation of Christian doctrine in existential terms. He rejected the idea of God as a supernatural being or an object of belief, instead describing God as the "Ground of Being"—the ultimate reality that underlies all existence. For Tillich, God was not a personal entity but the source of all meaning and value in the universe. This approach allowed Tillich to present Christianity in a way that was compatible with modern existentialism, emphasizing faith as an act of personal trust and commitment rather than intellectual assent to specific doctrines.

Tillich also made significant contributions to the philosophy of culture, particularly through his analysis of the relationship between religion and art. He believed that art, like religion, provides a way for individuals to express their ultimate concerns and to confront the deepest questions of existence. In works like Art and Ultimate Reality (1954), Tillich argued that modern art, despite its apparent fragmentation and abstraction, could serve as a vehicle for spiritual exploration and the discovery of meaning in a secular world.

Tillich's theology and philosophy had a profound influence on both religious thought and existential philosophy in the 20th century. His reinterpretation of God, his existential dimensions of faith, and his analysis of the relationship between culture and religion continue to inspire debates about the role of religion in a secular world and the search for meaning in the face of existential anxiety.

Ludwig Wittgenstein (1889 – 1951 CE)

Ludwig Wittgenstein was an Austrian-British philosopher who made groundbreaking contributions to the philosophy of language, logic, and the philosophy of mind. Born in Vienna to a wealthy family, Wittgenstein was initially trained as an engineer before turning to philosophy under the influence of Bertrand Russell at the University of Cambridge. His intellectual career unfolded during a time of significant developments in logic and analytic philosophy, and his work responded to the ideas of philosophers such as Gottlob Frege and Russell. Wittgenstein's two major works, Tractatus Logico-Philosophicus (1921) and Philosophical Investigations (1953), represent two distinct phases of his thought, often referred to as the "early" and "late" Wittgenstein.

Wittgenstein's early philosophy, as expressed in Tractatus Logico-Philosophicus, focused on the relationship between language and reality. He argued that the structure of language mirrors the structure of the world, with words functioning as "pictures" that correspond to states of affairs in the world. Wittgenstein famously claimed that "the limits of my language mean the limits of my world," suggesting that what can be meaningfully spoken about must correspond to what can be clearly pictured or represented. Anything beyond this, such as ethics or metaphysics, could only be shown but not spoken, marking a boundary to what language could express.

However, Wittgenstein later rejected many of the ideas he had presented in the Tractatus. In Philosophical Investigations, published posthumously, he introduced the concept of "language games" to describe the diverse ways in which language is used in different social contexts. For Wittgenstein, meaning is not determined by a correspondence between language and reality but by the way words are used in specific activities or forms of life. He argued that the meaning of a word is its use in language, emphasizing the pragmatic and context-dependent nature of language. This shift marked a move toward understanding language as a dynamic practice rather than a fixed system of representation.

Wittgenstein's later philosophy also explored the idea of "family resemblance" to describe how concepts function. Instead of rigid definitions, he argued that many concepts share overlapping features without having a single essence. This insight challenged traditional philosophical approaches that sought to define concepts through necessary and sufficient conditions. His rejection of essentialism and focus on ordinary language profoundly influenced later philosophers, particularly in the fields of philosophy of language, epistemology, and ethics.

Wittgenstein's influence on 20th-century philosophy was immense, particularly in the analytic tradition. His work inspired figures such as J.L. Austin and Gilbert Ryle, who emphasized looking at how language functions in everyday contexts. Wittgenstein's two major works remain foundational texts, with his later philosophy being regarded as a landmark contribution to understanding language, meaning, and philosophical problems.

Gabriel Marcel (1889 – 1973 CE)

Gabriel Marcel was a French existentialist philosopher, dramatist, and music critic, best known for his Christian existentialism and his focus on the themes of existence, faith, and human relationships. Born in Paris, Marcel was raised in a secular intellectual environment, but he later converted to Catholicism, which profoundly shaped his philosophical outlook. His philosophical development occurred in the context of early 20th-century European existentialism, particularly in response to the works of Jean-Paul Sartre and Martin Heidegger. Marcel's existentialism, however, was distinct in its emphasis on religious faith and the positive aspects of human experience, as opposed to the more atheistic existentialism of Sartre.

Central to Marcel's philosophy was the distinction between "being" and "having," a theme he explored in works such as Being and Having (1949). Marcel argued that modern life is characterized by a focus on possession and control, where individuals relate to the world and others through the lens of "having." This attitude reduces relationships and experiences to objects that can be owned or manipulated, leading to alienation and a loss of genuine connection. In contrast, Marcel advocated for an orientation of "being," where individuals engage with others in a more open, participatory, and loving manner. For Marcel, the focus on "being" leads to a deeper sense of fulfillment and an authentic engagement with life.

Marcel's existentialism was also characterized by his focus on the themes of presence, availability, and participation. He believed that true human relationships are grounded in the willingness to be present for others, to make oneself "available" in a way that transcends mere transactional interactions. This notion of availability is central to his concept of love, which he saw as a form of self-giving that creates a bond between individuals that is more profound than any contractual relationship. Marcel contrasted this form of love with the objectifying relationships he associated with modern technological society, where individuals are treated as means to an end rather than as unique beings with intrinsic value.

Faith played a crucial role in Marcel's philosophy, particularly in his understanding of hope and transcendence. Marcel viewed human existence as fundamentally characterized by a longing for transcendence and a recognition of the limits of human understanding. He argued that genuine faith is not a matter of intellectual certainty but of trust and openness to the mystery of being. Hope, for Marcel, is an existential act that affirms the possibility of meaning and redemption in the face of suffering and uncertainty. His Christian existentialism thus emphasized the importance of faith, love, and hope as essential elements of the human condition.

Gabriel Marcel's work had a significant impact on existentialist thought, particularly within the context of Christian existentialism. His focus on interpersonal relationships, love, and faith distinguished his philosophy from the more secular and pessimistic existentialism of Sartre and Heidegger. Marcel's ideas continue to resonate in contemporary discussions about the nature of human existence, the role of faith, and the importance of authentic relationships in an increasingly alienating world.

Rudolf Carnap (1891 – 1970 CE)

Rudolf Carnap was a German philosopher and one of the central figures of the Vienna Circle, a group of philosophers and scientists who developed the school of logical positivism in the early 20th century. Born in Ronsdorf, Germany, Carnap studied physics and philosophy at the universities of Jena and Freiburg. His intellectual context was shaped by the rise of analytic philosophy, particularly the works of Ludwig Wittgenstein and Bertrand Russell, as well as the scientific advancements of the time. Carnap's work was deeply influenced by the goal of creating a scientific, rigorous foundation for philosophy, which led him to focus on logic, language, and the philosophy of science.

Carnap's most significant contributions were in the areas of logic and the philosophy of language. In his early work, The Logical Structure of the World (1928), Carnap sought to demonstrate how all knowledge could be reduced to a formal, logical system. He developed the concept of "logical construction," whereby complex concepts could be defined in terms of simpler, more basic elements, ultimately grounding them in empirical observations. This project was part of the broader logical positivist effort to eliminate metaphysics and speculative philosophy, which Carnap and his colleagues regarded as meaningless because it could not be empirically verified.

Central to Carnap's philosophy was the principle of verification, which held that a statement is meaningful only if it can be empirically verified or is analytically true (i.e., true by definition). This principle was a key tenet of logical positivism and aimed to distinguish between meaningful scientific statements and metaphysical or ethical claims, which Carnap argued were not subject to verification and thus lacked cognitive content. This emphasis on empirical verification and the rejection of metaphysics placed Carnap at the forefront of the analytic tradition, influencing the development of philosophy of science and the philosophy of language.

Carnap's work also addressed the distinction between "syntax" and "semantics" in the philosophy of language. In his book Logical Syntax of Language (1934), he argued that the meaning of a statement could be understood in terms of its formal structure, or syntax, rather than its content or semantics. Carnap believed that by focusing on the syntactical rules governing language, philosophers could avoid the ambiguities and confusions associated with metaphysical debates. However, later in his career, Carnap shifted his attention to the study of semantics, acknowledging the importance of meaning and interpretation in language, as seen in his work Meaning and Necessity (1947).

Carnap's influence on 20th-century philosophy was profound, particularly in the areas of logic, philosophy of language, and philosophy of science. His commitment to scientific rigor and his efforts to create a formal, logical foundation for philosophy helped shape the direction of analytic philosophy, particularly in the philosophy of science. Although his strict adherence to the principle of verification was later criticized and abandoned by many philosophers, Carnap's work remains a foundational part of the analytic tradition, particularly in its focus on language, logic, and the elimination of metaphysical speculation.

Antonio Gramsci (1891 – 1937 CE)

Antonio Gramsci was an Italian Marxist philosopher, journalist, and politician, best known for his work on cultural hegemony and the role of intellectuals in society. Born in Sardinia, Gramsci grew up in poverty and later moved to Turin, where he became involved in socialist politics and joined the Italian Communist Party. Gramsci's intellectual development took place during a period of intense political conflict in Italy, particularly the rise of fascism under Benito Mussolini. Imprisoned by the fascist regime in 1926, Gramsci wrote much of his most important work, the Prison Notebooks, while incarcerated. These notebooks would later become some of the most influential texts in Marxist theory.

Gramsci's concept of cultural hegemony is central to his philosophy. He argued that the ruling class maintains power not only through economic control but also through the manipulation of cultural institutions, such as education, media, and religion. By shaping the dominant ideology and values of society, the ruling class secures the consent of the subordinate classes, making direct coercion less necessary. For Gramsci, cultural hegemony operates through the creation of a shared worldview that reflects the interests of the ruling class while appearing natural and inevitable to all members of society. This insight expanded traditional Marxist analysis by emphasizing the importance of culture and ideology in maintaining class dominance.

Gramsci's work also focused on the role of intellectuals in shaping cultural and political life. He distinguished between "traditional intellectuals," who serve as agents of the ruling class by reinforcing dominant ideologies, and "organic intellectuals," who emerge from the working class and challenge the status quo. Gramsci believed that organic intellectuals play a crucial role in fostering class consciousness and organizing resistance to capitalist hegemony. He argued that intellectuals should not be isolated from the masses but should work within social movements to build a counter-hegemony that could challenge the existing order and create the conditions for revolutionary change.

In addition to his work on cultural hegemony and intellectuals, Gramsci developed a theory of the state that distinguished between "political society" and "civil society." Political society refers to the institutions of coercion, such as the military and the police, that maintain order through force. Civil society, on the other hand, includes the institutions of culture, education, and ideology that shape people's beliefs and values. Gramsci argued that for revolutionary change to occur, it was necessary not only to seize control of political society but also to transform civil society by creating new cultural and ideological frameworks that reflect the interests of the working class.

Gramsci's influence on Marxist theory has been profound, particularly in the fields of political science, sociology, and cultural studies. His emphasis on the role of culture, ideology, and intellectuals in maintaining and challenging power structures has resonated with later thinkers, including those in the Frankfurt School and post-colonial theory. Gramsci's work continues to be a vital resource for understanding the complexities of power, resistance, and social change in modern capitalist societies.

Mikhail Bakhtin (1895 – 1975 CE)

Mikhail Bakhtin was a Russian philosopher and literary critic, best known for his work on dialogism, the philosophy of language, and the theory of the novel. Born in Orel, Russia, Bakhtin was educated at the University of St. Petersburg, where he studied philology and philosophy. His intellectual development took place during a period of intense political and social upheaval in Russia, particularly following the Russian Revolution and the rise of the Soviet Union. Although Bakhtin's early work was largely neglected by the official Soviet academic establishment, he continued to develop his ideas on language, literature, and culture, gaining significant influence in the latter half of the 20th century.

One of Bakhtin's most important contributions was his theory of dialogism, which he articulated in works such as Problems of Dostoevsky's Poetics (1929) and The Dialogic Imagination (1975). Dialogism refers to the idea that all language and thought are inherently dialogic, meaning they exist in relation to other voices, perspectives, and contexts. For Bakhtin, meaning is created through the interaction of multiple voices, each contributing to the development of understanding. This emphasis on dialogue contrasts with traditional views of language as a tool for conveying static truths, highlighting instead the dynamic, relational nature of meaning-making.

Bakhtin's concept of "heteroglossia" is central to his analysis of the novel as a literary form. He argued that novels, particularly those of authors like Fyodor Dostoevsky, represent a multiplicity of voices, perspectives, and social languages, all interacting and competing within a single text. This diversity of voices creates a rich, polyphonic structure in which no single viewpoint dominates, allowing for a nuanced exploration of social and ideological conflicts. For Bakhtin, the novel's ability to incorporate heteroglossia made it a uniquely dialogic form of literature, reflecting the complexity of human experience.

Bakhtin also developed the concept of "carnivalesque" to describe a literary mode that subverts and challenges established social hierarchies and norms. Drawing on the tradition of medieval carnival, Bakhtin argued that carnivalesque literature, through its use of humor, parody, and grotesque imagery, creates a space for the suspension of official rules and the inversion of social roles. This form of literature, he believed, allows for a temporary liberation from rigid structures of authority, providing a means of resistance and renewal. His analysis of the carnivalesque has been influential in studies of literature and culture, particularly in relation to subversive movements.

Bakhtin's work on dialogism, heteroglossia, and the carnivalesque has profoundly impacted literary theory, cultural studies, and the philosophy of language. His ideas about the relational nature of meaning and the importance of multiple perspectives have influenced a wide range of disciplines, from linguistics to political theory. Despite the constraints of Soviet censorship, Bakhtin's intellectual legacy has grown significantly, and he is now recognized as one of the most important thinkers of the 20th century.

R. Buckminster Fuller (1895 – 1983 CE)

R. Buckminster Fuller was an American architect, inventor, and philosopher whose work focused on sustainability, design, and the potential for technology to address global issues. Born in Milton, Massachusetts, Fuller's early education was unremarkable, and he struggled to find a direction until he developed his philosophy of "doing more with less." Fuller's career unfolded during a time of rapid technological change and global conflict, and he sought to develop innovative designs that would contribute to human survival and well-being. His work combined engineering, architecture, and systems thinking with a deep concern for the environment and humanity's place within it.

Fuller's most famous creation is the geodesic dome, a lightweight, efficient structure that distributes stress evenly, making it one of the strongest and most efficient designs relative to its weight. The dome became a symbol of Fuller's larger philosophical project, which he called "comprehensive anticipatory design science." This approach emphasized the importance of creating systems and designs that addressed not only current problems but also future needs, using minimal resources for maximum impact. Fuller believed that through innovative design, humanity could overcome challenges such as resource depletion and environmental degradation.

A central theme in Fuller's philosophy was his concept of "Spaceship Earth," which he developed in his 1969 book Operating Manual for Spaceship Earth. Fuller viewed Earth as a finite, self-contained system, much like a spaceship, where all resources are limited and must be carefully managed. He argued that humans have a responsibility to act as "crew" members, working to preserve and optimize the planet's resources for the benefit of all. This metaphor captured Fuller's belief that global cooperation, sustainability, and technological innovation were essential to ensuring the survival of humanity in the face of mounting ecological and social challenges.

Fuller's work also explored the potential for individual creativity and ingenuity to drive positive social change. He coined the term "Dymaxion," combining "dynamic," "maximum," and "ion," to describe his vision of maximizing efficiency and sustainability in everything from transportation to housing. His Dymaxion designs, such as the Dymaxion car and Dymaxion house, embodied his philosophy of doing more with less, emphasizing lightweight materials, energy efficiency, and affordability. Although many of Fuller's designs were never mass-produced, his ideas about sustainability and efficiency influenced fields ranging from architecture to environmental science.

Fuller's impact extended beyond his inventions and designs to his broader vision of global transformation. He was a strong advocate for the use of technology and design to solve world problems, believing that humanity had the capacity to create a future of abundance and sustainability if it embraced a holistic, systems-based approach. His work inspired generations of architects, environmentalists, and thinkers who saw in his vision a blueprint for a more just, sustainable, and innovative future.

Herbert Marcuse (1898 – 1979 CE)

Herbert Marcuse was a German-American philosopher and social theorist associated with the Frankfurt School of critical theory. Born in Berlin, Marcuse studied under prominent German philosophers such as Martin Heidegger, but his political leanings eventually led him to Marxist theory. Marcuse's philosophical development took place in the turbulent context of early 20th-century Europe, shaped by World War I, the Russian Revolution, and the rise of fascism. Fleeing Nazi Germany in 1934, Marcuse immigrated to the United States, where he became an influential figure in leftist intellectual circles, particularly during the social movements of the 1960s.

Marcuse's philosophy is best known for its critique of advanced industrial societies, which he argued were characterized by "one-dimensional" thinking that stifled human creativity and individuality. His most influential work, One-Dimensional Man (1964), critiqued both capitalist and communist societies for their repressive structures, which he believed served to integrate individuals into the system, reducing their capacity for critical thought and genuine freedom. Marcuse contended that modern technological societies created false needs—consumer desires and behaviors that serve the interests of the ruling elite rather than fulfilling true human potential.

Marcuse was also known for his re-interpretation of Marxism, incorporating insights from psychoanalysis and existentialism. He argued that the liberation of human beings from oppressive social structures would require not only economic change but also a transformation of consciousness. In works like Eros and Civilization (1955), Marcuse combined Freudian and Marxist theory to argue that modern societies repress human desires and instincts, leading to alienation and social control. He believed that a liberated society would enable the free expression of human creativity and desires, allowing for a more genuine form of freedom that goes beyond mere material well-being.

Marcuse's critique of modern society found a receptive audience among the New Left, particularly in the 1960s, when student movements and countercultural groups were challenging the established political and social order. His ideas about the repressive nature of consumer capitalism and the need for radical social change resonated with those seeking alternatives to both Western capitalism and Soviet-style communism. Marcuse became a key intellectual figure of the New Left, and his work influenced movements for civil rights, feminism, and anti-imperialism.

Although Marcuse's influence waned in the later decades of the 20th century, his critiques of consumerism, technology, and social repression remain relevant. His vision of human liberation—one that encompasses both economic justice and the freeing of human desires—continues to inspire discussions about the nature of freedom, individuality, and resistance in contemporary society.

Leo Strauss (1899 – 1973 CE)

Leo Strauss was a German-American political philosopher best known for his work on classical political theory and his critique of modernity. Born in Kirchhain, Germany, Strauss studied at the University of Marburg and later in Berlin, where he was influenced by thinkers such as Martin Heidegger and Edmund Husserl. Forced to flee Nazi Germany due to his Jewish heritage, Strauss moved to the United States in 1937, where he held academic positions at the New School for Social Research and the University of Chicago. Strauss's intellectual development occurred during a time of crisis in Europe, marked by the collapse of liberal democracies, the rise of totalitarianism, and the horrors of World War II.

Strauss's philosophy focused on the tension between ancient and modern political thought. He argued that modern political philosophy, beginning with figures like Machiavelli, Hobbes, and Locke, had abandoned the moral and ethical concerns of classical philosophy in favor of a more pragmatic, power-driven approach to politics. In works like Natural Right and History (1953), Strauss defended the classical notion of "natural right" as the basis for political order, arguing that modern relativism and historicism had undermined the possibility of objective moral standards. For Strauss, the recovery of classical philosophy—particularly the works of Plato and Aristotle—was essential to addressing the moral and political crises of the modern world.

One of Strauss's most influential ideas was his theory of esotericism, the belief that many philosophers wrote in a deliberately obscure or coded manner to protect themselves from political persecution or to ensure that only the most serious and thoughtful readers would grasp the full meaning of their work. Strauss argued that many of the great works of philosophy contain hidden meanings that can only be uncovered through careful, close reading. This method of interpretation, known as "Straussian reading," has been particularly influential in the study of classical and early modern political philosophy.

Strauss was also a strong critic of liberalism and modernity, which he believed had led to the decline of moral and political standards. He argued that modern liberal democracies, by prioritizing individual rights and freedoms, had lost sight of the common good and the need for virtuous leadership. While Strauss was not an advocate of authoritarianism, he believed that the health of a political community depended on the cultivation of virtue and wisdom among its leaders and citizens. His critique of liberalism, combined with his defense of classical philosophy, made him a controversial figure, particularly among proponents of modern democracy.

Strauss's influence extended far beyond academic philosophy, shaping political thought in the United States, particularly among conservative intellectuals. His ideas about natural right, esotericism, and the critique of modernity have been embraced by some as a defense of traditional values and criticized by others as an endorsement of elitism. Regardless of these debates, Strauss's work remains a significant force in political philosophy, particularly in discussions about the relationship between philosophy and politics, the nature of democracy, and the role of tradition in modern life.

Friedrich Hayek (1899 – 1992 CE)

Friedrich Hayek was an Austrian-British economist and philosopher, known for his contributions to political theory, economics, and the philosophy of law. He was born in Vienna, Austria, and studied under the Austrian School of economics, influenced by figures like Ludwig von Mises. Hayek's work emerged during a time of global economic crises, such as the Great Depression, which fueled debates over the role of government intervention in markets. He became a key figure in the defense of classical liberalism and free-market economics, opposing the rise of socialism and central planning.

Hayek's most influential philosophical contribution is his critique of central planning and socialism, laid out in his famous book The Road to Serfdom (1944). He argued that any attempt by the state to centrally control the economy would lead to a loss of individual freedoms and eventually to totalitarianism. Hayek believed that the complexity of economic systems made it impossible for central authorities to have enough knowledge to make informed decisions about resource allocation. Instead, he advocated for the free market as a decentralized system that uses prices to communicate information and coordinate economic activities.

At the core of Hayek's philosophy is the concept of spontaneous order, which he applied to economics, law, and society. He argued that complex social systems, such as economies and legal systems, emerge organically through individual actions rather than through central design. In a free market, prices act as signals that allow individuals to make informed decisions, leading to an efficient allocation of resources without the need for central control. This idea was an extension of classical liberal thought, emphasizing the importance of individual liberty and limited government intervention.

Hayek also made significant contributions to epistemology with his theory of knowledge. He argued that knowledge is decentralized and dispersed among individuals, meaning that no single authority can possess all the knowledge necessary to run an economy or society effectively. His concept of "the knowledge problem" highlighted the limitations of central planning and argued for the superiority of decentralized decision-making. This idea became a cornerstone of his defense of free markets, as he believed that individuals, operating within the framework of the market, are better equipped to make decisions based on their local knowledge.

Throughout his career, Hayek remained a staunch advocate of classical liberalism and free-market capitalism, influencing a wide range of disciplines beyond economics. His ideas played a pivotal role in shaping modern economic thought, particularly in the rise of neoliberal policies during the late 20th century. Hayek's influence can be seen in the policies of leaders like Margaret Thatcher and Ronald Reagan, and his work continues to be a touchstone in debates about government intervention, economic planning, and individual liberty.

Hans-Georg Gadamer (1900 – 2002 CE)

Hans-Georg Gadamer was a German philosopher best known for his work in hermeneutics, the theory and methodology of interpretation. Born in Marburg, Germany, Gadamer studied under prominent philosophers such as Martin Heidegger, Edmund Husserl, and Nicolai Hartmann. His intellectual career took shape during a period of intense philosophical debate in Germany, particularly surrounding existentialism, phenomenology, and the crisis of modernity. Gadamer's major work, Truth and Method (1960), emerged in this context, addressing the nature of human understanding and interpretation while drawing on the hermeneutic tradition of Wilhelm Dilthey and Friedrich Schleiermacher.

Gadamer's philosophy centers on the idea that understanding is not a methodical process but an event that occurs through the fusion of horizons. He argued that our historical and cultural contexts shape how we interpret texts, artworks, and other phenomena. Unlike traditional approaches that sought objective or fixed interpretations, Gadamer believed that all understanding is influenced by the interpreter's background, or "horizon." When we engage with a text or artwork, a dialogue occurs between our horizon and that of the text, leading to a fusion of perspectives that generates new meaning. This process is dynamic, with each encounter producing new understandings as contexts shift.

One of Gadamer's key contributions to hermeneutics was his critique of the Enlightenment's emphasis on scientific objectivity. In Truth and Method, he challenged the notion that knowledge is best obtained through detached, objective observation, as found in the natural sciences. Instead, he argued that understanding in the humanities is fundamentally dialogical, grounded in the interplay between the interpreter and the object of interpretation. Gadamer believed that truth could not be reduced to methodological certainty, as it is always contingent upon historical and cultural circumstances. This perspective highlighted the unique value of the humanities in shaping our understanding of the world.

Gadamer also emphasized the importance of tradition in shaping human understanding. He believed that we are always situated within a tradition and that our interpretations are influenced by the cultural, historical, and linguistic contexts in which we find ourselves. Rather than seeing tradition as a constraint, Gadamer viewed it as a necessary condition for understanding. Tradition provides the framework within which dialogue and interpretation occur, enabling us to engage meaningfully with texts and experiences from the past.

Gadamer's hermeneutics has had a profound influence on fields such as literary theory, theology, and legal interpretation. His insistence that understanding is always mediated by history and culture resonated with postmodern thinkers, while his defense of tradition and dialogue continues to shape debates about the nature of human understanding. Although initially overshadowed by figures like Heidegger, Gadamer's contributions to hermeneutics have secured him a place as one of the most significant philosophers of the 20th century.

Karl Popper (1902 – 1994 CE)

Karl Popper was an Austrian-British philosopher of science and political thinker, best known for his contributions to the philosophy of science and his critique of totalitarianism. Born in Vienna, Austria, Popper was educated at the University of Vienna, where he initially studied psychology but later turned his attention to philosophy. His intellectual development took place during a time of great scientific and political upheaval, particularly with the rise of fascism and communism in Europe. Popper's philosophy of science was shaped by his reaction against logical positivism and the prevailing views of scientific method that emphasized verification. He became a leading figure in the development of falsifiability as a criterion for scientific demarcation.

Popper's most famous contribution to the philosophy of science is his theory of falsifiability, which he introduced in The Logic of Scientific Discovery (1934). He argued that scientific theories cannot be conclusively verified because no amount of empirical evidence can ever prove a theory to be true in all cases. Instead, Popper proposed that scientific theories must be falsifiable, meaning that they can be tested and potentially refuted by empirical observation. This approach shifted the emphasis in the philosophy of science from verification to the critical testing and refinement of hypotheses, influencing how scientists and philosophers think about scientific progress.

Popper's philosophy extended beyond science into the realm of politics and social theory. In The Open Society and Its Enemies (1945), Popper critiqued totalitarian ideologies, particularly fascism and communism, which he saw as threats to individual freedom and rational inquiry. He argued that these ideologies were rooted in historicism, the belief that history follows a predetermined path, often leading to authoritarian rule. Popper championed an "open society," where political institutions are subject to constant critique and individuals are free to question and revise their beliefs. He believed that democracy, with its emphasis on transparency and accountability, was the best safeguard against totalitarianism.

Popper also rejected utopian social engineering, the idea that society could be perfected through large-scale, top-down interventions. He believed such attempts often led to unintended consequences and the concentration of power in the hands of a few. Instead, Popper advocated for "piecemeal social engineering," an approach focusing on incremental, reversible reforms aimed at solving specific problems. This view aligned with his broader philosophical commitment to fallibilism, the belief that human knowledge is always provisional and subject to revision.

Karl Popper's influence on the philosophy of science and political theory remains significant. His emphasis on falsifiability reshaped the understanding of scientific inquiry, while his defense of open societies and critique of totalitarianism continues to resonate with thinkers concerned with the preservation of freedom and rational discourse. Popper's work remains relevant in discussions about the nature of science, the role of democracy, and the limits of human knowledge.

Theodor W. Adorno (1903 – 1969 CE)

Theodor W. Adorno was a German philosopher, sociologist, and musicologist, and one of the leading figures of the Frankfurt School of critical theory. Born in Frankfurt, Germany, Adorno studied philosophy, sociology, and music, and his intellectual development was shaped by the political and social upheavals of early 20th-century Europe, including the rise of fascism and the aftermath of World War I. The Frankfurt School, with which Adorno was closely associated, sought to develop a critique of capitalist society that went beyond traditional Marxist analysis, incorporating insights from psychoanalysis, sociology, and aesthetics.

Adorno's most famous philosophical contribution is his critique of the "culture industry," a term he used to describe the mass production of culture under capitalism. In Dialectic of Enlightenment (1944), co-authored with Max Horkheimer, Adorno argued that the culture industry—represented by Hollywood films, popular music, and other forms of mass media—served to pacify and manipulate the public by promoting conformity and discouraging critical thought. The products of the culture industry, he claimed, offer superficial pleasure while reinforcing the status quo and distracting individuals from structural inequalities inherent in capitalist societies.

A key theme in Adorno's philosophy was his critique of instrumental reason, the idea that reason has been reduced to a mere tool for achieving technical and economic goals. He believed that in modern capitalist societies, reason had become subservient to the logic of domination and control, alienating individuals from their true needs and potential. This critique was part of a broader analysis of the Enlightenment, which Adorno and Horkheimer saw as having degenerated into a project of domination, both over nature and over human beings. For them, the Enlightenment's promise of human emancipation had been betrayed by its entanglement with capitalist exploitation and authoritarianism.

Adorno's work in aesthetics and musicology was also central to his philosophical project. He argued that autonomous art, which resists commodification and mass production, holds the potential to challenge the dominant ideology of capitalist society. In Aesthetic Theory (1970), Adorno explored how modernist art and music, through their formal complexity and refusal to conform to commercial demands, could offer a form of resistance to the culture industry. He believed that true art could reveal the contradictions of society and open up spaces for critical reflection and social change.

Adorno's influence extends across a wide range of disciplines, including philosophy, sociology, and cultural studies. His critique of the culture industry and his analysis of the relationship between reason, domination, and art continue to shape discussions about the role of culture in modern society. Although his work has been criticized for its pessimism and elitism, Adorno's contributions to critical theory remain foundational for understanding the complexities of modern capitalist societies and the possibilities for emancipation.

Hans Jonas (1903 – 1993 CE)

Hans Jonas was a German-born philosopher best known for his work on ethics, particularly in relation to technology, biology, and the environment. Born in Mönchengladbach, Germany, Jonas studied under leading figures in philosophy such as Martin Heidegger and Rudolf Bultmann. His intellectual development was influenced by existentialism, phenomenology, and Jewish philosophy, as well as the political upheavals of the 20th century, including the rise of Nazism, which led Jonas to emigrate from Germany. His later work focused on the ethical implications of technological and scientific advancements, which he believed posed new challenges for human responsibility and survival.

Jonas' most significant philosophical contribution is his development of an ethics of responsibility, articulated in his seminal work, The Imperative of Responsibility (1979). He argued that modern technology had fundamentally changed the nature of human action by extending its consequences far beyond immediate or local effects. Whereas traditional ethics focused on interpersonal relationships and actions with short-term impacts, Jonas believed that the far-reaching and potentially irreversible effects of technology—such as environmental degradation and nuclear war—required a new ethical framework. His guiding principle, the "heuristics of fear," suggests that humanity must err on the side of caution when dealing with technologies that could harm future generations.

In this context, Jonas introduced the idea of an ethical responsibility toward future generations, which had been largely absent from previous ethical systems. He argued that modern civilization's capacity for large-scale technological manipulation, especially in areas like biology and ecology, imposed an unprecedented moral obligation to consider the long-term effects of these actions. For Jonas, the traditional ethical focus on the present was inadequate in the face of ecological crises and technological risks that could jeopardize the future of humanity and life on Earth.

Jonas also contributed to the philosophy of biology, where he explored the relationship between life, technology, and human existence. In The Phenomenon of Life (1966), Jonas argued that life should be understood as an integrated process in which organisms strive to preserve their existence. He viewed this biological striving as a fundamental characteristic of life, and he believed that this insight had profound ethical implications. For Jonas, understanding life as a self-sustaining process underscored the importance of respecting and protecting the integrity of living systems in the face of technological interference.

Hans Jonas's work has had a lasting influence on environmental ethics, bioethics, and the philosophy of technology. His emphasis on responsibility and his concern for the future have resonated in contemporary discussions about sustainability, climate change, and the ethical challenges posed by biotechnological advancements. Jonas's philosophy serves as a call for greater caution and foresight in the face of human technological power, advocating for an ethical stance that prioritizes the protection of life and the environment for future generations.

Jean-Paul Sartre (1905 – 1980 CE)

Jean-Paul Sartre was a French philosopher, playwright, and novelist, widely regarded as one of the central figures in 20th-century existentialism. Born in Paris, Sartre studied philosophy at the École Normale Supérieure, where he became deeply influenced by the works of Edmund Husserl and Martin Heidegger. His intellectual development occurred during a period of political and social upheaval, particularly the rise of fascism and the Second World War. Sartre's experiences during the war, including his time as a prisoner of war, profoundly shaped his existentialist philosophy, which emphasized human freedom, responsibility, and the absurdity of existence.

Sartre's most influential philosophical work is Being and Nothingness (1943), in which he laid out the core tenets of existentialism. He argued that existence precedes essence, meaning that human beings are not born with a predetermined nature or purpose but must create their own identities through their actions. For Sartre, this radical freedom is both exhilarating and burdensome, as it places the responsibility for one's life entirely on the individual. He famously stated that "man is condemned to be free," highlighting the weight of responsibility that comes with this freedom. Sartre's philosophy rejected external authorities, such as religion or societal norms, emphasizing the need for authentic self-creation.

A key concept in Sartre's philosophy is "bad faith," which refers to the denial of one's own freedom and responsibility by conforming to societal expectations or external pressures. He believed that many individuals live in bad faith by deceiving themselves into thinking that they are bound by circumstances or roles rather than recognizing their freedom to act otherwise. For Sartre, living authentically requires acknowledging one's freedom and making choices that reflect one's true values, even in the face of uncertainty and anxiety. This focus on authenticity and personal responsibility became a central theme in existentialist thought.

Sartre's existentialism extended into his political philosophy, particularly his later commitment to Marxism and socialism. He believed that human freedom could only be fully realized in a society that eliminated economic and social inequalities. In works like Critique of Dialectical Reason (1960), Sartre attempted to reconcile existentialism with Marxist theory, arguing that individual freedom must be understood in the context of social and historical conditions. He rejected deterministic interpretations of Marxism, insisting that human action remained crucial in shaping history. His political activism, including his support for anti-colonial movements and workers' rights, reflected his belief in the importance of collective action in the pursuit of freedom.

Sartre's influence on philosophy, literature, and political thought was immense, particularly during the post-World War II period. His existentialism resonated with those grappling with the disillusionment and uncertainty of the modern world. His emphasis on freedom, responsibility, and authenticity continues to inspire and provoke debate, securing his place as a central figure in existentialist philosophy and its engagement with questions of meaning, identity, and social justice.

Hannah Arendt (1906 – 1975 CE)

Hannah Arendt was a German-American political theorist, renowned for her analysis of totalitarianism, authority, and the nature of power. Born in Hanover, Germany, Arendt studied philosophy under Martin Heidegger and Karl Jaspers, two figures who significantly influenced her early intellectual development. Fleeing Nazi persecution, Arendt emigrated first to France and then to the United States, where she became an influential public intellectual. Her experiences as a Jewish refugee and her observations of the totalitarian regimes of Nazi Germany and Stalinist Russia shaped much of her thinking about how such regimes could emerge and flourish in the modern world.

Arendt's most famous work, The Origins of Totalitarianism (1951), provides a comprehensive analysis of totalitarianism, which she distinguished from other forms of dictatorship or tyranny. Arendt argued that totalitarianism is characterized by its use of ideology and terror to dominate every aspect of life. She examined the roots of totalitarian regimes, tracing their origins to European anti-Semitism, imperialism, and the breakdown of traditional political structures. According to Arendt, totalitarianism is marked by its effort to isolate individuals from one another, destroying the fabric of social and political life. Her work illuminated the mechanisms that enabled such regimes to gain and maintain control.

A key theme in Arendt's political thought is the concept of vita activa, or active life, which she explored in The Human Condition (1958). In this work, Arendt distinguished between three fundamental human activities: labor, work, and action. Labor refers to the repetitive tasks necessary for biological survival, work involves the creation of lasting objects or institutions, and action is the political activity that takes place in the public sphere. For Arendt, action is the highest form of human activity because it involves individuals engaging with one another in dialogue, debate, and collective decision-making. She argued that the modern world had become increasingly dominated by labor and work, leading to the erosion of genuine political action.

Arendt also made significant contributions to the philosophy of judgment, particularly in her later work. She was deeply interested in how individuals form judgments in the absence of clear rules or guidelines. In her unfinished work The Life of the Mind, Arendt examined the nature of thinking and judging, drawing on the ideas of Immanuel Kant. She argued that judgment is inherently tied to imagining the perspectives of others and plays a crucial role in political life. Arendt believed judgment allows individuals to navigate complex moral and political dilemmas, making it essential for responsible citizenship.

Arendt's work has had a lasting impact on political theory, particularly her analyses of totalitarianism, authority, and political action. Her exploration of the conditions necessary for freedom and the role of judgment in political life continues to influence debates in philosophy, political science, and ethics. Arendt's ideas remain central to discussions about power, democracy, and the dangers of authoritarianism.

Emmanuel Levinas (1906 – 1995 CE)

Emmanuel Levinas was a French-Lithuanian philosopher best known for his work on ethics and the philosophy of the "Other." Born in Kaunas, Lithuania, Levinas was raised in a Jewish family and later moved to France, where he studied philosophy under Edmund Husserl and Martin Heidegger. The traumatic experience of World War II, including his imprisonment in a German labor camp and the murder of his family during the Holocaust, profoundly shaped his philosophy. Levinas's work sought to provide an ethical response to the violence and atrocities of the 20th century, offering a radical rethinking of ethics that placed the encounter with the "Other" at its core.

Levinas's central philosophical concept is the primacy of the ethical relation with the Other, which he explored in works such as Totality and Infinity (1961) and Otherwise than Being (1974). He argued that traditional Western philosophy, beginning with the Greeks, had focused too much on ontology—the study of being—and had neglected the ethical dimension of human existence. For Levinas, ethics precedes ontology, meaning that the most fundamental aspect of human life is not knowledge or self-awareness, but the ethical responsibility we have toward others. He believed that the face-to-face encounter with the Other imposes an infinite ethical demand, compelling us to respond with care and responsibility.

A key feature of Levinas's ethics is his notion of "infinity," which refers to the idea that the Other is always beyond full comprehension or understanding. The face of the Other, Levinas argued, expresses a vulnerability and a call for ethical responsibility that cannot be reduced to mere concepts or categories. This infinite nature of the Other means that our ethical obligation toward others is also infinite; it cannot be fully satisfied or completed. Levinas believed that this ethical relationship is the foundation of all human interaction and that it challenges the egocentric focus of much of Western philosophy, which tends to prioritize the self over the Other.

Levinas's critique of totalitarianism and violence is deeply tied to his ethical philosophy. He argued that totalitarian systems, such as those of Nazi Germany, seek to erase the individuality and alterity of others, reducing them to mere objects or categories within a larger system. For Levinas, true ethical behavior involves recognizing the irreducible uniqueness of each individual and responding to them as a subject rather than an object. This ethical stance stands in opposition to the dehumanizing tendencies of modern bureaucratic and totalitarian systems, which Levinas saw as rooted in the failure to recognize the ethical primacy of the Other.

Levinas's influence extends beyond philosophy to fields such as theology, politics, and literary theory. His emphasis on ethics as the foundation of human life, his focus on responsibility toward others, and his critique of traditional Western metaphysics have made him a central figure in contemporary ethical thought. Levinas's ideas continue to inspire discussions about the nature of morality, the limits of human understanding, and the ethical challenges of modernity.

Maurice Blanchot (1907 – 2003 CE)

Maurice Blanchot was a French philosopher, writer, and literary critic whose work is known for its exploration of language, literature, and the nature of existence. Born in Devrouze, France, Blanchot's intellectual development was shaped by existentialism, phenomenology, and his close relationships with figures like Georges Bataille and Emmanuel Levinas. Although he remained a private figure throughout his life, Blanchot's writings exerted a profound influence on post-war French thought, particularly in philosophy and literary theory. His enigmatic style and concern with the limits of language and representation characterize his philosophy.

Blanchot's philosophy revolves around the concept of literature as a space where traditional notions of meaning, identity, and presence are disrupted. In works like The Space of Literature (1955) and The Writing of the Disaster (1980), he explored the idea that literature operates in a realm of ambiguity and uncertainty, where the author's intention and the reader's interpretation can never fully coincide. He believed that literature reveals the essential absence at the heart of existence, an absence that cannot be fully captured or articulated by language. For Blanchot, writing is a process of confronting the unknown and the ungraspable, where meaning always escapes definitive understanding.

One of Blanchot's central themes is the relationship between death and writing. He argued that writing is intimately connected to death because it involves a withdrawal from the world of action and presence into a space of silence and absence. In his essay Literature and the Right to Death (1949), Blanchot claimed that literature allows individuals to confront the limits of existence by exposing the impossibility of fully representing life or death. This confrontation with death, Blanchot suggested, is a necessary part of the creative process, as it reveals the inherent limitations of language and the futility of trying to capture the essence of being in words.

Blanchot's work also engages with political and ethical themes, particularly in his reflections on community and responsibility. He was influenced by Levinas's ethics of the Other, and his later writings explore the idea of a community based not on shared identity or common goals, but on a shared experience of absence and fragmentation. In The Unavowable Community (1983), Blanchot argued that true community arises from the recognition of the other's irreducibility and the refusal to impose unity or identity, offering an alternative vision of human relationships based on openness and vulnerability.

Blanchot's influence on contemporary philosophy and literary theory has been far-reaching, particularly in the development of post-structuralism and deconstruction. His work on language, death, and absence has resonated with thinkers such as Jacques Derrida and Michel Foucault, and his philosophy remains a provocative contribution to 20th-century thought.

Simone de Beauvoir (1908 – 1986 CE)

Simone de Beauvoir was a French existentialist philosopher, feminist, and writer, best known for her work on the nature of gender and oppression. Born in Paris, de Beauvoir studied philosophy at the Sorbonne, where she formed a lifelong intellectual partnership with Jean-Paul Sartre. Her intellectual development occurred in the vibrant context of mid-20th century France, where existentialism and Marxism were central to philosophical discourse. De Beauvoir's philosophy was deeply influenced by her commitment to existentialism, particularly its emphasis on freedom, choice, and the human condition. However, she extended existentialist ideas into the realm of feminist theory, where her groundbreaking work would leave an enduring legacy.

De Beauvoir's most famous work, The Second Sex (1949), is a foundational text in feminist philosophy. In this book, she famously declared that "one is not born, but rather becomes, a woman," emphasizing that gender is not a natural, biological fact but a social construct. She argued that throughout history, women have been relegated to the status of the "Other," defined in opposition to men, who occupy the position of the "Self." De Beauvoir examined the ways in which this othering of women results in their oppression, denying them the autonomy and freedom that men enjoy. This analysis challenged traditional views of gender and paved the way for later feminist thought by revealing the deep-rooted structures of patriarchy.

A key element of de Beauvoir's existentialist feminism is her focus on freedom and transcendence. Like Sartre, she believed that human beings are condemned to freedom, meaning that individuals are responsible for creating meaning in their lives through their choices. However, de Beauvoir emphasized that women have historically been denied the opportunities to exercise their freedom fully. In patriarchal societies, women are often confined to roles that limit their ability to transcend their immediate circumstances and assert their individuality. De Beauvoir called for women to embrace their freedom and reject the roles imposed on them by society, advocating for greater equality between the sexes.

In addition to her work on gender, de Beauvoir made significant contributions to existentialist ethics. She explored the tension between individual freedom and the need for solidarity with others. In The Ethics of Ambiguity (1947), de Beauvoir argued that human existence is inherently ambiguous because individuals are both free and constrained by their relationships with others. She rejected both absolute individualism and collectivism, advocating for an ethics that recognizes the complexity of human life and the need to balance personal freedom with ethical responsibility toward others. This ethical framework, grounded in existentialist principles, informed her political activism and her engagement with issues of social justice.

Simone de Beauvoir's work has had a profound and lasting impact on feminist theory, existentialist philosophy, and ethics. Her analysis of the social construction of gender and her call for women's liberation continue to influence feminist discourse. Her existentialist approach to freedom, ethics, and the human condition remains a vital part of philosophical discussions about autonomy, oppression, and the possibilities for human flourishing.

Maurice Merleau-Ponty (1908 – 1961 CE)

Maurice Merleau-Ponty was a French phenomenologist and philosopher whose work focused on the nature of perception, embodiment, and human experience. Born in Rochefort-sur-Mer, France, Merleau-Ponty studied at the École Normale Supérieure in Paris, where he became closely associated with Jean-Paul Sartre and Simone de Beauvoir. His intellectual development occurred within the context of existentialism and phenomenology, particularly the influence of Edmund Husserl and Martin Heidegger. Merleau-Ponty's philosophy sought to expand on phenomenology by emphasizing the primacy of perception and the lived body in shaping human experience and knowledge.

Merleau-Ponty's major work, Phenomenology of Perception (1945), is a foundational text in phenomenology, where he argued that perception is the primary mode through which we engage with the world. Rejecting Cartesian dualism, which separates mind and body, Merleau-Ponty proposed that the body is not merely a vessel for the mind but the very means through which we perceive and interact with the world. He introduced the concept of the "lived body," emphasizing that our bodies are not objects of observation but subjects through which we experience reality. This view challenged traditional philosophical approaches that privileged abstract reasoning over embodied experience.

Central to Merleau-Ponty's philosophy is the notion of "embodiment," the idea that our consciousness is fundamentally rooted in our bodily experience. He argued that human beings do not encounter the world as disembodied minds but as embodied beings who are always situated in a particular context. For Merleau-Ponty, perception is not a passive process of receiving sensory data but an active, embodied engagement with the world. He believed that perception is shaped by the body's interactions with its environment, and that this embodied perception is the basis for all knowledge. This emphasis on the embodied nature of experience had a significant impact on later developments in phenomenology, cognitive science, and the philosophy of mind.

Merleau-Ponty also explored the concept of intersubjectivity, the idea that our understanding of the world is shaped by our relationships with others. He argued that we experience other people not as mere objects but as subjects with their own perspectives and experiences. This recognition of the other's subjectivity is essential for human interaction and social life. Merleau-Ponty's work on intersubjectivity influenced later existentialist and phenomenological discussions about the nature of selfhood, otherness, and the social dimensions of human experience.

Although his life was cut short, Merleau-Ponty's contributions to phenomenology, particularly his focus on perception, embodiment, and intersubjectivity, continue to influence a wide range of disciplines, from philosophy and psychology to the arts and political theory. His work remains central to contemporary discussions about the nature of human experience, the body, and the ways in which we engage with the world and with others.

Simone Weil (1909 – 1943 CE)

Simone Weil was a French philosopher, mystic, and political activist known for her reflections on suffering, justice, and spiritual redemption. Born in Paris to a secular Jewish family, Weil displayed an early talent for philosophy and attended the École Normale Supérieure, where she studied under prominent figures like Émile Chartier (Alain). Her intellectual development was shaped by her engagement with Marxism, social justice, and her experiences working in factories and participating in labor movements. Weil's short life was marked by her intense concern for the oppressed and her efforts to bridge philosophy, politics, and spirituality.

Weil's early philosophical work focused on the nature of oppression and justice. In her writings on labor and politics, such as Oppression and Liberty (published posthumously in 1955), Weil critiqued both capitalism and Marxism, arguing that both systems failed to address the spiritual and moral needs of the human soul. She believed that true justice must go beyond material conditions and economic equality to include the recognition of human dignity and the need for spiritual sustenance. Weil's commitment to the working class led her to work in factories and support workers' rights, experiences that deeply influenced her understanding of alienation and suffering.

A central theme in Weil's philosophy is the concept of attention, which she explored in both her ethical and spiritual writings. Weil believed that attention is the highest form of human engagement, requiring the individual to focus fully on the needs and suffering of others without selfish interference. In her essay Reflections on the Right Use of School Studies (1942), she argued that cultivating attention in education could develop a moral awareness that would extend beyond the classroom to the broader world. This notion of attention also played a key role in her religious thought, where she saw it as a form of prayer and a way to encounter the divine.

Weil's spirituality, which became increasingly important in her later life, was deeply influenced by her experiences of suffering and her encounters with Christianity, though she never formally converted. Her mystical writings, including Gravity and Grace (published posthumously in 1947), reflect her belief that human existence is marked by a tension between the forces of gravity (the material world and its burdens) and grace (the divine intervention that lifts the soul toward the good). Weil argued that true spiritual liberation requires a renunciation of the self and a willingness to accept suffering as a pathway to understanding divine love. Her vision of spirituality was marked by a profound sense of compassion for the oppressed and a commitment to social justice.

Simone Weil's work, though often overshadowed by her contemporaries, has had a lasting influence on political theory, theology, and existential philosophy. Her reflections on suffering, attention, and spiritual redemption continue to resonate with those seeking to understand the ethical and spiritual dimensions of human life. Weil's commitment to both the intellectual and the practical aspects of philosophy has made her a unique and enduring voice in 20th-century thought.

Alfred Ayer (1910 – 1989 CE)

Alfred Jules Ayer was a British philosopher best known for his promotion of logical positivism and his work in the philosophy of language, particularly his advocacy of verificationism. Born in London, Ayer was educated at Eton and then at Oxford, where he studied philosophy. After a period of study in Vienna, where he became associated with the Vienna Circle of logical positivists, Ayer returned to the UK and became a leading figure in the analytic philosophy tradition. His most influential book, Language, Truth, and Logic (1936), introduced logical positivism to the English-speaking world and marked the beginning of his prominent role in 20th-century philosophy.

Ayer's philosophy was deeply influenced by the logical positivists, particularly their focus on the principle of verification. This principle asserts that for a statement to be meaningful, it must be either empirically verifiable or logically necessary. In Language, Truth, and Logic, Ayer applied this principle to traditional metaphysical and theological claims, arguing that statements about God, ethics, or metaphysical realities are meaningless because they cannot be empirically tested. For Ayer, the only meaningful statements are those that can be verified through sense experience or logical deduction, reducing metaphysical speculation to non-sense in the positivist sense.

A central theme in Ayer's work is his rejection of metaphysics and religious belief. He argued that metaphysical propositions, such as those concerning the existence of God or the nature of reality beyond the empirical world, fail to meet the verification criterion and thus have no cognitive content. According to Ayer, debates about metaphysical issues are futile because they do not pertain to matters that can be observed or scientifically tested. This stance aligned with the logical positivists' broader goal of eliminating what they saw as unproductive speculation in philosophy, replacing it with a focus on language, science, and logical analysis.

Ayer also contributed significantly to the philosophy of language, particularly in his examination of the distinction between analytic and synthetic statements. Analytic statements are those that are true by definition, such as "All bachelors are unmarried," while synthetic statements require empirical verification. Ayer argued that much of traditional philosophy's confusion stemmed from a failure to recognize this distinction. By clarifying the difference between these types of statements, Ayer sought to demonstrate that many philosophical problems could be dissolved rather than solved, a hallmark of the logical positivist approach.

Despite the later decline of logical positivism, Ayer's influence on analytic philosophy, especially in the philosophy of language and epistemology, remained significant. His emphasis on clarity, logic, and the rejection of unverifiable claims helped shape mid-20th-century philosophical debates, even as the positivist movement lost momentum. Ayer's work continues to be studied, particularly for its rigorous approach to language and its critical stance on metaphysics and religious belief.

Marshall McLuhan (1911 – 1980)

Marshall McLuhan was a Canadian philosopher and media theorist whose work revolutionized the study of media and communication in the 20th century. Born in Edmonton, Alberta, McLuhan studied literature and became deeply interested in the relationship between media, technology, and culture. His work emerged during the rapid technological advancements of the mid-20th century, particularly the rise of mass media such as television and radio. McLuhan is best known for his aphorism "the medium is the message" and his analysis of how media shape human perception and society, which he explored in works such as Understanding Media (1964) and The Gutenberg Galaxy (1962).

McLuhan's concept of "the medium is the message" is central to his philosophy. He argued that the content delivered by a medium is less significant than the medium itself in shaping human experience. For McLuhan, each medium—whether print, radio, or television—affects the way people perceive the world and interact with it. For example, print media encourage linear, logical thinking, while electronic media like television foster more holistic, immediate modes of perception. McLuhan believed that understanding how different media affect society and culture was essential for understanding the broader effects of technological change on human consciousness.

A major focus of McLuhan's work was his exploration of how media shape human cognition and social organization. In The Gutenberg Galaxy, he examined the effects of the printing press on Western civilization, arguing that the shift from oral to print culture transformed human consciousness by emphasizing individualism, rationality, and visual perception. With the advent of electronic media, McLuhan believed that society was moving toward a "global village," where people would once again experience a more collective and holistic form of consciousness, similar to that of pre-literate societies. This shift, he argued, would have profound implications for how people communicate, think, and organize themselves socially.

McLuhan's ideas about media also extended into the realm of technology and its relationship to human senses. He introduced the concept of "extensions of man," suggesting that media and technologies extend human sensory capacities, often in ways that have unintended consequences. For instance, the telephone extends the voice, and the car extends the legs, but these extensions also alter human interactions and social dynamics. McLuhan's view of technology as an extension of human faculties helped pave the way for later theories about the relationship between technology, identity, and society.

Marshall McLuhan's work has had a lasting impact on media studies, communication theory, and cultural criticism. His insights into the transformative power of media and his foresight regarding the rise of electronic media in shaping society have continued to resonate in contemporary discussions about the digital age, the internet, and social media. McLuhan's work remains a critical lens through which scholars and thinkers analyze the ongoing interplay between technology, media, and human experience.

E. M. Cioran (1911 – 1995 CE)

Emil Cioran, known as E. M. Cioran, was a Romanian-born French philosopher and essayist, renowned for his pessimistic and aphoristic writings on despair, existentialism, and the futility of life. Born in Rășinari, Romania, Cioran studied philosophy at the University of Bucharest, where he was influenced by thinkers such as Friedrich Nietzsche and Arthur Schopenhauer. Cioran's early experiences with insomnia and existential crisis deeply shaped his outlook on life, leading him to develop a philosophy characterized by profound skepticism and nihilism. He later moved to France, where he wrote in French and became an influential figure in 20th-century existentialist and nihilist thought.

Cioran's work is marked by a relentless exploration of human suffering, mortality, and the meaninglessness of existence. In books such as The Trouble with Being Born (1973) and A Short History of Decay (1949), Cioran delves into the darker aspects of the human condition, expressing his belief that life is inherently filled with anguish and despair. He argued that existence itself is an affliction, and that the consciousness of mortality only heightens the absurdity of life. His writing, often composed in short, aphoristic bursts, reflects a deep sense of existential weariness and a rejection of any attempt to find ultimate meaning or redemption in life.

Cioran's philosophy also engages with themes of nihilism and pessimism, drawing on the influences of Nietzsche and Schopenhauer. Like Nietzsche, Cioran rejected the idea of transcendence and religious salvation, arguing that the search for meaning in a meaningless world is doomed to failure. He viewed nihilism as a logical response to the recognition that life is devoid of inherent purpose, and he embraced this bleak outlook as a form of liberation from the illusions of hope and progress. Cioran's pessimism, however, was not without a sense of irony or dark humor, as he often portrayed life's absurdity with a sharp, biting wit.

Despite his deep pessimism, Cioran also reflected on the possibilities of finding solace in solitude, contemplation, and a rejection of societal norms. He believed that the individual's awareness of life's absurdity could lead to a form of detachment or withdrawal from the expectations and pressures of the external world. Cioran's emphasis on solitude and introspection resonated with existentialist themes of authenticity and personal freedom, although his work remained distinctly more pessimistic than that of figures like Sartre or Camus.

Cioran's writing, while bleak and often unsettling, has had a significant influence on existentialist and nihilist thought, particularly in its exploration of the limits of human experience and the impossibility of escaping suffering. His aphoristic style and penetrating insights into the nature of despair continue to resonate with readers and thinkers grappling with questions of meaning, mortality, and the human condition. Cioran's work remains a vital contribution to 20th-century existential and philosophical literature.

Wilfrid Sellars (1912 – 1989 CE)

Wilfrid Sellars was an American philosopher known for his profound contributions to epistemology, philosophy of mind, and the philosophy of language. Born in Ann Arbor, Michigan, Sellars was the son of prominent philosopher Roy Wood Sellars. He studied at the University of Michigan, the University of Buffalo, and finally at Oxford, where he was influenced by both Anglo-American and Continental traditions. Sellars' intellectual career unfolded during a time when analytic philosophy was becoming increasingly dominant in the United States, and his work aimed to bridge the gap between empiricism and rationalism, offering a more integrated approach to understanding knowledge and perception.

Sellars is most famous for his critique of the "myth of the given," which he articulated in his essay Empiricism and the Philosophy of Mind (1956). The "myth of the given" refers to the assumption that certain forms of knowledge, such as sensory experiences, are directly given to us and serve as a foundation for all other knowledge. Sellars challenged this notion, arguing that all knowledge, even that which appears to be immediate, is mediated by conceptual frameworks. According to Sellars, perception and experience are not simply passive receptions of data but are shaped by our prior understanding, language, and cultural background. His rejection of the "given" marked a significant departure from traditional empiricism.

A key aspect of Sellars' philosophy is his distinction between the "manifest image" and the "scientific image" of the world. The manifest image refers to the world as it appears to us in everyday experience, with its objects, people, and values. In contrast, the scientific image is the view of the world presented by science, which often reveals realities that are not directly perceivable, such as atoms, forces, and physical laws. Sellars argued that both images are valid but that they must be reconciled within a coherent philosophical framework. He believed that philosophy's task was to integrate these two perspectives to form a comprehensive understanding of reality.

Sellars also made significant contributions to the philosophy of language, particularly in his account of how language and thought are interconnected. He argued that language is not merely a tool for expressing pre-existing thoughts but is essential to the very structure of thinking. For Sellars, human cognition is fundamentally linguistic, and our capacity for abstract reasoning and knowledge depends on our ability to use language. This view placed him in opposition to theories that treated language as secondary to thought, positioning him as a central figure in debates about the nature of meaning and representation.

Sellars' influence on contemporary philosophy is substantial, particularly in the areas of epistemology, philosophy of mind, and the philosophy of science. His work laid the groundwork for later developments in functionalism and representationalism in the philosophy of mind, and his critique of foundationalism continues to shape discussions about the nature of knowledge and perception. His philosophical legacy endures, particularly in his efforts to reconcile scientific and everyday understandings of the world.

Paul Ricoeur (1913 – 2005 CE)

Paul Ricoeur was a French philosopher renowned for his contributions to phenomenology, hermeneutics, and existentialism. Born in Valence, France, Ricoeur's early life was marked by tragedy—his parents died when he was a child, and he was raised by his grandparents. Ricoeur pursued his education at the University of Rennes and the Sorbonne, where he was deeply influenced by the existentialist and phenomenological traditions, particularly the work of Edmund Husserl and Gabriel Marcel. Ricoeur's philosophical career spanned a period of political and social upheaval, including World War II, during which he was a prisoner of war. These experiences informed his reflections on memory, narrative, and the human condition.

Ricoeur's philosophy centers on the idea of interpretation, particularly the role of hermeneutics in understanding human experience. His work sought to reconcile two traditions: the existentialist focus on individual existence and the hermeneutic tradition, which emphasizes the interpretation of texts and symbols. In his early work, such as Freedom and Nature (1950), Ricoeur explored the tension between human freedom and the constraints of the natural world, examining how individuals navigate between these forces. He argued that human freedom is always mediated by our interpretation of the world, and that this process of interpretation is shaped by our historical and cultural contexts.

Ricoeur's later work extended his exploration of hermeneutics to the interpretation of texts, particularly in relation to language, narrative, and history. In Time and Narrative (1983-1985), Ricoeur examined the role of narrative in shaping human identity and experience. He argued that narrative is not merely a way of recounting events but is fundamental to how we understand ourselves and our place in the world. For Ricoeur, human identity is inherently narrative; we construct our sense of self through the stories we tell about our lives. This view positioned him in conversation with existentialist thinkers like Jean-Paul Sartre but emphasized the social and interpretive dimensions of selfhood.

Memory and forgiveness are also central themes in Ricoeur's philosophy, particularly in his later work. In Memory, History, Forgetting (2000), Ricoeur investigated the complex relationship between personal memory, collective history, and the ethics of remembrance. He was deeply concerned with the question of how societies and individuals come to terms with traumatic pasts, particularly in the context of war and political violence. Ricoeur argued that memory is never a straightforward recollection of the past but is always shaped by interpretation and the passage of time. He also explored the potential for forgiveness, viewing it as a way to transcend the burden of the past while acknowledging the suffering it has caused.

Paul Ricoeur's contributions to hermeneutics, phenomenology, and narrative theory have had a profound impact on contemporary philosophy. His work on interpretation, memory, and identity continues to influence fields as diverse as literary theory, history, and theology. Ricoeur's philosophy remains central to discussions about the nature of human experience, the role of narrative in shaping identity, and the ethics of memory and forgiveness.

David Bohm (1917 – 1992 CE)

David Bohm was an American theoretical physicist and philosopher whose work spanned the fields of quantum mechanics, consciousness, and the philosophy of science. Born in Wilkes-Barre, Pennsylvania, Bohm studied under prominent physicists such as Robert Oppenheimer and became involved in early research on quantum theory. However, his career was disrupted by political persecution during the McCarthy era, forcing him to leave the United States. He settled in Brazil and later in the United Kingdom, where he continued his research and developed his philosophical ideas. Bohm's work arose during significant advancements in physics, particularly in the interpretation of quantum mechanics, and he sought to reconcile these discoveries with broader questions about reality and consciousness.

Bohm's most significant contribution to physics is his interpretation of quantum mechanics, known as the "Bohmian interpretation" or "Bohmian mechanics." Unlike the Copenhagen interpretation, which posits that particles do not have definite properties until they are measured, Bohm's theory suggested that particles have well-defined trajectories, guided by an underlying "quantum potential." This interpretation reintroduced a form of determinism into quantum mechanics, challenging the prevailing view that quantum phenomena are inherently probabilistic. While not widely accepted by the mainstream physics community, Bohm's theory offered a novel way of thinking about the relationship between matter and information at the quantum level.

In his book Wholeness and the Implicate Order (1980), Bohm introduced the idea of the "implicate order," challenging the traditional view of reality as composed of discrete, independent parts. Instead, Bohm argued that the universe is fundamentally interconnected, with all phenomena unfolding from a deeper, hidden order. This implicate order is "unfolded" into the explicate order of everyday experience, but the two are inextricably linked. Bohm believed this holistic perspective could provide a more integrated understanding of the universe, moving beyond the fragmented, mechanistic worldview of classical physics.

Bohm was also deeply interested in the nature of consciousness and its relationship to the physical world. He argued that consciousness and matter are not separate entities but aspects of the same underlying reality. His dialogues with the Indian philosopher Jiddu Krishnamurti and work on the dialogue process reflected his belief that fragmentation in human thought and perception was a source of conflict and misunderstanding. Bohm advocated for a more holistic, non-dualistic approach to understanding consciousness.

David Bohm's contributions to physics and philosophy have left a lasting impact on discussions about the nature of reality, quantum mechanics, and consciousness. His ideas about the implicate order and the interconnectedness of all things continue to inspire debates in fields ranging from theoretical physics to metaphysics, offering a bridge between science and philosophy in the quest to understand existence.

Elizabeth Anscombe (1919 – 2001 CE)

Elizabeth Anscombe was a British analytic philosopher, renowned for her work in moral philosophy, philosophy of mind, and philosophy of action. Born in Limerick, Ireland, and educated at Oxford University, Anscombe became a key figure in the mid-20th-century revival of virtue ethics. She studied under Ludwig Wittgenstein and later became one of his most important interpreters and defenders, contributing to his work's dissemination in the English-speaking world. Her work emerged in an intellectual environment dominated by logical positivism and utilitarianism, and she sought to offer alternatives through her deep engagement with the classical tradition, particularly Aristotle and Thomas Aquinas.

Anscombe's most influential work, Intention (1957), is considered one of the seminal texts in the philosophy of action. In this work, she analyzed the concept of intentional action, arguing that understanding human behavior requires a careful examination of the intentions behind actions. Anscombe rejected the dominant behaviorist and consequentialist models of human action, which focused on external behaviors or outcomes. Instead, she argued that an action's moral significance is rooted in the agent's intentions. Her insights into how actions are understood and explained remain a cornerstone in discussions of action theory and the philosophy of mind.

Another of Anscombe's significant contributions to philosophy was her critique of consequentialism, particularly in her essay Modern Moral Philosophy (1958). In this essay, she attacked utilitarianism and other consequentialist ethical theories, arguing that they placed too much emphasis on the outcomes of actions rather than the moral character of the agents themselves. Anscombe called for a return to a virtue ethics approach, rooted in classical moral theory, particularly that of Aristotle. She argued that modern moral philosophy was fundamentally flawed because it attempted to derive moral rules and obligations in the absence of a coherent concept of human flourishing or virtue.

A staunch critic of nuclear warfare, Anscombe famously protested Oxford's decision to grant an honorary degree to U.S. President Harry Truman, condemning the atomic bombings of Hiroshima and Nagasaki. She argued that intentional killing of innocent civilians, even in wartime, could never be morally justified. This stance reflects her broader commitment to deontological ethics, where certain actions are considered morally wrong regardless of their consequences. Her work on moral absolutes, particularly regarding the ethics of war and the sanctity of life, became a critical part of 20th-century moral philosophy debates.

Anscombe's influence extended beyond her own writings to her role as an interpreter of Wittgenstein's later work. Her translation and editing of Philosophical Investigations brought Wittgenstein's ideas about language, meaning, and the philosophy of mind to a wider audience. Through both her original work and her role as Wittgenstein's intellectual heir, Elizabeth Anscombe remains one of the most significant figures in 20th-century analytic philosophy, particularly in the areas of ethics and the philosophy of action.

John Rawls (1921 – 2002 CE)

John Rawls was an American political philosopher, best known for his work on justice and political liberalism. Born in Baltimore, Maryland, Rawls studied at Princeton University and later at Oxford as a Rhodes Scholar, where he was influenced by the ethical theories of Immanuel Kant and utilitarian thinkers. His intellectual development occurred during a time of social and political upheaval in the mid-20th century, particularly surrounding issues of civil rights and economic inequality. Rawls sought to develop a comprehensive theory of justice that could address these concerns and provide a framework for a fair and just society.

Rawls' most famous work, A Theory of Justice (1971), introduced the concept of "justice as fairness" and established him as one of the leading political philosophers of the 20th century. In this book, Rawls proposed a thought experiment called the "original position," in which individuals are placed behind a "veil of ignorance." Behind this veil, people do not know their place in society, their social status, or their natural talents. Rawls argued that under these conditions, rational individuals would choose principles of justice that ensure fairness for all, particularly the least advantaged. This led to his two principles of justice: the principle of equal basic liberties and the difference principle, which allows social and economic inequalities only if they benefit the least advantaged members of society.

Rawls' theory was a response to utilitarianism, which he believed failed to adequately protect individual rights. Utilitarianism, which advocates for actions that maximize overall happiness, could, in Rawls' view, justify sacrificing the rights of minorities for the greater good. In contrast, Rawls' justice as fairness sought to safeguard individual liberties while still allowing for economic and social inequalities, as long as they contributed to the overall benefit of society's most vulnerable members. His work provided a moral justification for the welfare state and influenced debates about distributive justice, civil rights, and democratic governance.

In his later work, Political Liberalism (1993), Rawls addressed the question of how a pluralistic society, composed of individuals with differing values and beliefs, could reach consensus on principles of justice. He introduced the idea of an "overlapping consensus," where people from different moral and religious backgrounds could agree on basic principles of justice, even if they disagreed on deeper ethical or metaphysical questions. Rawls' focus on public reason and political dialogue aimed to provide a framework for peaceful coexistence in diverse, democratic societies.

John Rawls' contributions to political philosophy, particularly his theory of justice, continue to shape contemporary debates about equality, fairness, and the role of government. His work remains a cornerstone of modern political theory, influencing discussions about human rights, social welfare, and the ethical foundations of liberal democracy. Rawls' vision of a just society, grounded in fairness and respect for individual liberties, continues to resonate with philosophers, policymakers, and activists seeking to address the challenges of inequality and social justice.

Gilles Deleuze (1925 – 1995 CE)

Gilles Deleuze was a French philosopher known for his radical rethinking of traditional metaphysics, philosophy of difference, and the relationship between philosophy and creativity. Born in Paris, Deleuze studied philosophy at the Sorbonne, where he was influenced by thinkers like Henri Bergson and Friedrich Nietzsche. His intellectual development took place during a time of post-World War II reconstruction, when French intellectual life was grappling with existentialism, Marxism, and structuralism. Deleuze's work stands out for its resistance to fixed categories and its exploration of the fluidity of being, knowledge, and experience.

Deleuze's early work, such as Difference and Repetition (1968), focused on the concept of difference and the rejection of the traditional philosophical emphasis on identity and sameness. He argued that Western philosophy, particularly through thinkers like Plato and Aristotle, had privileged stable, identical forms over processes of becoming and difference. For Deleuze, difference is not a deviation from an underlying identity but is fundamental to reality itself. This philosophy of difference rejects the idea of a fixed essence or identity underlying things, proposing instead that being is always dynamic and in flux, constantly producing new forms and structures.

Deleuze's collaboration with psychoanalyst Félix Guattari, particularly in Anti-Oedipus (1972) and A Thousand Plateaus (1980), further developed his critique of traditional structures, both philosophical and social. These works introduced the concept of "rhizomes" as a metaphor for non-hierarchical, decentralized structures of thought and society, in contrast to the "tree" model of knowledge that assumes a central origin and branching derivations. Deleuze and Guattari applied this idea to critique capitalist society, psychoanalysis, and political institutions, arguing that power structures operate through rigid hierarchies and controls that suppress the creative forces of desire and becoming.

A key concept in Deleuze's philosophy is the idea of "becoming," which emphasizes the process of transformation over static being. In A Thousand Plateaus, Deleuze and Guattari explored different forms of becoming, such as becoming-animal, becoming-woman, or becoming-imperceptible, as ways of escaping rigid social roles and identities. They viewed these processes as modes of liberation that challenge dominant structures of power and open up new possibilities for life and thought. This focus on becoming and multiplicity is central to Deleuze's anti-essentialist, anti-hierarchical approach to philosophy.

Deleuze's work has had a significant impact on fields such as literary theory, political philosophy, and cultural studies. His rejection of fixed categories and his emphasis on creativity, difference, and becoming have influenced post-structuralist thought and postmodernism. Deleuze's philosophical legacy continues to inspire debates about the nature of identity, knowledge, and power, and his ideas remain relevant in contemporary discussions about politics, culture, and the possibilities for radical change.

Frantz Fanon (1925 – 1961 CE)

Frantz Fanon was a Martinican psychiatrist, philosopher, and revolutionary thinker, best known for his analysis of colonialism and its psychological effects on both colonized and colonizers. Born in Fort-de-France, Martinique, Fanon studied in France, where he became a psychiatrist and was deeply influenced by existentialism and Marxism. His philosophical development took place during a time of decolonization movements in Africa, Asia, and the Caribbean, and Fanon became a leading voice in the struggle against colonial oppression. His work provided a psychological, political, and philosophical critique of colonialism and racism, offering a framework for understanding the dynamics of power, resistance, and liberation.

Fanon's most famous work, The Wretched of the Earth (1961), is a foundational text in postcolonial theory. In this book, Fanon argued that colonialism dehumanizes both the colonized and the colonizers, creating a relationship based on violence and domination. He emphasized that colonialism exploits the material resources of colonized peoples while imposing a psychological form of domination, in which the colonized internalize their own inferiority. Fanon believed that decolonization could not be achieved through peaceful means, as the violence of colonization must be met with a violent struggle for liberation. His analysis of violence and its role in decolonization became one of the most controversial aspects of his philosophy.

In Black Skin, White Masks (1952), Fanon explored the psychological effects of racism and colonialism on the individual. He examined how colonized peoples internalize the values of the colonizers, leading to a form of alienation from their own identity and culture. Fanon described this process as the adoption of a "white mask," in which the colonized person attempts to conform to the standards and expectations of the colonizer. This psychological alienation, according to Fanon, results in deep feelings of inferiority and self-hatred among the colonized. Drawing on psychoanalysis, particularly the ideas of Freud and Lacan, Fanon analyzed the psychological dimensions of racial oppression.

Fanon was also deeply concerned with the role of culture in the decolonization process. He believed that the recovery and affirmation of indigenous cultures were essential to the liberation of colonized peoples. In The Wretched of the Earth, he argued that the colonized must reject the cultural impositions of the colonizer and rediscover their own cultural traditions as a source of strength and identity. Fanon saw culture as a dynamic force, evolving in response to historical conditions, and emphasized the importance of creativity and cultural production in the struggle for freedom.

Frantz Fanon's work has had a lasting impact on postcolonial studies, critical race theory, and revolutionary politics. His analysis of the psychological, cultural, and political dimensions of colonialism continues to resonate with scholars and activists engaged in struggles against racism, imperialism, and oppression. Fanon's work remains a powerful critique of colonialism's lasting effects and a call for radical political and social transformation.

Michel Foucault (1926 – 1984 CE)

Michel Foucault was a French philosopher and historian whose work focused on the relationships between power, knowledge, and social institutions. Born in Poitiers, France, Foucault was educated at the École Normale Supérieure in Paris, where he became associated with the structuralist and post-structuralist movements. His intellectual development took place during a period of political and social upheaval in France, particularly during the student protests of 1968. Foucault's work challenged traditional understandings of power and authority, offering a new way of thinking about how knowledge and power are intertwined in the shaping of human behavior and social structures.

Foucault's early work, such as Madness and Civilization (1961), examined the history of mental illness and the treatment of the insane in Western society. He argued that the concept of madness is not an objective fact but a social construct that has changed over time in response to shifts in power and knowledge. Foucault traced the ways in which the treatment of the insane evolved from medieval times, when madness was seen as a form of divine inspiration or punishment, to the modern era, when it became a medical condition to be controlled and institutionalized. This analysis laid the groundwork for Foucault's broader critique of the ways in which power operates through institutions and discourses.

One of Foucault's most influential concepts is the idea of "biopower," which he introduced in The History of Sexuality (1976). Biopower refers to the ways in which modern states exert control over the bodies and lives of individuals, particularly through the regulation of sexuality, reproduction, and health. Foucault argued that, in modern societies, power is exercised not primarily through laws or force but through the management of life itself, including the disciplining of bodies and the normalization of behaviors. This focus on the body and its regulation marked a shift from traditional theories of power, which had emphasized legal and political structures.

Foucault's work on disciplinary power, particularly in Discipline and Punish (1975), explored how modern institutions such as prisons, schools, and hospitals function as mechanisms of control and surveillance. He argued that the shift from public executions and corporal punishment to incarceration and surveillance marked a fundamental transformation in the exercise of power. In modern societies, power operates not through direct violence but through the internalization of norms and the regulation of behavior. Foucault's analysis of surveillance, particularly the concept of the "panopticon," has had a profound influence on discussions of modern society, power, and control.

Michel Foucault's work continues to shape debates in philosophy, political theory, and cultural studies. His insights into the nature of power, knowledge, and the body have influenced fields as diverse as sociology, gender studies, and critical theory. Foucault's philosophy remains central to contemporary discussions about authority, governance, and the ways in which social institutions shape human identity and behavior.

Thich Nhat Hanh (1926 – 2022 CE)

Thich Nhat Hanh was a Vietnamese Zen Buddhist monk, peace activist, and prolific author, renowned for his teachings on mindfulness, compassion, and nonviolent conflict resolution. Born in Quang Ngai Province, Vietnam, Nhat Hanh entered the monastery at the age of 16 and became a central figure in the development of socially engaged Buddhism. His philosophy was shaped by the turmoil of the Vietnam War, during which he advocated for peace and reconciliation. Nhat Hanh's blend of traditional Buddhist teachings with modern ideas on social justice and peace resonated globally, influencing both Eastern and Western audiences.

Nhat Hanh is best known for his teachings on mindfulness, which he presented as a means of cultivating inner peace and awareness in everyday life. In his writings, including The Miracle of Mindfulness (1975), he emphasized the importance of being fully present in the moment, whether eating, walking, or breathing. His approach to mindfulness is deeply rooted in Buddhist principles of non-attachment and interdependence, but he adapted these teachings for modern contexts, making them accessible to lay practitioners and those from non-Buddhist backgrounds. For Nhat Hanh, mindfulness was not only a personal practice but also a way to create a more peaceful and compassionate society.

A key element of Nhat Hanh's philosophy is the concept of "interbeing," which refers to the interconnectedness of all things. He taught that nothing exists independently and that all phenomena are interrelated, a view grounded in the Buddhist doctrine of dependent origination. This understanding of interbeing encourages a deep sense of responsibility for the well-being of others and the planet. Nhat Hanh used this concept to address social and environmental issues, arguing that mindfulness and compassion must extend beyond the individual to encompass society and the environment. His ecological awareness and advocacy for global peace positioned him as a leading voice in both spiritual and activist circles.

Thich Nhat Hanh's commitment to nonviolence and peace activism was evident throughout his life. During the Vietnam War, he founded the "School of Youth for Social Services," which provided aid to war victims, and worked tirelessly for reconciliation between the warring factions. His philosophy of nonviolent resistance was influenced by both Buddhist teachings and figures like Mahatma Gandhi and Martin Luther King Jr., whom he met in 1966. Exiled from Vietnam for his peace efforts, Nhat Hanh continued to advocate for global peace and conflict resolution, emphasizing that peace must begin within individuals through mindfulness and compassion.

Nhat Hanh's legacy as a teacher and activist continues to inspire millions worldwide. His integration of mindfulness with social engagement, environmentalism, and peace activism has had a lasting impact on contemporary Buddhism and global peace movements. His teachings on mindfulness, interbeing, and compassionate living remain central to modern spiritual practice and continue to guide individuals seeking a path of peace, awareness, and social justice.

Noam Chomsky (1928 – present)

Noam Chomsky is an American linguist, cognitive scientist, philosopher, and political activist, widely regarded as one of the most influential intellectuals of the 20th and 21st centuries. Born in Philadelphia, Pennsylvania, Chomsky's early interest in language and philosophy led him to study at the University of Pennsylvania, where he developed his groundbreaking theories in linguistics. His work in linguistics, particularly his theory of generative grammar, revolutionized the field and laid the foundation for modern cognitive science. Chomsky's political activism, particularly his critiques of U.S. foreign policy and mass media, also became central to his intellectual identity.

Chomsky's most famous contribution to linguistics is his theory of generative grammar, introduced in Syntactic Structures (1957). He argued that humans possess an innate linguistic ability, a "universal grammar" shared by all languages. According to Chomsky, the human brain is hardwired with a set of grammatical principles that enable us to generate and understand an infinite number of sentences. This theory challenged the prevailing behaviorist view, which held that language was acquired through conditioning and learning. Chomsky's work shifted the focus of linguistics from surface-level language patterns to the deep, underlying structures of language.

In addition to his contributions to linguistics, Chomsky is renowned for his political philosophy, particularly his critiques of U.S. imperialism and corporate influence in the media. In works like Manufacturing Consent (1988), co-authored with Edward S. Herman, Chomsky argued that the mass media serves the interests of powerful elites by shaping public opinion and limiting dissent. He introduced the concept of the "propaganda model," which posits that media organizations, driven by corporate interests, systematically filter information in ways that maintain the status quo. Chomsky's analysis of media and power structures remains influential in discussions of democracy, freedom of speech, and corporate control of information.

Chomsky's political activism has also focused on U.S. foreign policy, particularly its interventions in Latin America, Southeast Asia, and the Middle East. In works such as Hegemony or Survival (2003), Chomsky argued that the U.S. government's pursuit of global dominance has led to widespread suffering and instability. He has been a vocal critic of both Republican and Democratic administrations, condemning their involvement in covert operations, regime changes, and military interventions. Chomsky's anti-imperialist stance and defense of human rights have made him a leading figure in left-wing political thought and activism.

Noam Chomsky's intellectual legacy spans multiple fields, from linguistics to political philosophy. His theory of generative grammar transformed our understanding of language and cognition, while his critiques of U.S. imperialism and mass media have shaped political discourse for decades. Chomsky remains an influential voice in both academic and political spheres, continuing to challenge established power structures and advocating for social justice, human rights, and intellectual freedom.

Alasdair MacIntyre (1929 – present)

Alasdair MacIntyre is a Scottish philosopher known for his work in moral and political philosophy, particularly his critique of modernity and his revival of Aristotelian ethics. Born in Glasgow, Scotland, MacIntyre studied at the University of London and Oxford University, where he was initially influenced by Marxism, existentialism, and Christian thought. Over the course of his career, he became increasingly critical of contemporary moral philosophy, particularly the dominance of liberal individualism and its focus on subjective moral choice. MacIntyre's work is characterized by its call for a return to virtue ethics, rooted in the classical tradition of Aristotle and Thomas Aquinas.

MacIntyre's most influential work, After Virtue (1981), is a critique of modern moral philosophy and an argument for the revival of Aristotelian ethics. In this book, MacIntyre argues that the moral framework of modernity is fragmented and incoherent, having lost its connection to a shared understanding of human purpose or telos. He contends that modern ethical systems, such as utilitarianism and deontology, are inadequate because they fail to provide a coherent account of human flourishing. MacIntyre's solution is a return to virtue ethics, where moral evaluation is grounded in the cultivation of virtues and the pursuit of the common good within a community.

A central theme in MacIntyre's philosophy is his critique of liberal individualism. He argues that the modern emphasis on individual autonomy and subjective choice has led to a breakdown in moral discourse. Without a shared conception of the good life, moral debates become arbitrary and disconnected from any objective standards. MacIntyre contrasts this with the Aristotelian tradition, which views human beings as fundamentally social creatures whose flourishing is tied to their participation in a community and the cultivation of virtues. For MacIntyre, virtues such as justice, courage, and wisdom are essential for achieving the good life, both for individuals and for society as a whole.

MacIntyre's work also emphasizes the importance of tradition in moral reasoning. He argues that moral knowledge is not derived from abstract principles but is developed within particular historical and cultural traditions. In Whose Justice? Which Rationality? (1988), MacIntyre explores how different traditions—such as Aristotelian, Thomistic, and Enlightenment thought—offer competing conceptions of justice and rationality. He contends that moral progress can only occur within a living tradition that provides the context for ethical inquiry and development. This emphasis on tradition challenges the modern Enlightenment project of universal, context-independent moral reasoning.

Alasdair MacIntyre's critique of modernity and his defense of virtue ethics have had a profound influence on contemporary moral and political philosophy. His work has inspired a renewed interest in Aristotelian ethics and has contributed to ongoing debates about the role of community, tradition, and virtue in moral life. MacIntyre's call for a return to a more integrated and holistic approach to ethics continues to resonate with scholars and thinkers seeking alternatives to the fragmented moral landscape of modernity.

Jacques Derrida (1930 – 2004 CE)

Jacques Derrida was a French philosopher born in Algiers, then a part of French Algeria. He became one of the most influential figures in 20th-century continental philosophy, particularly known for founding the school of thought known as deconstruction. Derrida's philosophical work arose in the context of post-World War II intellectual life in France, which saw a resurgence of interest in structuralism, phenomenology, and existentialism. He studied under figures like Michel Foucault and Louis Althusser, but his work took a different trajectory, critiquing the structures of language and meaning.

Deconstruction, Derrida's most famous contribution, is a method of philosophical analysis that seeks to reveal the inherent contradictions in texts and ideas. Derrida argued that language is inherently unstable and that meanings are never fixed. He proposed that texts contain internal tensions and ambiguities that undermine their apparent coherence. By analyzing these contradictions, deconstruction shows how meaning is always deferred and never fully graspable. This concept, called "différance," suggests that meaning is produced through the play of differences between words rather than through clear definitions.

Derrida's philosophy also involved a critique of Western metaphysics, particularly its reliance on binary oppositions, such as presence/absence, speech/writing, and reason/emotion. He argued that these oppositions privilege one term over the other, creating hierarchies that shape thought and culture. Deconstruction seeks to subvert these hierarchies by showing that the supposedly privileged term is dependent on the suppressed term. For instance, Derrida challenged the idea that speech is primary and writing is secondary, arguing that writing is not merely a derivative form of communication but an integral part of how language operates.

Another central theme in Derrida's work is his critique of the concept of "logocentrism," the belief that there is a fundamental, unchanging truth or meaning underlying language and thought. Derrida argued that this belief in a stable, foundational truth is a fallacy because all meaning is contingent and shaped by historical and cultural contexts. In works like Of Grammatology, Derrida demonstrated how texts, even those that appear to convey clear meanings, are subject to endless interpretation and reinterpretation, making definitive readings impossible.

Derrida's influence extended far beyond philosophy, impacting fields like literary theory, legal studies, and architecture. His work, though often seen as difficult and controversial, opened up new ways of thinking about language, meaning, and power. Deconstruction became a central methodology in critical theory, and Derrida's critiques of structures of meaning continue to resonate in debates about politics, ethics, and culture.

Michel Serres (1930 – 2019 CE)

Michel Serres was a French philosopher and historian of science known for his interdisciplinary approach, blending science, literature, and philosophy. Born in Agen, France, Serres was educated at the École Normale Supérieure and later became a professor at the Sorbonne. His early work was influenced by structuralism, but he soon diverged from it, forging his own path that embraced complexity, fluidity, and the interconnectedness of knowledge. In post-World War II France, where science and the humanities were often seen as separate, Serres sought to build bridges between these fields, creating a unique philosophy of communication and networks.

Serres' philosophy is perhaps best captured in his concept of "messenger" or "the parasite," which he explores in works like The Parasite (1980). The term "parasite" in Serres' work refers to both an actual parasite and a metaphorical one, a figure who disrupts and mediates communication. He argued that all communication, whether in nature, society, or science, involves a third party—a mediator—who changes the nature of the message. This mediation is not just a disturbance but a necessary part of any system, applying to everything from thermodynamics to social relations and suggesting that disruption and noise are intrinsic to the flow of information and meaning.

A central theme in Serres' philosophy is the idea of "relation" and "complexity." He believed that the world is not composed of isolated objects but of relationships between things, challenging traditional notions of knowledge that sought to categorize and simplify. In works like Hermes (1969-1980) and The Natural Contract (1990), Serres emphasized the importance of interconnections—between nature and culture, and between the sciences and the humanities—while criticizing reductive approaches that fail to account for the complexity of the world.

Serres was also a pioneer in environmental philosophy, addressing the relationship between humans and nature long before it became a widespread concern in the humanities. In The Natural Contract, he proposed that humanity should rethink its relationship with the Earth by entering into a "contract" with nature, akin to Rousseau's social contract. He argued that humans have treated the Earth as an object to be exploited and called for a shift toward a more symbiotic and responsible relationship.

Michel Serres' influence extended across multiple disciplines, including philosophy, science, literature, and environmental studies. His unique ability to weave together disparate fields into a coherent vision of complexity and relationship has had a lasting impact on how scholars approach the intersections between science, culture, and the environment. His emphasis on mediation, complexity, and the importance of environmental ethics remains highly relevant in contemporary philosophical discourse.

Richard Rorty (1931 – 2007 CE)

Richard Rorty was an American philosopher known for his contributions to pragmatism and his critique of traditional philosophy. Born in New York City, Rorty studied at the University of Chicago and Yale University, where he became deeply influenced by the American pragmatist tradition, particularly the works of John Dewey, William James, and Charles Sanders Peirce. Rorty's intellectual context emerged during the post-World War II era, when analytic philosophy was dominant in the United States. However, Rorty's philosophy diverged from this tradition, advocating for a more pluralistic, anti-essentialist approach to philosophical inquiry.

Rorty's most influential work, Philosophy and the Mirror of Nature (1979), challenged the traditional view of philosophy as a discipline that aims to discover objective truths about the world. He rejected the idea that philosophy could serve as a "mirror" of reality, offering a definitive, objective account of the world's structure. Instead, Rorty argued that knowledge is contingent, shaped by historical and cultural contexts, and that philosophical problems are often the result of misguided attempts to find universal foundations for knowledge. His approach was influenced by pragmatism, which emphasizes the practical consequences of ideas and the contingent nature of truth.

A key element of Rorty's philosophy is his rejection of the "correspondence theory of truth," which holds that statements are true if they correspond to an independent reality. Rorty argued that truth is not about accurately representing the world but about what works in practice for a given community. This led to his famous statement that truth is "what our peers let us get away with saying." For Rorty, philosophy should not be concerned with discovering absolute truths but with fostering conversation and solidarity within communities. This rejection of foundationalism and essentialism placed Rorty in opposition to traditional analytic philosophy, but it also connected him to the broader tradition of pragmatism.

Rorty was also known for his critique of the idea that philosophy could provide a neutral, objective ground for political or ethical principles. In works like Contingency, Irony, and Solidarity (1989), he argued that liberal democratic societies do not need universal foundations for justice or morality. Instead, he advocated for a form of liberalism based on historical contingency and cultural pluralism. Rorty believed that societies should focus on creating conditions for human solidarity and reducing cruelty, rather than seeking metaphysical or epistemological justifications for their values. His political thought emphasized the importance of narrative, literature, and shared experiences in building solidarity.

Richard Rorty's work had a profound impact on philosophy, particularly in his rejection of traditional metaphysical and epistemological concerns. His pragmatic approach, with its emphasis on conversation, contingency, and solidarity, challenged the foundations of modern philosophy and offered a vision of intellectual life grounded in pluralism and democratic values. Rorty remains an influential figure in debates about the role of philosophy in public life and the nature of truth and knowledge.

Charles Taylor (1931 – present)

Charles Taylor is a Canadian philosopher whose work has spanned political philosophy, ethics, and the philosophy of social science. Born in Montreal, Quebec, Taylor studied at McGill University and later at Oxford as a Rhodes Scholar, where he was influenced by figures like Isaiah Berlin and Ludwig Wittgenstein. His intellectual development took place during a time when analytic philosophy was dominant, but Taylor's work was characterized by its engagement with both analytic and continental traditions. He sought to address questions of human identity, political theory, and modernity, emphasizing the importance of cultural and historical contexts in shaping human experience.

Taylor's most influential work, Sources of the Self (1989), explores the development of modern notions of identity and the self. In this book, Taylor traces the history of Western conceptions of the self, from ancient Greek philosophy to modernity, arguing that the modern sense of individual identity is rooted in a complex interplay of cultural, religious, and philosophical traditions. He contends that the modern self is shaped by what he calls "moral sources"—the ethical frameworks and values that individuals draw upon to make sense of their lives. Taylor's exploration of the self is deeply connected to his broader interest in how culture and history shape human experience.

A central theme in Taylor's philosophy is his critique of what he calls the "disenchantment" of the modern world. In A Secular Age (2007), Taylor examines the shift from a world in which belief in God and the supernatural was taken for granted to one in which secularism and disenchantment dominate. He argues that modernity has led to a loss of meaning and a narrowing of human experience, as traditional sources of spiritual and communal life have been replaced by individualism and instrumental reason. However, Taylor does not advocate a return to pre-modern religious worldviews; instead, he seeks to explore new ways of finding meaning in a secular, pluralistic world.

Taylor is also a prominent figure in political philosophy, particularly in his work on multiculturalism and the politics of recognition. In Multiculturalism: Examining the Politics of Recognition (1994), he argues that modern liberal societies must recognize the diverse cultural identities of their citizens. Taylor contends that individual identity is deeply shaped by culture, and that societies must allow for the expression of different cultural identities if they are to achieve justice and equality. His work on the politics of recognition has been influential in debates about multiculturalism, identity politics, and the rights of minority groups in liberal democracies.

Charles Taylor's contributions to philosophy have had a lasting impact on discussions of modernity, identity, and politics. His emphasis on the role of culture and history in shaping human experience challenges the more abstract, individualistic approaches of much modern philosophy. Taylor's work continues to influence debates about the nature of the self, the meaning of secularism, and the challenges of multiculturalism in contemporary societies.

Amartya Sen (1933 – present)

Amartya Sen is an Indian economist and philosopher who has made significant contributions to welfare economics, development studies, and social justice theory. Born in Santiniketan, India, Sen was educated at Presidency College in Calcutta and later at Trinity College, Cambridge, where he developed a deep interest in economics and philosophy. Sen's intellectual journey unfolded in the context of post-colonial India, where issues of poverty, inequality, and human development were pressing concerns. His work is characterized by a commitment to improving the lives of the world's poorest people through both economic analysis and moral reasoning.

Sen is perhaps best known for his capability approach, introduced in his book Development as Freedom (1999). This framework shifts the focus of development economics from income and wealth to individual freedoms and capabilities. According to Sen, traditional economic measures like Gross Domestic Product (GDP) are inadequate indicators of human well-being because they fail to capture whether people have the real freedoms necessary to lead lives they value. Instead, Sen argues that development should be understood in terms of expanding individuals' capabilities—their opportunities to achieve well-being, participate in society, and exercise autonomy. This approach has had a profound impact on international development policy, including the United Nations Human Development Index (HDI).

Sen's work also engages deeply with issues of justice, particularly through his critique of utilitarianism and the dominant models of distributive justice. In his book The Idea of Justice (2009), Sen offers a more pragmatic, comparative approach to justice than that of John Rawls. Rather than seeking ideal principles of justice that are universally applicable, Sen advocates for addressing injustices through concrete comparisons of different societal arrangements. His approach is rooted in public reasoning and the idea that justice is not a final state to be achieved but an ongoing process of reducing injustices wherever they are found. Sen's focus on real-world applications and public participation in discussions of justice sets him apart from more abstract theories of justice.

Sen is also a vocal advocate for gender equality and the rights of women, particularly in the context of developing countries. He famously coined the term "missing women" to describe the demographic imbalance caused by gender discrimination in countries like India and China. His analysis revealed that millions of women were "missing" due to sex-selective abortions, infanticide, and unequal access to healthcare and nutrition. Sen's work on gender inequality has brought attention to the intersection of economic development, cultural practices, and human rights, highlighting the need for policies that address these complex factors.

Amartya Sen's interdisciplinary approach, blending economics, philosophy, and social policy, has had a transformative impact on how we think about development, justice, and human well-being. His capability approach continues to shape global discussions on poverty, inequality, and freedom, making him one of the most influential thinkers in contemporary social and economic philosophy.

Richard Swinburne (1934 – present)

Richard Swinburne is a British philosopher of religion known for his rigorous defense of theism and Christian theology through the application of analytic philosophy. Born in Smethwick, England, Swinburne was educated at Exeter College, Oxford, and has spent much of his academic career teaching at universities such as the University of Oxford. His work arose in a context where analytic philosophy was often secular, focusing on logic, language, and empiricism. Swinburne, however, used these tools to argue for the rationality of religious belief, particularly the existence of God, contributing to a resurgence of interest in the philosophy of religion.

Swinburne's most significant contribution is his cumulative case argument for theism. In his trilogy—The Coherence of Theism (1977), The Existence of God (1979), and Faith and Reason (1981)—he systematically defends belief in God using principles of probability and inductive reasoning. He argues that various classical arguments for God's existence, such as the cosmological, teleological, and moral arguments, all provide evidence that, when combined, make the existence of God highly probable. Swinburne asserts that although no single argument may conclusively prove theism, the cumulative effect of all these arguments together presents a strong case for belief in God.

One of Swinburne's most innovative contributions is his application of Bayesian probability to arguments for the existence of God. In The Existence of God, he employs Bayesian probability to assess how the existence of the universe, its fine-tuning for life, and human experiences like religious phenomena increase the likelihood of theism over naturalism. He argues that the coherence and explanatory power of theism provide a better explanation for the existence of the universe and its intricate order than atheistic accounts. This probabilistic framework sets his work apart from earlier, more traditional approaches to natural theology.

Swinburne is also known for defending the coherence of core Christian doctrines, such as the Trinity and the Incarnation. In The Christian God (1994), he addresses the intellectual challenges posed by these doctrines and uses analytic philosophy to demonstrate their logical consistency. He argues that Christian beliefs, when examined philosophically, are compatible with reason, significantly impacting contemporary discussions about faith and reason within analytic philosophy.

In addition to his work on theism, Swinburne has contributed to debates in the philosophy of mind, particularly in relation to dualism. In The Evolution of the Soul (1986), he defends substance dualism, arguing that humans consist of both a physical body and an immaterial soul. Swinburne maintains that consciousness and personal identity cannot be fully explained by physical processes alone, positioning him as a leading voice in discussions about the nature of consciousness and the human person.

Sarah Kofman (1934 – 1994 CE)

Sarah Kofman was a French philosopher and literary critic whose work intersected with psychoanalysis, feminist theory, and deconstruction. Born in Paris to a Jewish family, Kofman's early life was marked by the trauma of World War II, during which her father was arrested and deported to Auschwitz, where he was killed. Kofman's experiences with loss and displacement would later influence her philosophical inquiries, particularly her focus on identity, trauma, and the relationship between language and power. She studied under Jacques Derrida and was heavily influenced by his deconstructive approach, which shaped much of her own intellectual trajectory.

Kofman's work is notable for its deep engagement with the writings of Friedrich Nietzsche and Sigmund Freud. In Nietzsche and Metaphor (1983), Kofman examined Nietzsche's use of language, particularly his reliance on metaphor, to critique the foundations of Western metaphysics. She argued that Nietzsche's philosophical project sought to dismantle traditional metaphysical binaries, such as truth and falsity, through a style of writing that embraced ambiguity and instability. Kofman's analysis of Nietzsche reflected her broader interest in how language constructs and deconstructs meaning, a theme she would continue to explore in her work on psychoanalysis and feminism.

Psychoanalysis was another central focus of Kofman's work, particularly in her study of Freud. In The Enigma of Woman (1985), Kofman offered a feminist reading of Freud, exploring his theories of femininity and sexuality. While Kofman was critical of Freud's often reductive and patriarchal views on women, she also sought to uncover the complexities and contradictions within his writings. She argued that Freud's theories reveal deeper uncertainties about gender and desire, suggesting that psychoanalysis, when critically examined, could provide insights into the instability of gender identity. Kofman's work in this area contributed to the growing body of feminist psychoanalytic theory.

Kofman was also known for her engagement with the concept of the "philosophical subject," particularly in relation to questions of identity and difference. In Smothered Words (1998), a reflection on the Holocaust and her own experiences of loss, Kofman explored the limits of language in representing trauma. She questioned the ability of philosophy to adequately address the horrors of history, arguing that certain experiences, such as the Holocaust, resist rational explanation or representation. Kofman's work in this area aligned her with post-structuralist thinkers who critiqued the Enlightenment's faith in reason and progress.

Throughout her career, Kofman maintained a critical stance toward traditional philosophical concepts, using deconstruction and psychoanalysis to challenge fixed notions of identity, language, and power. Her work continues to be influential in feminist philosophy, literary theory, and post-structuralism. Kofman's tragic death by suicide in 1994 marked the loss of a deeply original thinker whose contributions to philosophy remain significant.

Alain Badiou (1937 – present)

Alain Badiou is a contemporary French philosopher known for his work on ontology, politics, and mathematics. Born in Rabat, Morocco, Badiou was educated at the prestigious École Normale Supérieure in Paris, where he studied under prominent figures such as Louis Althusser. Badiou's philosophical development took place during the politically charged atmosphere of post-war France, particularly in the context of May 1968's student uprisings. These events, alongside his engagement with Marxism and Maoism, profoundly shaped his thinking on politics and revolution. His work ambitiously seeks to reconcile politics, mathematics, and metaphysics.

Badiou's most significant philosophical contribution is his theory of the "event," elaborated in Being and Event (1988). In this work, Badiou rethinks the relationship between being and becoming, drawing on set theory from mathematics to formulate his ontology. He argues that reality consists of multiplicities within a structured order, or "situation," and that an event occurs when something radically new emerges, disrupting this order and revealing previously unseen possibilities. For Badiou, events such as revolutions or scientific discoveries are moments of profound change that provide opportunities for individuals to commit to new truths.

Badiou's political philosophy is deeply connected to his theory of the event. He advocates for revolutionary politics that create new possibilities for collective life, rather than merely reforming existing systems. Drawing on his Marxist background, Badiou moves beyond traditional class analysis to focus on the transformative potential of political events. In works like The Communist Hypothesis (2009), he defends communism as an emancipatory project, arguing that despite the failures of 20th-century communism, the ideas of collective equality and justice remain vital goals. He critiques the liberal-democratic order as complacent and incapable of generating meaningful change.

Another key aspect of Badiou's philosophy is his emphasis on mathematics in understanding ontology. Drawing heavily on set theory, particularly the work of Paul Cohen, he argues that mathematics provides the most accurate description of being as multiplicity. For Badiou, mathematics is not simply a tool for understanding the physical world but is foundational to ontology itself. His insistence on the primacy of mathematics as a philosophical discipline sets him apart from other contemporary thinkers, marking a unique fusion of metaphysical inquiry and mathematical formalism.

Alain Badiou's work has been influential in fields ranging from political theory to aesthetics and metaphysics. His ideas about the event, the role of mathematics in ontology, and his commitment to revolutionary politics continue to inspire debates within contemporary philosophy. Badiou remains a provocative and influential figure, challenging traditional assumptions while offering new ways of thinking about change, truth, and collective action.

Quentin Skinner (1940 – present)

Quentin Skinner is a British intellectual historian and philosopher, best known for his contributions to the history of political thought and his development of the "Cambridge School" of intellectual history. Born in Oldham, England, Skinner was educated at Gonville and Caius College, Cambridge, where he later became a prominent professor. His work emerged in post-World War II Britain, where the study of political philosophy was dominated by abstract, theoretical approaches. Skinner sought to ground political thought in its historical context, emphasizing the importance of understanding the language and intentions of political actors in their own time.

Skinner's methodological approach, articulated in works such as The Foundations of Modern Political Thought (1978), focuses on the idea that political theories cannot be properly understood without examining the historical context in which they were produced. He argues that political thinkers are not abstract theorists but participants in political debates who use language strategically to advance their positions. For Skinner, political philosophy must be studied as a form of political action, with attention to the historical circumstances, institutions, and discourses that shape it. This perspective has become a hallmark of the Cambridge School.

One of Skinner's major contributions is his work on the concept of liberty, particularly in Renaissance and early modern political thought. In Liberty Before Liberalism (1998), Skinner challenges the liberal understanding of freedom as non-interference, associated with thinkers like John Locke and Isaiah Berlin. Instead, he revives the republican tradition of liberty, which defines freedom as non-domination. Rooted in Renaissance republican writings such as those of Machiavelli, this view holds that liberty arises not when individuals are merely left alone by the state, but when they are protected from arbitrary power. Skinner's work has sparked renewed interest in republican liberty and its relevance to contemporary political theory.

Skinner has also contributed significant studies of early modern thinkers, particularly Thomas Hobbes and Niccolò Machiavelli. His analysis of Hobbes challenges the traditional view of him as a proponent of authoritarianism, showing that Hobbes' philosophy contains nuanced ideas about political obligation and consent. Similarly, Skinner's work on Machiavelli has helped rehabilitate the Florentine thinker, framing his realism as a defense of republican liberty rather than mere power politics.

Quentin Skinner's historical approach to political philosophy has transformed the field, encouraging scholars to engage with political texts in their historical contexts rather than treating them as abstract, timeless theories. His work continues to shape debates about political theory, historiography, and the nature of liberty in both historical and contemporary contexts.

Daniel Dennett (1942 - Present)

Daniel Dennett was born on March 28, 1942, in Boston, Massachusetts. He studied philosophy at Harvard University, earning his bachelor's degree in 1963, and completed his doctorate at Oxford University in 1965 under Gilbert Ryle, an influential figure in the philosophy of mind. Dennett's academic work has focused on consciousness, cognitive science, free will, and evolutionary biology, bridging philosophy with scientific inquiry. Over his long career, he has taught at several institutions and is currently a professor at Tufts University, where he continues to influence philosophical and scientific communities.

Dennett's theories are rooted in his rejection of Cartesian dualism, the idea that the mind and body are separate. Instead, he advocates for a materialist understanding of consciousness, arguing that the mind can be fully explained by physical brain processes. This perspective emerged alongside mid-20th-century advancements in neuroscience and cognitive psychology, which challenged metaphysical views of consciousness. By the 1960s and 1970s, Dennett embraced the growing movement toward understanding the brain through biological and computational models, a view that underpins much of his work.

One of Dennett's most notable contributions is his theory of consciousness, detailed in Consciousness Explained (1991). He challenges the idea of a "Cartesian Theater," where conscious experiences converge, proposing instead the "multiple drafts" model. In this framework, mental processes occur simultaneously in different brain regions without a single point of convergence. Dennett demystifies consciousness, presenting it as a collection of mental events across neural circuits, making it accessible to scientific investigation rather than abstract metaphysical speculation.

Dennett's compatibilist view of free will, elaborated in Freedom Evolves (2003), argues that free will can exist in a deterministic universe. He suggests that evolution has endowed humans with complex decision-making abilities, allowing for meaningful choices within deterministic frameworks. By redefining free will as a natural phenomenon arising from biological complexity, Dennett offers a middle ground that challenges the traditional free will versus determinism binary, shaping contemporary discussions on moral responsibility.

In Breaking the Spell (2006), Dennett applies evolutionary psychology to examine why humans developed religious systems. He argues that religion is a byproduct of evolutionary mechanisms that helped early humans survive and cooperate as social beings. By advocating for the objective, scientific study of religion, Dennett has sparked debates within the philosophy of religion. His naturalistic approach has impacted philosophy and psychology while contributing to cultural discussions on science, morality, and belief systems.

Julia Kristeva (1941 – present)

Julia Kristeva is a Bulgarian-French philosopher, psychoanalyst, and literary critic, known for her work on language, subjectivity, and the intersection of psychoanalysis with feminist theory. Born in Sliven, Bulgaria, Kristeva moved to France in the mid-1960s to study linguistics at the University of Paris, where she became associated with prominent intellectuals such as Roland Barthes, Michel Foucault, and Jacques Lacan. Her intellectual career unfolded in the context of French structuralism and post-structuralism, and she became an influential figure in feminist philosophy, psychoanalytic theory, and semiotics.

Kristeva's work is perhaps best known for her theory of abjection, introduced in Powers of Horror (1980). Abjection refers to the psychological process by which individuals establish boundaries between themselves and what they perceive as impure or threatening, such as bodily fluids, waste, or death. Kristeva argues that abjection plays a fundamental role in shaping human identity, as it helps define the self in opposition to what is considered "other." This process is central to both individual psychology and the construction of cultural norms, particularly those related to purity and exclusion. Her theory of abjection has significantly influenced feminist theory, particularly in its exploration of the body and its relation to social structures.

Another major aspect of Kristeva's philosophy is her exploration of language and semiotics, particularly her development of the concept of the "semiotic" as distinct from the "symbolic." In Revolution in Poetic Language (1974), Kristeva argues that language operates on two levels: the symbolic, referring to the structured, rule-governed aspect of language that relates to social order, and the semiotic, the pre-linguistic, bodily, and emotional dimension of communication. The semiotic, often associated with the maternal body, is typically repressed in favor of the symbolic order, but Kristeva contends that it is essential to creative expression and subject formation.

Kristeva's contributions to feminist theory are central to her intellectual legacy. In The Feminine and the Sacred (2000), she explores the role of motherhood and maternity in shaping female subjectivity, arguing that feminist critiques of patriarchy often overlook the complexity of the maternal experience. Kristeva seeks to reconcile feminist thought with psychoanalysis, emphasizing that motherhood, far from being a source of oppression, can be a site of creativity and transformation. Her nuanced understanding of gender, identity, and the body has influenced both feminist philosophy and psychoanalytic theory, offering new perspectives on the relationship between the personal and the political.

In addition to her work on abjection and semiotics, Kristeva has extensively examined the intersection of psychoanalysis and literature, analyzing writers such as Dostoevsky, Proust, and Céline. Using psychoanalytic concepts, she explores themes of identity, trauma, and the unconscious in literary texts. Her interdisciplinary approach, combining philosophy, psychoanalysis, and literary criticism, has established her as a leading figure in post-structuralist and feminist theory. Julia Kristeva's work continues to inspire debates on language, identity, and gender.

Giorgio Agamben (1942 – present)

Giorgio Agamben is an Italian philosopher known for his work on political philosophy, theology, and biopolitics. Born in Rome, Agamben studied law and philosophy at the University of Rome and later became associated with prominent thinkers such as Martin Heidegger and Hannah Arendt. His intellectual development occurred in post-war Europe, where debates about sovereignty, state power, and human rights were central to political thought. Agamben's work has influenced fields ranging from legal theory to critical theory, with his exploration of "bare life" and its implications for modern political systems being particularly notable.

Agamben's most significant contribution to political philosophy is his theory of "biopolitics," elaborated in Homo Sacer: Sovereign Power and Bare Life (1995). Building on Michel Foucault's work, Agamben examines how modern states exert control over individuals by reducing them to "bare life"—existence stripped of political significance and reduced to mere biology. He argues that the distinction between political life (bios) and bare life (zoe) has been foundational to Western political systems and that modern states increasingly govern through the management of life itself. For Agamben, the concentration camp serves as the ultimate paradigm of this biopolitical order, where individuals are subjected to total state control.

A central concept in Agamben's philosophy is the "state of exception," referring to the suspension of law in the name of protecting the state. He argues that the state of exception, once seen as a temporary measure during crises, has become a permanent feature of modern governance. In works like State of Exception (2003), he traces how governments invoke emergency powers to bypass legal norms and exert unchecked authority. Agamben links this phenomenon to biopolitical control, where managing life and death becomes central to sovereign power. His critique of this dynamic resonates with concerns about authoritarianism, surveillance, and human rights.

Agamben's engagement with theology is also central to his work, particularly his analysis of the relationship between religion and politics. In The Kingdom and the Glory (2007), he explores the Christian concept of the "economy" of salvation and its influence on political and economic systems. He argues that theological concepts, such as the division between God's kingdom and government, have profoundly shaped Western ideas of sovereignty and authority. This exploration reveals the continuity between religious and secular forms of power, showing how theological frameworks underpin modern political structures.

Giorgio Agamben's interdisciplinary approach, combining political philosophy, theology, and legal theory, has made him a leading figure in contemporary political thought. His analysis of biopolitics, sovereignty, and the state of exception continues to inform debates about power, law, and human rights, offering critical insights into the intersection of politics, life, and authority in modern society.

Aung San Suu Kyi (1945 – present)

Aung San Suu Kyi is a Burmese political leader, philosopher, and human rights activist who became an international symbol of the struggle for democracy in Myanmar. Born in Rangoon (now Yangon), Myanmar, Suu Kyi is the daughter of Aung San, the country's independence hero. She was educated at the University of Oxford, where she studied philosophy, politics, and economics, and later worked for the United Nations in New York. Her political philosophy developed in the context of Myanmar's military dictatorship, and she emerged as a leading figure in the pro-democracy movement during the 1988 uprisings against military rule. Suu Kyi's commitment to nonviolent resistance and democratic reform drew inspiration from figures such as Mahatma Gandhi and Martin Luther King Jr.

Suu Kyi's political philosophy is grounded in the principles of nonviolent resistance, human rights, and the rule of law. In her writings and speeches, including the collection Freedom from Fear (1991), she argues that true political freedom cannot be achieved through violence or authoritarianism. Instead, she advocates for a peaceful transition to democracy, where the rights of all citizens are respected, and the government is accountable to the people. Suu Kyi's commitment to nonviolence is rooted in Buddhist principles of compassion and moral integrity, which she sees as essential to both personal and political life. Her philosophy emphasizes the moral responsibility of individuals to stand up for justice, even in the face of repression.

A key element of Suu Kyi's thought is her emphasis on the rule of law and the importance of democratic institutions. She has argued that without strong legal frameworks and transparent governance, no society can achieve true freedom. In her efforts to reform Myanmar's political system, she has called for constitutional changes to limit the power of the military and establish a democratic system of checks and balances. Suu Kyi's vision of democracy is not merely procedural but is grounded in a deep respect for human dignity and the belief that political power must always be exercised in service of the common good.

Suu Kyi's political career has been marked by long periods of house arrest and imprisonment, during which she became a global symbol of peaceful resistance against tyranny. Her struggle for democracy and human rights in Myanmar earned her numerous international accolades, including the Nobel Peace Prize in 1991. However, her leadership has been criticized in recent years, particularly over her handling of the Rohingya crisis, in which Myanmar's military was accused of committing atrocities against the Rohingya Muslim population. Suu Kyi's defense of the military's actions at the International Court of Justice in 2019 led to widespread condemnation, raising complex questions about her legacy as a human rights advocate.

Despite the controversies surrounding her leadership, Aung San Suu Kyi's influence on the global discourse of democracy and nonviolent resistance remains significant. Her philosophy, deeply rooted in the ideals of human rights, moral integrity, and the rule of law, continues to inspire pro-democracy movements around the world. Her complex political career serves as a case study in the challenges of maintaining moral principles in the face of political realities and power.

Peter Singer (1946 – present)

Peter Singer is an Australian philosopher who has made groundbreaking contributions to ethics, particularly in the areas of animal rights, bioethics, and global poverty. Born in Melbourne, Australia, Singer studied at the University of Melbourne and later at the University of Oxford, where he was influenced by utilitarian philosophers such as Jeremy Bentham and John Stuart Mill. His work emerged during a period of growing awareness about animal welfare, environmental issues, and the ethical implications of global inequality, which shaped his approach to applied ethics.

Singer is best known for his work on animal rights, particularly his book Animal Liberation (1975), which is often considered the foundational text of the modern animal rights movement. In this work, Singer applies utilitarian ethics to argue that animals deserve equal consideration of their interests, particularly in avoiding suffering. He criticizes practices like factory farming and animal experimentation, arguing that they cause immense suffering to animals and that there is no moral justification for treating animals as mere resources. Singer's philosophy challenges traditional views that prioritize human interests over those of other sentient beings.

A key aspect of Singer's philosophy is his commitment to utilitarianism, the ethical theory that actions should be judged based on their consequences in promoting the greatest overall happiness or minimizing suffering. Singer's version of utilitarianism extends beyond human interests to include the interests of all sentient beings, including animals. He argues that the capacity to suffer, rather than species membership, should be the basis for moral consideration. This position challenges anthropocentric views of ethics and has had a profound impact on debates about animal welfare and human dietary practices.

Singer has also contributed significantly to discussions of global poverty and bioethics. In his essay Famine, Affluence, and Morality (1972), he argues that individuals in affluent countries have a moral obligation to donate a significant portion of their income to alleviate global poverty. Using utilitarian reasoning, he claims that the suffering caused by poverty far outweighs the minor inconveniences of reducing personal wealth. This argument has influenced global philanthropy movements, such as effective altruism, which encourages individuals to give in ways that have the most significant positive impact.

In bioethics, Singer has tackled controversial issues such as euthanasia, infanticide, and the moral status of embryos. He advocates for what he calls "preference utilitarianism," where moral decisions should be made based on the preferences of individuals who are capable of having interests, including the preference to avoid suffering or to die with dignity. His positions, particularly on euthanasia and infanticide, have sparked significant debate, but his influence on modern ethics is undeniable. Singer's utilitarian approach has shaped discussions on how to balance competing moral claims in a world of limited resources and diverse forms of life.

Homi K. Bhabha (1949 – present)

Homi K. Bhabha is an Indian-born British scholar known for his work in postcolonial theory and cultural criticism. Born in Mumbai, India, Bhabha was educated at the University of Mumbai and later at Christ Church, Oxford. He has taught at several prestigious universities, including Harvard, where he has played a central role in shaping the academic discourse around postcolonial studies. Bhabha's intellectual work emerged in the late 20th century, a time when scholars were re-examining the cultural and political legacies of colonialism and the complex relationships between colonizers and colonized peoples.

Bhabha's most influential work is The Location of Culture (1994), in which he introduces key concepts that have become foundational in postcolonial theory. One of his central ideas is the concept of "hybridity," which refers to the mixing and merging of cultural identities in colonial and postcolonial contexts. Bhabha argues that colonialism does not produce a simple binary opposition between the colonizer and the colonized but rather a space of cultural negotiation and transformation. Hybridity, according to Bhabha, destabilizes the power dynamics of colonialism by creating new, in-between identities that challenge rigid cultural boundaries.

Another significant contribution from Bhabha is his idea of "mimicry," which he explores as a strategy used by colonized people to resist colonial authority. Mimicry involves the colonized adopting the customs, behaviors, and languages of the colonizers but in a way that subtly undermines their dominance. Bhabha suggests that mimicry exposes the ambivalence of colonial power, as the colonized subject appears to conform but simultaneously disrupts the authority of the colonizer through parody or imitation. This concept has been particularly influential in analyzing the complexities of identity and power in postcolonial societies.

Bhabha also emphasizes the importance of the "Third Space" in his theoretical framework. The Third Space is a space of cultural interaction and negotiation that goes beyond binary oppositions such as East/West or colonizer/colonized. It is a space where new meanings and identities are produced, allowing for cultural exchange that transcends fixed categories. Bhabha's concept of the Third Space has been widely applied in discussions of diaspora, migration, and global culture, as it offers a way to understand how cultural identities are formed through processes of interaction and negotiation rather than through static definitions.

Bhabha's work on hybridity, mimicry, and the Third Space has had a profound impact on postcolonial studies, literary theory, and cultural criticism. His emphasis on the fluidity of cultural identity and the ambivalence of colonial power has challenged traditional notions of power and resistance, offering a more nuanced understanding of the colonial encounter. Bhabha's ideas continue to influence scholars and activists seeking to understand the complexities of cultural identity in an increasingly globalized world.

Vandana Shiva (1952 – present)

Vandana Shiva is an Indian scholar, environmental activist, and philosopher known for her work on ecofeminism, sustainable agriculture, and the rights of indigenous peoples. Born in Dehradun, India, Shiva was educated in physics, earning a PhD in philosophy of science from the University of Western Ontario. Her intellectual development coincided with the rise of environmental movements and the growing awareness of ecological degradation, particularly in the Global South. Deeply influenced by the environmental and social impacts of Western industrial practices, Shiva has become a leading advocate for environmental justice.

Shiva is best known for her work on ecofeminism, a philosophy linking the exploitation of women and nature under patriarchal systems. In books like Staying Alive: Women, Ecology, and Development (1988), she argues that the marginalization of women and environmental degradation are interconnected phenomena rooted in colonialism and capitalist development. Critiquing the Western model of economic growth for prioritizing profit over sustainability, Shiva highlights the role of rural and indigenous women as central to the struggle for environmental justice, given their direct exposure to biodiversity loss and ecological harm.

A central focus of Shiva's work is her opposition to industrial agriculture and genetically modified organisms (GMOs). She has been a vocal critic of multinational corporations like Monsanto for promoting monoculture farming and patented seeds, which she argues undermine biodiversity and food sovereignty. In The Violence of the Green Revolution (1991), Shiva critiques the environmental and social consequences of the Green Revolution in India, highlighting issues like soil depletion, water scarcity, and the displacement of small farmers. She advocates for a return to traditional organic farming practices that sustain biodiversity and empower local communities.

Shiva's philosophy emphasizes the value of indigenous knowledge systems in environmental conservation. She argues that indigenous communities have developed sustainable practices over generations, based on a holistic understanding of ecosystems and the interdependence of living beings. In contrast to Western scientific approaches that treat nature as a resource, indigenous knowledge recognizes the intrinsic value of the environment. Shiva calls for the protection of indigenous rights and the recognition of their wisdom as essential to achieving global environmental sustainability.

Vandana Shiva's contributions to ecofeminism, environmental activism, and sustainable agriculture have made her a prominent figure in the global environmental movement. Her critiques of industrial agriculture and her advocacy for biodiversity and indigenous rights have influenced environmental policy and activism, particularly in the Global South. Shiva's work continues to inspire movements for ecological justice and the protection of the planet's biodiversity in the face of ongoing environmental challenges.

Judith Butler (1956 – present)

Judith Butler is an American philosopher and gender theorist, known for her groundbreaking work in feminist theory, queer theory, and critical theory. Born in Cleveland, Ohio, Butler studied at Yale University, where she earned a PhD in philosophy. Her academic development took place during a time of significant debates about identity, power, and social norms within feminist and queer movements. Butler became a leading figure in these intellectual currents by challenging essentialist notions of gender and identity, offering a more fluid and performative understanding of these concepts.

Butler's most influential work is Gender Trouble (1990), in which she introduced the concept of gender performativity. She argued that gender is not an innate, biological reality but rather a set of behaviors, norms, and roles that individuals enact repeatedly. According to Butler, gender identity is constructed through performative acts that align with societal expectations. These performances are neither natural nor stable; they are subject to change and contestation. Butler's theory of performativity challenges traditional binary notions of male and female, suggesting that gender is not something one is, but something one does.

A central element of Butler's philosophy is her critique of the binary opposition between sex and gender. Traditionally, sex was understood as a biological fact, while gender was seen as a cultural or social construct. Butler, however, argues that sex itself is also socially constructed, as it is always interpreted through cultural norms and discourses. This idea is explored in Bodies That Matter (1993), where Butler critiques the notion that bodies are neutral, pre-discursive entities. Instead, she posits that bodies are shaped by discourses of power and knowledge, particularly those that regulate sexuality and gender. This radical rethinking of sex and gender has had a profound impact on feminist theory and queer studies.

Butler is also known for her work on the politics of recognition and the role of language in shaping identity. In Excitable Speech (1997), she examines how language, especially hate speech and censorship, operates to both empower and constrain individuals. She argues that language is not a simple tool of communication but a medium of power that shapes identities and social realities. This analysis of language extends to her discussions of gender and sexuality, where Butler explores how certain identities are rendered invisible or unintelligible by dominant cultural norms.

Butler's contributions to feminist and queer theory have significantly influenced discussions about identity, power, and social norms. Her work on gender performativity has provided a framework for understanding gender as fluid and contingent, rather than fixed and essential. In addition, her exploration of language, power, and embodiment continues to resonate in fields such as critical theory, political philosophy, and cultural studies. Judith Butler remains a leading figure in contemporary philosophy, known for her challenging and provocative ideas about identity, gender, and the body.

David Chalmers (1966 – present)

David Chalmers is an Australian philosopher best known for his work in philosophy of mind, particularly his contributions to discussions about consciousness and the "hard problem" of consciousness. Born in Sydney, Australia, Chalmers studied mathematics and computer science at the University of Adelaide before pursuing philosophy at Indiana University, where he earned his PhD. His work emerged during a period of renewed interest in the nature of consciousness and the limits of physicalist explanations of the mind. Chalmers has become a prominent figure in contemporary philosophy of mind for his exploration of the explanatory gap between physical processes and conscious experience.

Chalmers gained widespread recognition with his 1996 book The Conscious Mind: In Search of a Fundamental Theory, where he introduces the distinction between the "easy" and "hard" problems of consciousness. The "easy" problems involve explaining cognitive functions such as perception, memory, and behavior in terms of neural mechanisms. The "hard" problem concerns why and how physical processes in the brain give rise to subjective, conscious experiences—what philosophers call "qualia." Chalmers argues that physicalist explanations of the mind, while addressing the easy problems, cannot fully explain the existence of subjective experience.

Chalmers' work challenges reductionist approaches that seek to explain consciousness solely in terms of physical processes. He advocates for "naturalistic dualism," treating consciousness as a fundamental aspect of the universe, similar to space or time. Chalmers suggests that consciousness may require its own set of fundamental principles to be understood, going beyond the scope of current physical science. His dual-aspect theory posits that consciousness has both a physical and a non-physical dimension, positioning him as a leading voice opposing strict physicalist views of the mind.

In addition to his work on consciousness, Chalmers has contributed to the philosophy of artificial intelligence (AI) and virtual reality. He explores how advances in AI and virtual reality technologies might reshape our understanding of consciousness and personal identity. Chalmers examines whether artificial systems could ever possess genuine consciousness and the ethical implications if they did. His work touches on the nature of intelligence, the possibility of machine consciousness, and the philosophical implications of simulated environments.

David Chalmers' contributions to philosophy of mind have reshaped discussions about consciousness, challenging physicalist accounts and proposing new ways to explore subjective experience. His work on the hard problem of consciousness has sparked ongoing debates in philosophy and neuroscience, solidifying his status as one of the most influential figures in the study of mind and consciousness today.